Local Talent

Susanna C. Sheehy

©2009 Susanna C. Sheehy

This novel is a work of fiction. Any references to historical events; to real people, living or dead; or to real locales are intended only to give the fiction a sense of reality and authenticity. Names, characters, places, and incidents either are the product of the author's imagination or are used fictitiously, and their resemblance, if any, to real live counterparts is entirely coincidental.

All rights reserved. This book is printed in the United States of America. No part of this book may be used or reproduced in any manner whatsoever without written permission except in the case of brief quotations embodied in critical articles and reviews. For information address inquires to:

Elden Publishing, LLC
P.O. Box 421803
Atlanta, GA 30342
susannasheehy@susannasheehy.com

Book cover design by Elden Publishing, LLC
Editing by Emily Sheehy

ISBN: 9780978927141
LCCN: 2009933391
Copyright information available upon request

Other books by Susanna Sheehy

The Second Half Trilogy

Marking Time
Book one
Second Half
Book two
Crossed Lines
Book three

Plastic Diamonds
A novella: expected publication date is March, 2010

Novels are available at Amazon.com, BarnesAndNoble.com, and are also available for order at local book stores.

Visit Susanna at:
www.susannasheehy.com

Chapter One

Gwen pulled her bottom lip between her teeth. She could hear her husband storming around in the basement slamming doors and swearing. She had hoped he'd be supportive of her idea but he wasn't. He didn't think she could succeed.

About a year ago, she'd started making her own soap. She had just wanted to have a hobby, something to fill her time now that the kids were grown and gone. Well they weren't exactly gone. They did keep showing up to ask for help with something or the other.

She had actually done very well with the soap. She'd formulated a shampoo bar that left even the driest hair feeling silky and it lubricated the very driest scalp. That one had come first since she had very dry hair and scalp, probably due to the fact that she had been dyeing it for thirty years. But she also had formulated a shampoo bar for oily hair and scalp and one for those few people who were blessed with normal oil production.

She had a line of skin products and even bath salts. All of her friends used them and she had a very small but promising internet business.

She'd approached her husband of thirty years about opening a small shop with her friend Helen who had started making chocolates at about the same time she had started making soap, for about the same reason with about the same success.

"Soap and Chocolate," Phillip said. "It won't work, sweetheart. It's not a good combination."

"It isn't going to be just soap and chocolate, Phil. We're going to make it a gift shop. We'll carry other things too. I've researched it. We buy wholesale and sell at a profit. I have some ideas for other things that I'll produce and we're planning to publish an ad magazine that will go out locally and promote us. We'll sell ads in it for people who want to sell their products in our shop. With Sandy Springs just achieving city status it's the perfect time."

"Gwen," Phillip said. "We're almost retirement age. We don't want to borrow the kind of money we'd need to start a business like that right now. It's gambling our retirement."

"We're fifty five years old, Phil, retirement is ten years away and we've prepared well." She'd crossed her arms in defiance then uncrossed them when they collided with her uncomfortably thickened waist. "Besides," she said. "What are you planning to do after retirement, just sit around and watch TV?"

"No, but I don't want to be forced to keep working because I have to pay off a lot of your debts."

"Well then," she said. "I'll just borrow the money myself. I don't need you."

The evening had ended with Phillip watching a baseball game and Gwen seething in her soap workshop.

*

"I guess it just isn't going to happen, Helen," Gwen said the next day at lunch with her friend. "He doesn't believe in me."

"That's what Matt said too, Gwen, but I'm going to do it anyway. I work too and I have credit. I'll get a loan without him." She reached across the table and put her hand on Gwen's arm. "Come on Gwen. Don't let them stop us. I think it's just some kind of male menopause." She sat back and picked up her veggie burger. "I don't know about Phillip, but Matt's been really hysterical lately. He frets about the kids. I mean they're grown and gone. He didn't worry about them this much when they were teens."

"Yeah, you're right. Phil is worrying about work all the time now. He used to tell me that worrying was a waste of time." Gwen started to eat her salad then looked at her friend. "Helen, how come you still look so slim? I seem to be getting thick in the middle." She looked down at her belly.

"I'm having the same problem, but I just never had as full a figure as you so it isn't as noticeable."

"So it's noticeable?"

"Only because I know you so well." She took a bite of her burger and chewed thoughtfully. "Let's join a gym and hire a personal trainer."

"Phil will have a fit."

"We won't tell him."

*

"I can't believe we just did that," Gwen said as they left the bank.

"Don't tell me you're having second thoughts. You wrote a fantastic prospectus. They were really impressed," Helen said.

"They must have been. They gave us the loan. Are you sure you want to do this, Helen?" Gwen looked sideways at her friend. "I mean you're the only one that actually has a paying job."

"You have a paying job. You get paid for your soap. After all it was your tax ID number that really convinced them."

"I hardly make anything."

"You make enough to pay tax on it. Besides we're going to do great. I believe in us even if our husbands don't."

"Me too." Gwen raised her chin. "I think."

*

"What's this, Phil?" Gwen asked that evening when she brought in the mail. There was a credit card bill for an account they hadn't used in probably ten years. "Did you use this card? There's a two hundred dollar balance on it."

"Shit!" Phil took the bill out of her hand, studied it for a minute and picked up the phone. He dialed the eight hundred number and started talking. Gwen left the room to take the dog out and water the garden.

"I put a fraud alert on our credit," Phillip said when she came back into the kitchen.

"You did what?"

Phillip looked at her startled. "Someone used our credit card, Gwen, an account that hadn't been used for years. That could just be the start of identity theft. I had to do something."

"If this interferes with our small business loan, I'll really be mad at you."

"What small business loan?"

"Helen and I got one this afternoon. We've been working on it for a while. If this messes it up I'll never forgive you."

"You did that without telling me? Why didn't you talk to me about it?"

"I did. I told you I'd do it on my own since you didn't believe in me." Gwen's hands were fisted at her side.

Phillip glared at her then turned toward the basement. "I can't believe you did that without me." He stormed down the steps. "I had to do something about our credit." He called from the basement then went through the door to the garage slamming it loudly. "Someone stole our credit card number!"

Gwen heard him shout through the floor of the kitchen and retreated to her soap workshop. They didn't speak when they went to bed or when they got up the next morning.

*

"I really want this, Helen, but not at the expense of my marriage," Gwen said on the telephone the next day.

"It won't cost you your marriage. Maybe things need a little shaking up there anyway. That's what I'm hoping. Matt didn't speak to me after I told him either," Helen said. "Listen, I've got a location lined up to look at this afternoon after I get off work. Can you meet me there? It's right next to that new shopping and living complex in the middle of the strip. It's an older building, but I think it might profit from the new mall without costing too much."

"Sounds great, you get off at four o'clock, right? That'll give me enough time to look the place over and still put something on the table for Phil. If he even comes home, that is."

"He'll come home."

Gwen hung up the phone and went out the back door to look for Sandy. The dog was sixteen years old and couldn't hear a thing. Her vision wasn't good either but she was still pretty fit. They had steps that led from their back deck to the fenced yard below. Sandy could still get up those steps. The only problem for her was finding them.

The dog was a shaggy speckled mutt that Frankie, their middle child, had brought home when he was about ten years old with the proverbial 'she followed me home' story. Gwen had a pair of standard poodles at the time, her favorite breed, and a couple of Siamese cats. She hadn't wanted any more pets. But the scruffy little mutt had stolen everyone's hearts and had been with them ever since. The poodles had long since died and so had the two Siamese cats, but Sandy just kept on going.

"Sandy!" she called, laughing at herself for doing it. The dog couldn't hear. She looked around the wooded back yard and spotted the dog in the far corner behind an old azalea bush. "Sandy, I'm going to have to come up there and get you aren't I." She laughed at her conversation with the deaf dog then looked closer. Sandy wasn't moving at all. Was she sitting up or lying down? Gwen started to run. The terrain was rough. They had let the yard go fairly wild and the ivy had taken over. She reached the dog in seconds and sank to her knees where Sandy lay on her side.

Gwen knew the dog was dead without touching her. "Oh, Sandy," she put her head down on the furry body. It was still warm and not at all stiff yet. She could smell the sweet doggy scent of her. She didn't know when the tears started to drop on the soft hair. She was unaware of her sobs, but after a point she sat up and stroked Sandy's speckled face.

"I love you, baby," she whispered. "I'll miss you so much." She stood, stooped down to pick up the empty body and carried it back to the house.

"Gwen!" She heard Phillip's voice from the open kitchen door.

He must have come home for lunch. "I'm out back," she called.

Phillip appeared at the top of the steps. "What happened?" He started down toward her. "She's too heavy for you to be carrying," he reached for the dog.

"She's dead." Gwen's voice broke as Phillip helped her ease the body to the ground.

"Oh, Gwen," he put his arm around her as they stood and pulled her close.

She cried against his shoulder for a minute then felt the shudders of his own grief and looked up at him. "You loved her too," she said as she wiped her tears with her hand.

"We all loved her." Phillip looked down at their family pet lying on the deck. "What should we do with her? She's too big to bury."

"We'll cremate her like we did the others," Gwen said. "Help me get her into a plastic bag and I'll take her to Final Rest Pet Care."

"I didn't know we cremated the others," Phillip said as they lifted the stiffening dog into a bag. "Are they in the house somewhere?" He looked over his shoulder warily.

"No," Gwen smiled at his discomfort. "I always scatter them some place meaningful. Sometimes it takes me a little while to figure out where, but I always do."

They put the large dog into the trunk of Gwen's car then went upstairs to the kitchen. "Why are you here in the middle of the day, Phil?" Gwen asked washing her hands at the sink. "You don't usually come home for lunch. Do you want me to fix you something?"

"No, I'll get something on my way back to the office," he said approaching her from behind. He put his arms around her waist and pulled her back against him. "I felt bad about the way things went last night. I wanted to talk to you about it."

Gwen relaxed in his arms. They fit together so nicely. She was five feet four inches tall and he was five feet ten, average height for a woman; average height for a man. When he held her like this his husky voice was close to her ear. "What did you want to talk about?" She dried her hands on the dish towel.

"I'm sorry I didn't support you," he said. "I still wish you could have waited a while until you'd made a little more from your internet business and didn't have to borrow so much, but now that you've done it. I'm behind you all the way."

Gwen pulled away from him and walked over to hang the dish towel on the stove. She turned around and looked at him. "I didn't want to wait any longer, Phil."

"I see that."

"Helen and I are going to look at a rental space this afternoon. I'm hoping it will be the one."

"What time?"

"Four thirty."

"Can I meet you there? I'd like to see it."

"Only if you can behave."

Phillip approached her with a smile pulling at the corners of his mouth. "I'll behave." He kissed her lightly on the mouth then sobered. "Gwen, do you want me to take Sandy?" He glanced at the stairs that led down to the garage.

"No, I know the way."

"Are you sure you're up to looking at property today?" He brushed her shoulder with his hand. "I mean after…"

"Yeah, it's better for me to get busy. It helps with the grief."

*

"Phil?" He recognized the voice on the line as Matthew Riddick, Helen's husband and his own best friend. Phillip was engrossed in a project at the accounting firm where he worked.

"Hey, Matt," He checked his watch hoping that he hadn't worked through his appointment with Gwen. It was only three o'clock so he breathed a sigh of relief.

"Are you going to the shop sight?" Matthew asked.

"Yeah, are you?"

"Oh yeah, I tried to explain to Helen that our credit isn't separate but she insists that she's doing this without me." He paused. "I don't mean to be unsupportive, but this is a really bad time to borrow money."

"I feel that way too," Phillip said. "But you know what, Matt? This is really important to them. I wish I'd been a little more reasonable. Then maybe we could have reached some kind of a compromise."

"I just can't believe she did this without me." Matthew was angry.

"I can't either," Phillip said "But she tried to involve me and I said no."

Matthew was quiet on the other end of the line. Then he said, "I did the same thing."

"I guess we need to be supportive now; after all, their credit is our credit."

"Yeah, I guess I'll see you in an hour or so."

Phillip hung up the phone and thought of his wife and the loss of their family pet. He swallowed the lump in his throat. He'd been fighting it all afternoon.

"I'm off, Sarah," he said to the receptionist on his way out the door half an hour later. "I've got an appointment. See you tomorrow."

"What time will you be in? Mr. Brampton asked me to set up a meeting with everyone at seven."

"I guess I'll be in at seven then." He smiled at her and went outside. Phillip Desmond had worked for this accounting firm in this part of Atlanta, Georgia for twenty five years. He had always loved his job. The people he worked with were great, even though they changed on a regular basis.

Some of the same people he'd started with were still there, but for the most part the place turned people over in about five years, sometimes faster. Phillip just didn't like to change direction. He made a good living, lived only a few miles from his work, and enjoyed the work. Why rock the boat?

Retirement was looking better and better all the time, though. He just hoped he'd prepared for it well enough. He had been working as an auto mechanic when he met Gwen thirty some years ago. That work was fun too. In fact, he still tinkered with cars. He had an old Austin Healey in the garage that he was rebuilding a motor on. It would have been nice if he could make a living at that but he'd just thought he should do something more with his life, especially after he married Gwen and they started having kids.

Unfortunately he hadn't taken everyone's advice and started saving for retirement right away. It was tough working his way through school, attending classes at night and still trying to spend a little time with his growing family.

Gwen had helped of course. She'd worked out of the house typing papers for students and publications for faculty. She'd managed to help with the income and take care of the kids at the same time.

He pulled his car into the parking lot at the address Gwen had given him and got out. Gwen's car was there and so was Matthew's. Helen pulled in behind him in a blur and slammed her car to a stop in the space next to his.

"Helen!" He called jumping back. "Do you always drive like that? I don't think I want Gwen riding with you if you do."

"It looks to me like you don't dictate to Gwen, Phil." Helen jumped out of the car and laughed at his reprimand. Their relationship had always consisted of this teasing banter.

"Well, I might have some influence at least," he said putting his arm across her shoulder and walking toward the building. It was a row of shops just off Roswell Road in the heart of Sandy Springs, a suburb of Atlanta, Georgia.

"Which one of these places is it?"

"It's this one here." Helen guided him to a shop with a tattered green awning. "It will definitely need some renovating."

The strip of stores was around the corner from the new shopping complex, but not more than half a block and situated in such a way that with a little work it could almost look like an extension.

"Where are Gwen and Matthew?" Helen asked. "Their cars are here."

"I guess they're inside." Phillip opened the door for Helen and gestured for her to go in. Matthew and Gwen were standing at the end of the long narrow shop looking cautiously through an open door to the back. Gwen dabbed at her eyes with a Kleenex. "Oh I forgot to ask if she told you that Sandy died." He looked at Helen.

"No, she didn't, poor thing. She didn't have to come. We could have looked at the place tomorrow." Helen spoke quietly.

"Oh, there you are," Gwen said turning and hurrying toward them. "Helen, this place is going to need so much work. I'm not sure it's worth the lower rent. I'm actually afraid to go into the storage room." She dabbed at her eyes and sniffed. "I think Matt is too."

"Gwen, sweetie," Helen said hugging her friend fiercely. "I'm so sorry about Sandy. We didn't have to do this today."

"What happened to Sandy?" Matthew asked.

Phillip looked at him for the first time and noticed that he looked pale. "She died today."

"Oh well, I guess that explains the tears," Matthew said. "I thought she was upset about the shop. It just didn't seem worth crying about to me."

"Well the shop didn't help." Gwen sniffled again and hiccupping. "I dare you to go into that storage room." She looked at Matthew.

"Where is the landlord?" Helen asked.

"He said he'd just let us look around by ourselves and then disappeared. I think he's afraid of the place, too," Matthew said turning toward the back room. "I just wish I had a flashlight. There has to be a light in there, but I sure can't find it inside the door or outside for that matter."

"Here, I've got a pen light on my key chain." Phillip followed him over to the open door with the ominous looking darkness behind it. He went through the door and started systematically moving his light up and down the wall. "Here it is," he said after a minute and flipped the switch to turn on the light.

"The two of you can stop holding your breath now," Matthew called through the door. "Come on in. It's not that bad."

Helen and Gwen came reluctantly into the back room. Gwen was in front. Helen's hands were on Gwen shoulders holding her like a shield.

"It's not that bad in here." Phillip laughed. "What do you think Gwen's going to do to save you, Helen, if the boogie man jumps out?"

"Boo!" Matthew boomed suddenly.

"AAAAAhhhh." Both women squealed then dissolved into laughter.

"Matthew Riddick, that's not funny," Helen said. "At our age, that could be the end of us." She looked around. "You know, this place isn't that bad. It really needs some renovation, but we'll negotiate that with the landlord. I'm sure it won't be hard to relocate that light switch anyway."

"I don't know, Helen," Gwen said. "Those look like rat droppings to me." She pointed to the corner of the room under a wall of shelves.

"We'll definitely need an exterminator, but that sounds like something we need to negotiate with the landlord, too," Helen said. "Other than that I think it just might do. Where is that landlord? I need to talk to him." She hurried from the room.

"If you really don't like it, Gwen," Matthew said. "You'd better plan your resistance. I recognize that look in her eyes. She likes this place."

"I think I'll just wait and see what happens with the landlord," Gwen said as they left the room.

Phillip smiled and flicked off the light then guided himself out of the dark with his penlight.

*

"You said you were planning some renovations." Helen said as they all sat around a table in the office at the back of the strip mall. "What do you have planned?"

"We're putting a whole new face on it, a façade. The awning will come down and the display windows will be replaced by windows that blend with the new mall." The man who had introduced himself as Mr. Robins said. "We're also completely renovating the plumbing and electrical system and we're putting in a new HVAC system, that is, Heating Ventilating and Air Conditioning." He looked proud.

"What about paint," Helen said. "Those walls are a hideous combination of colors, all that pink and blue. What kind of a shop was in there before? I've lived here all my life and I can't remember."

"It wasn't there very long," Mr. Robins said. "It was a specialty toy store. They just couldn't compete with those new toy warehouses. Before that, though, it was a health food store. They did really well, were in there for thirty years, but the owner retired and shut it down."

"Oh," Helen said feigning interest. "Well, anyway, what about paint?"

"We always paint for the new tenant."

"Good," Helen said. "We'll need a window in the back room and…"

"No window," Mr. Robins said firmly.

"Why not? It's gloomy back there. We need some light."

"No window."

Helen looked at him for a minute then took a deep breath. "Alright, we'll need the shelves taken off the walls and new ones put up. Those have rotten places in them and some of them are so tilted I doubt that anything will stay on them."

"The shelves stay."

"Oh, come on," Helen said.

"I was lucky to convince the owner to do what he's doing." Mr. Robins looked strained. "Even so I had to agree to a five year lease."

"Five years!" Gwen howled. "Why? The new mall only wants a year." Until now Helen had done all the talking. All eyes turned to Gwen and she blushed.

"It was the only way we could spread the renovations out over the five shops and still rent for this much less." The man's upper lip and forehead were breaking into a sweat.

"I see," Helen said. She looked at Gwen then at Phillip and Matthew. "So you're not the owner."

"No, I'm his agent."

Helen tapped her fingers on the table thoughtfully. "Can we renovate ourselves?"

"I'd have to ask the owner, but I'm pretty sure he wouldn't mind if you did it at your own expense."

"Good, ask him. We'd like to get a couple of quotes on the work we want done before we sign a lease," Helen said. "We'll also want our lawyer to look over the lease before we sign it."

"That's fair, but the place is still available until you sign that lease."

"I don't think that will be a problem." Helen stood up and signaled the rest of the group to stand. "One more thing, Mr. Robins, can we sublease it if we want to."

"Yes, but the owner would want to approve the new tenants."

"Thank you, Mr. Robins. We'll wait to hear from you about those renovations."

*

Matthew Riddick leaned back in his chair and watched his wife work. She was really something. How did she know what questions to ask about leasing a store space? She's obviously done her homework, he thought.

He smiled as he watched the sweat break out on Mr. Robins' upper lip and had to suppress a laugh when the poor man reached into his pocket for a handkerchief to mop his brow.

She's beautiful when she's animated like this. Matthew looked at her profile while she focused on the agent. Her features weren't much different than they'd been thirty years ago when he married her. Her jaw line wasn't quite as straight, but the creases by her mouth were beautiful to him. He could see the pull of her smile and slant of her frown in the lines that had formed there.

I love her hair, he thought as he noticed the streaks of white lacing through the chestnut hair that fell in curls to her shoulders. Something stirred in his lower abdomen and he sat up straight and cleared his throat. No one noticed. He took a relieved breath.

Everyone was standing now. Matthew had been so lost in admiration for his wife he hadn't heard what went on. He stood with the others and followed them out onto the sidewalk.

"Come to dinner at our house, you two," Gwen said. "I'll grill some chicken and corn on the cob. We can talk about what we think."

"Sounds good," Helen looked at Matthew. "Is it alright with you, Matt? You look tired."

"I am tired, but I think I can keep my head up for dinner." He smiled weakly. "I'd like to go home and change first."

"It's settled, then," Gwen said. "You'll come to dinner at our house. See you in a while."

They were all in separate cars, so they divided up and went their separate ways. Matthew watched Helen get into hers and peel away from the curb like a bat out of hell. Smiling, he shook his head. She was always in such a hurry. He wanted to go home and go to sleep. He just couldn't seem to get rested these days.

"Matt," Helen called from the bedroom when he came into the house. "Come on back here and change your clothes."

He moved down the hall to the bedroom and opened the door. Helen stood in the middle of the room completely naked. She was still beautiful naked. There were scars from child bearing and her belly was no longer completely flat but she'd really aged well.

"That was exciting, wasn't it?" she said as she came toward him. "I'm all stimulated." She put her arms around his neck. "I liked your idea about coming home first. I think we have time for a little fun, don't you?" She kissed him.

He put his hands on her breasts. They were small but full and still firm even though she'd nursed twins. He remembered the stirring in his loins at the shop just a short while ago and wondered where it was now that he was actually in a position to do something about it.

"I'm too tired, Helen. I'm sorry. I just can't do it."

She stepped away from him and turned around. "You're always too tired, Matt. What's the matter with you? You're only fifty six years old. You'd think your were eighty." She disappeared into her walk-in closet and Matthew sat down on the bed and took off his shoes.

"You're right. I don't know what the problem is but I have no energy."

"You need to stop smoking for one thing," she said coming back out of her closet fully dressed. She sat down on the bed to pull her sandals on. "You quit for so long. Why did you start back up?"

"I don't know but I don't smoke very much." He pulled off his pants.

Helen looked at him with his pants off and his shirt hanging loose over his belly. He'd gotten so flabby. Talk about thick in the middle. She rolled her eyes and left the room. "Do you want to ride over with me?" She called as she walked down the hall to the kitchen.

"Yeah, just give me a minute. I'll be right there."

*

"Matt doesn't look so good," Phillip said to Gwen when they had gotten home and gone out on the deck to start the grill. "He's not only let his conditioning go but he looks pale, just not healthy."

"I noticed that too," Gwen said. "I'm not much better." She patted her belly and turned around to look at Phil. "You might as well know, Phil, I joined a gym. I joined you too. I think we're at an age where we can either really lose our conditioning or we can start working on it and feel pretty good in our old age."

"We can't afford a gym, Gwen," he said. "What's with this spending spree you've gone on?" Phillip's voice was rising with agitation.

"We can't afford not to join a gym and I signed you up so you'd better use it or we'll just be throwing away money." She turned back to the grill and closed the lid to let it warm up. "Helen joined for herself and Matt, too. So it'll be a group project."

"I can't believe this." Phillip turned to go inside when the front doorbell rang.

"Hey," Gwen said when he returned a minute later with Helen and Matthew in tow. "Would you like something to drink?"

"I'd love a martini if you've got one," Matthew said.

"You shouldn't drink so much either, Matt." Helen sat down at the patio table. "He feels terrible all the time." She turned to Gwen. "And small wonder when he smokes and drinks and eats like a pig."

"Hey, Helen," Matthew sat down. "Back off, okay."

"So tell me what you think about the shop." Gwen changed the subject.

Helen took a deep breath and turned to Gwen. "I think, if we can get a good price on the renovations we need, we should take it."

"Really? I just don't know, Helen, a five year lease." Gwen took the glass of wine that Phillip handed her and took a sip. "What if..."

"Don't be negative, Gwen. We're going to succeed." She sipped the glass of wine Phillip handed to her and watched angrily as he set a frosty martini in front of Matthew. "Besides we can sublease if we want out. I just think that we can't pass up the rent at that low price. In a way, a five year lease works in our favor." She turned back to Gwen.

"Well, we'll have to find out about the renovations. I just think we have to have a window in the office and storage space."

"Absolutely," Helen started to relax then stiffened as Matthew lit a cigarette. "Come on, Matt, cut it out. I swear if you don't do something about yourself, I'm going to leave you. I mean it."

"Helen, we're at dinner with friends. This isn't the place to be having this conversation," Matthew said. "I'm sorry, Gwen, Phil. She's been sniping at me all afternoon."

"Matt," Gwen said. "Put the cigarette out. I agree with Helen. You don't look too good. I'm worried about your health."

"Me too," Phillip said. "And Gwen just told me about the gym she and Helen signed us up for. I guess we're all going on a health kick."

"A gym! What the hell, Helen? You didn't even ask me." Matthew snuffed out the cigarette and stood up.

"You're right. I didn't ask you," Helen said. "What's the point of me asking you for anything these days? You're always too damn tired." She stood up and picked up her purse. "I'm sorry, Gwen, we need to go. I forgot Matthew has to be in bed early or he can't function." She stormed through the door and a minute later they heard the front door slam.

"I'm sorry." Matthew followed her.

They heard a car horn blow then the front door shut again and Phillip turned to Gwen. "I wonder if we're about to watch our best friends break up after thirty years of marriage."

Gwen turned to the grill and started placing chicken pieces. "I have to say, though, Helen has a point. Matt looks and acts like an old man."

"Do I do that, Gwen?" Phillip asked.

"Sometimes," Gwen basted the chicken and put on the ears of corn. "You worry a lot more than you did before, mostly about money."

"Do I really?"

"Yeah, sometimes I think you're going to worry so much about our retirement money that you'll die before we ever get there."

"I hope not." He put his arm around her waist.

She closed the grill, turned in his arms and rested her head on his shoulder. "I still love you, though. I'm not sure Helen still feels that way about Matt."

"I'm not sure either. It'll be tough if she leaves him, because he's still completely in love with her."

"He needs to do something about himself, then. I can't blame Helen for not wanting to let him weigh her down."

*

"So where is this damn gym you joined?" Matthew said as Helen screeched around a corner causing him to grab the handle above the door for support.

"It's over by the mall, why? Don't tell me you're thinking about using it."

"Helen, your sarcasm is getting old, so just stop it. You don't have to be sniping at me all the time. You've made your point."

"Have I?" She pulled into their driveway and pressed the button to raise the garage door. "Matt, I really don't think I want to be with you anymore." She jumped out of the car and slammed the door.

Matthew got out too and followed her into the kitchen. "Are you serious about this? I love you," he said putting his hand on her arm. "We're just going through a tough spell. Don't throw away thirty one years of marriage for a tough spell."

"Matt." She turned around and looked at him. "Look, I know you love me. You always have, but I'm not sure I love you anymore." She took a deep breath and softened at the hurt look in his eyes. "Look, Matt, you may love me, but you can't make love to me. Why is that?"

"I don't know. Maybe there's something wrong with me. Maybe I'm sick."

"Then go to the doctor and find out what it is so we can fix it."

"I hate doctors."

"You hate everything that might compel you to take care of yourself." She turned around and stormed down the hall to the guest room.

"So we're sleeping in separate rooms now?"

"Yes. I don't want to sleep with you anymore. You smell like smoke and liquor, and what's the point anyway. You won't touch me. As soon as you hit the bed you're out cold," she said. "Matt, you don't love me. You can't care about anyone if you can't care about yourself, and you obviously don't care about yourself."

He looked at her sadly and she softened again. Taking a deep breath she said, "I don't want to continue this right now. I'm upset and I'll say things I shouldn't. Go to bed. You need the rest." She shut the door while he was still standing in the hall and sat down on the bed.

Helen heard him move off toward the room they'd shared for thirty one years. She felt terrible about the hurt in his eyes. She'd said some really mean things. "But I can't watch you kill yourself, Matt," she whispered. "I used to love you and I loved you for a very long time."

*

"Gwen," Phil said. They were lying in bed watching the news on TV. "Should we get another dog? We could get a small one this time, train it really well then it could go with us wherever we go."

"No," she said. "I'm finished with pets. It's just too hard to lose them." She pointed the remote control at the television and turned it off. She switched off the lamp beside her bed, threw her sit-up pillow on the floor and lay down stretching out her legs.

"I don't think we've ever been without a pet. You brought cats with you when we got married and we were always adding them before their predecessors were gone. Are you sure?"

"I'm sure. I've been fighting tears all day. I have better things to do."

He stretched out on his side of the bed and reached for her hand. Squeezing it, he said, "You don't think the sixteen years we had with Sandy were worth it? The grief comes at the end and it doesn't last that long."

"Those years were worth it, but I'm not doing it again." She squeezed his hand and pulled away, rolling over on her side with her back to him.

"What about a cat? They're easy."

"No more pets."

Chapter Two

"You're not going to believe it, Helen," Gwen said into the telephone. "Remember Mitzi Rice from the kid's elementary school?"

"Mitzi Rice?"

"Yeah, she had that squirrely little girl with the limp brown hair and freckles. She was in Frankie and the twin's class." She paused thoughtfully. "The little girl's name was Linda. You wouldn't believe how pretty she is now. She's grown into such a beautiful woman. I guess it's the ugly duckling story again."

"Good for her," Helen said. "What about it?"

"Well, I remembered that Mitzi was an interior decorator, so I called her to see if she'd look at the shop for us and guess what?"

"What?"

"I talked her into looking at the place and giving us an estimate for free, and if we like her ideas, she'll give them to us for one year of advertising in the ad flyer and putting her name and cards in the shop."

"That's great, Gwen!" Helen sounded excited for the first time in their conversation. "You've really gotten into this new business."

"I'm really excited about it," she said and paused. "Is everything alright with you? I worried about you and Matt after you left last night."

"No, things aren't alright. We slept in separate rooms last night and ...I don't know ...I don't feel anything for him anymore." She sighed. "I'm not sure if I really just don't love him anymore or if I've just distanced myself from him because I can't stand to watch him kill himself."

"I can't stand it either, Helen, but I love him anyway."

"So you see it, too? It isn't just me?"

"No, and Phil has commented on it, too."

There was silence on the telephone line for a minute. Helen was thinking about watching Matthew get undressed and how it seemed to tire him. She also thought about the sag of his body and the lack of libido.

Gwen was recalling Phil's comment on how tired Matt looked and the fact that they drew her attention to the nagging feeling of concern she'd had when Matthew had arrived at the store and they'd spent some time alone together.

"Well," Helen broke their silence. "This morning he left the house before I got up and one of the key tags for the gym was gone. Maybe he's planning to do something about it."

"I hope so," Gwen said. "Anyway, I'm meeting Mitzi at the shop this afternoon at four thirty. I planned it so that you could join us if you wanted to."

"Great, I'll be there."

"Oh and, Helen," she said before they hung up. "I was thinking of going to city hall to file the name of the shop. I thought of a good name and wanted to run it by you."

"Run it by me," Helen said.

"Well at the top of the sign we would have 'Helen's and Gwen's shop', and then underneath would be 'Local Talent'. I guess 'Local Talent' would be the official name of the shop. What do you think?"

Helen was silent for a minute. "I love it. Go to City Hall." She paused and Gwen heard the sound of the other line in Helen's office ringing. "I need to go, Gwen. I have another call coming in and it's Dandy."

"Give her my love. Bye."

"Hey, honey," Helen said after she'd pressed the button to end her conversation with Gwen and picked up the line her daughter was on.

"Hey, Mama!" Dandy was twenty six years old. She had a twin brother named Danny. Their real names were Daniel and Delia, but they had been dubbed 'Danny and Dandy' shortly after birth and, though they both used their real names in the world outside, they would always be Danny and Dandy to their mother.

"How's everything?" Helen tried to sound upbeat. It didn't matter, though, Dandy was so focused on herself she wouldn't notice any tension in Helen's voice.

"Great!" she said. "I love my job and I love being married to Greg."

"I'm so glad, honey. It's important to like the work you do. I wish I did."

"I guess you'll be able to quit selling insurance soon with your shop opening up."

"I think it'll be about six months before we'll be ready to open, but as soon as we do, I'm putting in my notice and going full time to the shop," Helen said.

"That's great, Mama," Delia said obviously ready to change the subject. "Listen, I called to ask you something. I was hoping you wouldn't mind if Greg and I moved into the house with you for a couple of months."

"What!?"

"Gosh, you don't sound too happy about it. I thought you might enjoy having us around for a while."

"I'm sorry. I was just startled, Dandy, explain it to me."

"We've almost saved enough money for a down payment on a house. I'm just dying to have my own house, Mama. So I suggested that we give up our apartment in two months when the lease is up and move in with you. That way we'd be able to save faster."

"Because we'd be supporting you."

Dandy was silent on the other end of the line.

"I'm sorry, honey, that wasn't a nice thing to say. It's just that if I'm going to quit my job, we'll be a little strapped for a while until the store really gets going."

"We'll pay for our own food and any difference in the utilities." Dandy's voice was stiff.

"How does Greg feel about this?"

"He's alright with it, if it doesn't go on for very long. I mean you have that basement apartment. We wouldn't be in your way. Mama, I want to be settled in a house before we start a family."

"You're thinking of starting a family?"

"Yes, I'll continue to work, of course. I wouldn't want to give up my nursing, but we're thinking maybe in another year."

"Well," Helen said. "I think we can help out. Let me talk to Dad about it before you give your notice, but I know he'll agree. You know, now that I'm used to the idea it's growing on me. It would be fun to have young happy people around."

"Good."

"Dandy, have you heard anything from your brother lately?" Helen questioned cautiously.

"He's alright, Mama. We keep in touch."

"He still won't let you tell me his cell phone number?"

"No, Mama. He'll come around, just be patient."

Daniel hadn't spoken to her in over a year and when he'd spoken to her then, he was openly hostile.

"Maybe if he'd tell me why he's so mad at me we could work it out. Does he tell you?"

"Yes, but I can't talk to you about it. That would be a betrayal of trust." Delia paused. "I will tell you that he's in love. I think he's finally found the right girl."

"Do you think I'll ever get to meet her or will they just get married and live happily ever after without ever seeing me again?"

"I think he'll come around. Well, I've got to go. I'm at work and my break is over."

*

"Hello?" Phillip said into the telephone.

"Dad, this is Frankie."

"Hey, son, what's up?"

"I'm at the house and I can't find Sandy."

"Oh, Frankie, I'm sorry. I guess Mom hasn't had the time to call you. Sandy died yesterday."

The line was silent.

"Frankie..."

"I can't believe you didn't call me right away. How did it happen?"

"She just went up into the woods and died. I guess she knew it was her time. Your mom took her body to be cremated. She plans to scatter the ashes someplace meaningful."

"Don't you think that's something I should do?"

"Of course, I guess we had just started thinking of her as our dog. I'm sure your Mom will agree."

"Where is Mom anyway? I can never find her anymore." Frank sniffed.

"She's busy starting up a gift shop in Sandy Springs, but you're right. We should have contacted you right away," Phillip said. "Frankie, are you okay?"

"No! My dog is dead. How can I be alright?" He sniffed again and started to sob into the receiver.

"Do you want me to come home, Son?"

"No! I'm a grown man, Dad. I can handle this." The phone went dead as Frankie hung it up.

"Damn!" Phillip said as he hung up the phone. "We really should have called him." Frankie had always been the most volatile of their children. Andrea who was just barely a year older than him had been born sensible. He smiled thinking about her. She'd just taken life a step at a time and was living happily in Charleston, South

Carolina with her husband, Tom and son, Trevor, the first grandchild.

Then there was Rodney, the baby. He'd been an afterthought. They had really not expected to find themselves having another child five years after Frank. But he'd been a good kid and was in his junior year in college at Georgia Tech. They hadn't seen much of him lately. He lived in an apartment with a group of other students. Phillip suspected they did a lot of partying, but his grades were still good, so he wouldn't complain.

But Frankie had never gone to college after high school. He'd graduated high in his class, but didn't want to continue his education. He'd floated around for a long time delivering pizza and doing this and that. Now he was doing an HVAC apprenticeship.

"I hope he gets through it."

"You hope who gets through what?" Sarah said from behind him.

He jumped and turned to find her standing at the opening of his cubicle. "Frankie, I hope he gets through his apprenticeship."

"How far does he have to go?"

"Two more years, it's five years." Phillip shook his head. "The kid doesn't have much attention span."

"I think he'll do okay. Last time I talked to him he seemed to be enjoying it."

"Yeah, anyway, Sarah, I think I'll go home now. He's at home and he's upset. His dog died yesterday and we didn't call to tell him about it." He started packing up his computer. "He went home and couldn't find her."

*

Gwen let herself in the front door and called out to Frankie. She knew he was there because his car was parked at the curb. He didn't answer so she went to the base of the stairs that led to the kid's rooms.

"Frankie, are you up there?" There was still no answer so she started up the stairs. It was about half way up that she heard the sound of him crying. "Honey," she said as she opened the door to his room. "I guess you know that Sandy died."

"I can't believe you didn't call me."

"I thought about it Frankie, but I didn't want to do it over the phone. I hoped I'd be here when you came by."

"Well, you weren't," he said standing up from where he was sitting in a chair at the window. He went into the bathroom that joined his room with Rodney's and rinsed his face. "You're never here anymore. Most of the times when I come home you're nowhere to be found, or else you're in your soap workshop."

"Well, I'm glad to know you notice." She smiled and went over to where he stood in the bathroom door drying his face with a towel. "Frankie, I'm sorry about Sandy. I know it hurts. It hurt me too." She put her arms around his shoulders and hugged him. He was so tall. She couldn't imagine why. She and Phil weren't tall. Andrea was only five foot two. Rodney was six feet, but Frankie was six foot two. "You're so tall. I can hardly hug you anymore."

He let her hold him a minute longer then sniffed and stepped back. "So tell me about this shop. Dad said you were opening one."

"Helen and I are opening it. I need something to occupy my time now that you kids don't really need me anymore."

"I guess you're going to sell your soap and Helen's chocolates," he said. "It's kind of an odd combination."

"That's what Dad said. We'll sell other things too. I'm going to the Sandy Springs festival this weekend to look for some more local talent," she said. "Come on down to the kitchen and I'll fix you a sandwich."

He followed her out of the room and down the stairs. "I'm not hungry Mom, but I'd love a glass of water. I just ran around the park and I have to go to class tonight."

"How's class going?" Gwen filled a glass with ice and water, put it down on the table where Frankie was sitting then sat across from him.

"Great! Believe it or not, Mom, I really like the work. It's better for me than a desk job. This way I'm going from job to job. I hardly ever spend a whole day in one place."

"Good, honey, maybe you've found your niche."

"I think I have." He drank half the glass of water in one move then put the glass down. "What about needle point and cross stitch and things like that? Do you think you'd want to sell needle point?"

Gwen looked at him puzzled. "Are you doing needle point these days?"

"No," Frankie laughed. "My girlfriend does, though. You should see our apartment it's full of those things. She's even got stacks of them in the closet. She can't afford to frame them all and even if she did. We couldn't hang them all in our apartment. We haven't got that much wall space."

"You're living with her?" Gwen's eyes opened wide.

"Yeah, didn't I tell you about Grace?"

"I'm pretty sure you didn't, Frankie. I think I'd remember a thing like that."

"Well, we've been living together for a couple of months. Her name is Grace." He smiled. "Isn't that a nice name? It's so traditional."

Gwen smiled at the expression on his face. Maybe he's found the right girl. She thought.

"Anyway, what about the needle work?"

"Yes, that's exactly the kind of thing I'm looking for. But do you think she'd want to sell it? Isn't that kind of thing personal?"

"No more than any other art form and she was saying the other day she wished she could sell it. Grace is going to medical school and her parents are paying for it but she needs to make spending money."

"You're going to marry a doctor?!"

"I didn't say anything about marriage, Mom! Jeeeeze, you're as bad as Grace!" Frankie stood up. "I've got to go. I need to get showered before class. I'll tell Grace to call you." He walked around the table and kissed her cheek. "I'm sorry I got so upset about Sandy but she was such a great dog."

"Don't apologize, honey, there's nothing wrong with grieving and she was a great dog."

Gwen stood as Frankie left and went back over to the kitchen counter. She was planning to barbecue again tonight. Phil would be home soon and they'd have a glass of wine on the back deck. It was early May and the weather in Sandy Springs was still pleasant enough to cook outside. Soon it would be too hot so she was determined to enjoy it while she could. She heard the garage door open and knew Phil was home.

"Hey, baby," he said as he came up the stairs. He kissed her cheek and went back to their bedroom to change. "I stopped at the top of the hill to talk to Frankie," he said coming back into the kitchen a few minutes later. "I felt bad for him. He called me at work to ask where Sandy was."

"I know. I guess we should have called him. I thought about it but I didn't want to do it over the phone."

"So I ended up doing it over the phone," he said going to the refrigerator to get a beer. "You know, Gwen, it made me think. With you being in and out so much these days. I think you need a cell phone."

"I don't want a cell phone," she said firmly. "I've told you that. I won't remember to charge it or take it with me! No! I don't want a cell phone."

"You need one, baby, what if you get stranded on the road or something. Don't you see it's foolish not to take advantage of this technology?" Phillip said pulling a phone out of his pocket. "So I got you one."

"Take it back!"

"No, I want you to have it. Now come over here and let me show you how to use it."

"I can't. I'm marinating the meat."

"Gwen, you've put the meat in the marinade. That's all the work you have to do. The meat does the rest." He laughed. "Come on. I insist."

She went to the table where he was sitting and let him show her the basics of the phone.

"Phil," she said after her brief lesson. "Did you know that Frankie was living with a girl named Grace?"

"No, I didn't."

"She's a medical student."

"You're kidding." He laughed. "Our little Frankie is going to marry a doctor?"

"That's what I said and he protested. Said he hadn't said anything about marriage but judging from the look on his face. He's definitely in love with her."

"Hmmm," Phillip said. "Imagine that."

*

"So, Matt, how did it go with the personal trainer at the Gym?" Helen asked when they sat down to dinner. "This is the day you and Phil were going, isn't it?"

"Yeah, it was really pretty much of a sales pitch, but we signed up for three months of it." He laughed. "I guess he was a pretty good salesman."

"You didn't work out at all?"

"He evaluated us, so yes, he made us do some things to see how bad off we were." He sipped on his martini.

"I'm hoping you'll cut back on those, too, Matt. I'm sure you drink too much."

"One step at time, Helen."

She leaned back in her chair and took a deep breath. Matthew was irritating her again. She wasn't sure how long they could go on like this before she lost her temper and said something she'd regret.

"I'm trying, Helen, give me a break!"

"You're right." She pushed her salad around on her plate with a fork. "So how bad off were you?"

"Pretty bad," he laughed. "Phil could do more on every machine and he's just a little guy."

"He's not that small, Matt, you're just big."

"Yeah," he said leaning back and patting his bulging middle.

"I was talking about height."

"Remember how we used to call Phil and Gwen Mr. and Mrs. Short and us Mr. and Mrs. Tall?" Matthew grinned at the memory.

"Umhm, when our friendship was first starting."

"Anyway, the trainer wants us both to get a physical to be sure we're okay to start this project. I was thinking of skipping it. Phil said he had one last month."

"No, I think he's right, Matt. I'll make you an appointment with my doctor."

"I don't need an OB/GYN."

"Neither do I anymore, stupid, my doctor is an internist." She bit her tongue.

"Okay, if you insist, but I don't think it's necessary."

*

"It's like he's just determined to destroy himself," Helen said to Gwen at lunch. It was a

Saturday in late May and they were eating together at their favorite café.

"He's not that bad, Helen. He's going to the Gym."

"Yeah, he was so proud of himself for going to that trainer that he had a double martini with dinner and smoked about five cigarettes after going back for seconds and thirds. He's growing into a mountain and I don't think I can watch it anymore."

"I'm sorry, Helen," Gwen said as she concentrated on her lunch. "I wish I could do something to help."

"There isn't anything anyone can do." She took a deep breath. "Enough of this, if I don't stop going on about Matt, people will stop wanting to be with me. Tell me about Mitzi's plan for the shop. Has she shown it to you yet?"

"No, she's actually coming over to the house this afternoon to show them to me. I asked her if we could do it on the weekend so you could be involved. I hope you don't have plans."

"No, I don't."

"Good, because Frankie's girl friend is coming over too and I'm a little nervous. We haven't met before."

"Maybe this isn't a good time for store business, then, I mean the first time you meet Frankie's girl."

"It is business. I wonder if we'd ever have met her if she didn't want to be part of the business."

"I thought she was a doctor."

"She's a medical student."

"So how can she be a part of the gift shop?" Helen laughed.

"Apparently she does needle work. Frankie says it calms her nerves and she has so much of it she can't use it all. They don't have enough wall space and she can't afford to frame them all. He says there are stacks of them in the closet." Gwen pushed her half eaten lunch away. "I can't eat anymore. I'm too nervous."

"Why are you nervous? You're the future mother-in-law."

"Frankie didn't want to talk about marriage, remember?"

"That's right. I won't talk about it to him. But you do think that's the way things are going don't you?" Helen said.

"I guess I'm kind of hoping so. She seems to have grounded him a little."

"Well," Helen patted Gwen's arm. "I'm sure she's more nervous than you are. So when do we sign the lease on the new space."

"Well, I went ahead and put the earnest money down on it. We won't get that back if we decide against it but I wanted to wait until we get an estimate on the renovations before we sign a five year lease." She sipped her water and signaled for the waiter to bring the check. "That reminds me, Helen. Will Matt's company give us a good price? He does work for a construction company."

"I asked him about that. He's a project manager but he can estimate the job. He says he'll give us a good price but he can't give it away." She frowned. "He says he can't take men off paying jobs to work on personal stuff."

"Of course he can't. I didn't expect him to."

"I did. Well, anyway it'll probably be a better price than we'd get anywhere else."

"Good, I'll call him and arrange to get together with him and Mitzi at the shop." She signed her part of the check and put her card back in her purse. "This is so exciting, Helen. I can't wait to open up. I'm hoping to make October first the grand opening."

"That's only four and a half months away, Gwen, can we work that fast?"

"Probably not, but I'm going to try."

*

"Hello, Helen," Phillip said as he opened the door to her. He kissed her cheek and put his arm across her shoulders as they went into the living room. Phillip noticed again how tall she was. With Helen at five foot eight and him five foot ten; they were eye to eye with each other. "You know when we first became friends. It made me uncomfortable that you were so tall."

"I remember." She laughed. "You always stood up very straight when you were around me."

"It doesn't bother me anymore. I'm used to the fact that you're a giant."

"I'm not a Giant, you're a runt." She elbowed him playfully in the ribs and went to the dining room where Gwen and Mitzi had plans spread out on the table. "What have I missed?"

"These are great, Helen. I wish you could have come straight here from lunch. I don't know if I can explain them to you and Mitzi has to go."

"I'm sorry but I had something I had to do. Can you just give me a brief rundown of it, Mitzi?"

"Helen, it's good to see you." Mitzi gave her a hug. "How're the twins?"

"Doing fine," Helen said dismissing the subject. "Now, let me take a look at these plans."

Helen listened as Mitzi briefly went over the drawings. Then she said she had to go but they could keep the plans and study them for a while before they made their decision.

"I've decided," Gwen said when the front door had closed behind Mitzi. "They're good, exactly what I wanted. Don't you think so, Helen?"

"Yes, absolutely, can I take them home and let Matt look at them. Maybe we could go ahead and get the estimating process started."

"As long as it doesn't interfere with our run tomorrow," Phillip said coming into the dining room with two glasses of lemonade. He handed one to Helen.

"Your run? Why would Matt looking at the plans interfere with you and Gwen running?"

"Not me and Gwen, me and Matt."

"You're kidding!" Helen exclaimed. "You're going to get that fat old smoker to run. I don't think you'll get very far."

"Don't sell him too short, Helen. We've run together a couple of times since we started at the Gym. He can do a mile and a half now then he has to walk the last half mile. But he couldn't do a mile when we started."

"You're kidding! When do you run? He hasn't told me about it."

"He says you're not speaking to him these days," Phillip said looking out the window at the road. "Oh look, Frankie and the doctor are here."

"Oh, gosh, I should go to the bathroom." Gwen hurried down the hall.

"She's a nervous wreck." Phillip laughed as he and Helen walked to the front door to greet Frankie and Grace. Phillip opened the door and stepped back so they could come in. "Hey Frank," he said and turned to the tiny woman next to him. "This must be Grace." He smiled and took her hand.

She stood certainly no more than five feet tall. Her hair was long and straight and fell to the middle of her back. It was very dark and her eyes were a vibrant blue. "It's so nice to meet you, Mr. Desmond," She turned to Helen. "Frank, you didn't tell me your mother was so tall."

"This isn't my mother," Frankie said. "This is her best friend and partner in the shop, Helen. Hey, Helen, it's good to see you."

"Good to see you, too, sweetie." She hugged him and stepped back, her hands still on his shoulders. "Have you grown more since the last time I saw you? I swear you're as tall as Danny."

"No. Danny's still got a couple of inches on me." Frankie smiled. "Is he speaking to you yet?"

"Not a word, but I'm glad to know you're still in touch with him."

"Yeah, he'll come around." Frankie soothed. "Helen, this is Grace."

She turned to the small woman beside him. "It's nice to meet you, Grace. I hope my height didn't put you off."

"Oh no, I'm pretty used to being short but it might have been scary if you were his mother." She lowered her voice. "I'm nervous. I hope she likes me."

"She's nervous, too." Helen whispered. "Let's go into the living room." She guided Grace to a chair. "You two go watch baseball," she said over her shoulder to Phillip and Frank.

"Gladly," they said together, laughed and went down the hall to the den.

"Sit down, Grace, and let's see what you have in that bag." Helen sat down on the couch across from the chair Grace was in.

"Hello," Gwen bustled into the room with a glass of lemonade. "I'm sorry I wasn't here to greet you. Would you like some lemonade?" She extended her hand and Helen noticed that it was shaking. "I'm Frankie's mom, Gwen."

"Thank you, it's nice to meet you," Grace said taking the glass only seconds before it would have sloshed lemonade in her lap. She took a sip and set the glass on a coaster on the table beside her. Helen noticed that Grace's hand was shaking too.

"I was just asking Grace to show me what was in that big bag of hers."

"Yes, please do." Gwen sat on the couch next to Helen.

"Well," Grace said reaching into the large bag she'd brought. "I do this mostly to manage stress. Medical school is hard and I'm not sure I'm really smart enough. But I want to be a doctor so much." She pulled out a frame and held it against her chest. "This is what a framed piece of my work looks like." She turned it around.

Gwen sucked in her breath. It was a picture of Frankie, the likeness was impressive, done within the confines of cross stitch, but even the shadows on the cheekbones were perfect. "That's beautiful!" Gwen leaned forward and gently took the frame from her hand. "How did you get the pattern?"

"I made it. I have a computer program that will create a pattern from a scanned drawing or photo. I sketched this one." She took another sip of her lemonade and carefully set it back down. "Frank is a very good subject. It makes me feel good to look at him."

Gwen looked up. "You love my son, don't you?"

"Yes I do, very much." They looked at each other in silence for a minute.

"Can we see what else you have in the bag, Grace?" Helen said.

"Oh yes, of course," She reached into the bag and started pulling out pieces. "I thought I could maybe get a loan to frame some of these." She hurried on. "I mean so they would be easier to sell, and I also thought that maybe I could provide a service for people who wanted to do more custom patterns."

"That sounds great," Helen said. "But will you have the time and energy to do this while going to medical school?"

"I do it now. It keeps me from stressing out."

"You might as well make some money from it, then," Gwen said. "I think there is definitely a place in our shop for this, don't you Helen?" Gwen held the frame with Frankie's face in it at arm's length.

"Absolutely,"

"I don't suppose you'd give this to me, would you?"

"No," Grace said quietly but firmly. She reached for the picture and gently pulled it from Gwen's grasp.

"I didn't think so."

*

"So, when do you and Phil run?" Helen asked Matthew at dinner that night.

He looked up from his meal. "In the morning, why?"

"I hadn't noticed you were gone."

"Well, with you sleeping in the other room and me going to work so much earlier than you, that isn't really surprising is it?" he said taking another bite of his salad.

"No, I guess not. What did Dr. Simon say yesterday? You did go, didn't you? You didn't just skip it." She tried to look bored but she did wonder about his physical.

"No I went. Everything was alright. I mean the blood work won't come back for a couple of weeks, of course, but other than that, my blood pressure was high, but she said they can control that with medication. She gave me some samples and a prescription."

"How high was it?"

"She didn't seem too concerned. I took a pill this morning and it didn't seem to make any difference in the way I feel."

"What did she say about exercise?" Helen picked up her plate and Matthews.

He stopped her with a hand on her wrist. "I'm not finished."

"Oh, sorry," she put the plate back down.

"She said it was a good idea but to start slow. She's sending a letter in the mail to show to my trainer. I knew I didn't need to see a doctor." He took another bite of beef stew.

"You did too. You have high blood pressure."

"Yeah, yeah," he said scraping the gravy off his plate and getting up to take it to the sink. "So where are these plans? I'd like to take a look. Maybe I can get started on the estimate tomorrow after Phil and I run."

"They're back in your office." She rinsed the dishes and loaded the dishwasher. "Matt," She stopped him as he was leaving the room. "I'm glad you're doing so well on this exercising."

"You're happy with me about something?" he said. "Good."

*

"So Matt is taking his medication and exercising. He still smokes like a chimney and he won't go an evening without at least one martini but I think he's eating a little less because I can see him losing weight," Helen said.

"I wish I was losing weight," Gwen said as her upper thighs collided with her belly. They were at the Gym exercising. It was mid-June and they had been working out faithfully for six weeks. "I even joined weight watchers. Four weeks I've been on the diet and I've only lost five pounds. It's frustrating."

"I've heard it's better to lose it slowly," Helen said from the nautilus machine next to Gwen.

"What would you know about losing weight?"

"Nothing I guess. I'm just trying to be encouraging." She stood and wiped the sweat from her brow and neck with a damp cloth. "So Gwen, tell me how things are going on your end with the shop."

"Well, it's been a little frustrating with the landlord. He won't let us get in there until they've done their renovations and they seem to be dragging their feet." Gwen stood and changed machines with Helen. "It does look pretty good, though. The new store fronts really do blend with the new mall next door. Have you been by to see it lately?"

"Yeah, it does look good."

"All they have to do now is finish the HVAC system, that's Heating Ventilation and Air Conditioning, and then finish the plumbing. I just wish they'd hurry up so we could get the construction team started. Matt's got one lined up tentatively to start work on July first, but at this rate I'm not sure we'll be in there by then."

"You've talked to Matt?"

"Of course, we're doing a job together. I can see a big difference in him. The exercise is doing him good."

"Hmmm, can't they all work in there together?"

"I guess they could, but Mr. Robins wouldn't let me sign the lease on June first because the work wasn't done. I don't know if he'll let me on July first if it still isn't finished." Gwen stopped and mopped her face. "I've had enough of this, Helen. I'm going to take a shower."

"I'll stop now too," Helen said as she followed her to the locker room. "You know, Gwen, you've done a great job of pulling this all together. I haven't been much help, I'm afraid." They went into shower stalls beside each other and turned on the water.

"You've done a lot Helen. You lined up a printer for the ad magazine. Bye the way, I found a local freelance writer who would like to write a focus article for the magazine on the city of Sandy Springs."

"I thought it was just an advertising production."

"It was but I think we'll be more effective if we add a little community interest to it, don't you?"

"I guess that's a pretty good idea," Helen said thoughtfully as they stepped out of the shower and both started to towel off. "Anyway, Gwen, I think I'll pay Mr. Robins a visit. I just want to give a little prod."

"I was hoping you'd do that. You're a little more effective than me."

"Just pushier, that's all. Gwen, have you ever met the landlord?"

"No. Why?"

"No reason, I just wondered why he doesn't do any of this himself."

"He probably has a lot of commercial properties. I think he's rich and he just buys the properties then pays someone to run them."

"You're probably right."

*

"Gwen, who is keeping your books?" Phillip asked as they were getting ready for bed.

"I am."

He turned around and looked at her. "Do you think that's a good idea? Remember when you tried to do the family budget?"

"You just got hysterical, Phil, everything was fine," she said as she pulled her blouse off over her head. "Besides I got a computer program."

"Everything was not fine and I didn't think you knew anything about computers." Phillip crossed the room to where she was unfastening her bra. "You look great," he said rubbing his hand over her round bottom.

"I do not. You're just trying to get something from me. I can't stand how fat I am."

"I am trying to get something." He kissed her and ran his hand up her back. "But you do look great. I think the exercise is working."

"I haven't lost but five pounds and I've been so good. I'm afraid I'm going to look like this for the rest of my life."

"Suites me, I think you're beautiful." He propelled her backward to the bed.

"Phil, I'm not sure I'm in the mood for this."

"I'm sure I am. Let me talk you into it." He rolled her backwards onto the bed and crawled up over her, straddling her with his knees. He nibbled her breast then kissed her mouth. Why doesn't she know how beautiful she is? He thought as he rolled to the bed beside her and ran his hand the length of her body.

"Anyway, what does this have to do with keeping my books?"

"I want to keep your books," he said leaning down to nibble at her other breast.

"You don't think that I can do it." She stiffened and tried to roll away.

He pulled her back to him and kissed her mouth again running his thumb around her nipple as he did. "I just think I can do it better. I'm an accountant you know."

"I can't afford you. B. B. and James is way too expensive a firm for me." Gasping as he ran his hand down her belly and over her pelvic mound.

"I won't be working for B. B. and James. I'll be working for you, independently from them." He inserted a finger in the moist warm spot between her legs and began to massage her as he nibbled her neck.

Gwen gasped as he moved down her body with his mouth and began to lick the tender spot above his hand. "Ohhhh..." She whispered as the sensations engulfed her. "Can you do that?"

"Only if you want me to," he whispered and raised his eyes to meet hers.

"I mean work for me independently from them," she said on a moan.

Phillip moved up to her face and kissed her. "That too," He positioned himself between her legs and eased gently inside then stopped and looking down at her he kissed her again.

She tasted the tartness of herself on his lips and raised her hips to him. He pulled back only slightly. "Are you blackmailing me?" She asked her eyes widening.

"No, you know I won't stop now unless you want me to." He pushed further inside only slightly, desperately resisting the urge to plunge.

"Please don't stop now." She whispered and gasped as he buried himself inside of her and started the movement that never failed to delight her.

"Can I keep your books?" Phillip asked when they lay beaded with sweat and sated.

"Why do you want to?"

"I want to be a part of your new business."

"Well, alright then."

Chapter Three

"Hellllooo."

"Dad!" Helen yelled into the phone. "It's me, Helen. I was hoping to come and see you tomorrow about mid-morning," she said.

"Why?"

"Just a visit and I have a few little things I bought for you."

"I already have everything I want." He spoke loudly. "And your brother was visiting all week from Texas. I'm not in the mood for more company."

Helen winced. Her father could be so brutal. "Well, Dad, it's the only chance I'll have all week and I'd like to see you. Don't eat breakfast. I'm bringing English muffins and a surprise to put on them. You'll love it."

"I only eat fruit for breakfast."

"I'll come about ten o'clock then. This will be brunch, so don't eat too much fruit." She hung up the phone and put her face in her hands. She rubbed her eyes and then looked up at the small basket she had prepared to take to visit her father at his assisted living apartment.

"Going to see your dad?" Matt said as he came into the room. He went to the sink and washed his hands.

"Where did you come from? I thought you'd gone to the Gym."

"I got back a while ago. I was just outside pruning some of the azaleas up front." He dried his hands on a towel and looked inside the basket she was holding. "Fixed up a goody bag for him?"

"Yeah, I'm going tomorrow morning."

"Do you want me to come? Phil and I are going running, but we have to get up pretty early to beat the summer heat. I could be ready to go by nine thirty or ten."

"I know he'd love to see you but I want to go by myself. I made this apple ginger jelly from my mom's recipe and I want it to be kind of a special thing between him and me," she said holding the jar of jelly up and smiling.

"That's nice, honey, I'm sure he'll appreciate it." Matt looked at her with concern. Helen always tried to please her father but since her mother died a few years back, nothing anyone did ever pleased him. He knew the old man was lonely for his wife but he hated the way Helen kept getting hurt by it. "Tell him I'll come by later in the week. I have a job over that way. I can take a few minutes to visit with him."

"I'll tell him. So, Matt, you seem to have really gotten into running with Phil, I mean to get up early on a Sunday morning. That's commitment. How far are you running now?" Helen asked.

"Two miles, you know I'm almost starting to enjoy it. I think the weight training helps with the running, too. If your muscles are toned it's less painful, even if your chest and lungs need work."

"Do you get short of breath?"

"Sometimes, but if I do, I just slow down a little."

"Maybe if you stopped smoking?"

"Leave it alone, Helen. I've cut back to only five cigarettes a day. I'm doing well," Matt said as he turned to leave the room.

"Yes you are," she said quietly.

*

Helen stood outside the door to her father's apartment. She could hear the television blasting on the other side of the door but it wasn't any louder than the music coming from the apartment across the hall. She knocked on the door and waited but there was no response.

"Dad!" She called opening the door a crack and peeking in to be sure he was dressed and ready for her. He sat in his recliner with his head slumped to the side. A chill ran up her spine as she studied him then she relaxed as she saw his chest rising and falling and heard the rumble of a low snore.

She put the basket down on the table and went into the living room to find the remote control. She located it on the chair next to him and pressed the button to turn off the television set.

"Hey," he said. "I was watching that."

"You were asleep, Dad," she said as she bent to kiss his forehead.

"I was not." He looked up at her and smiled reluctantly. "I was just resting my eyes."

Helen swallowed the lump in her throat that she felt every time she saw her father. He was so withered. He had been a tall handsome man. She could still see a shadow of the man he'd been but his wavy white hair barely covered his head now and his broad shoulders sagged with weariness.

"Look what I brought you, Dad." Helen pulled the jar of jelly out of her basket.

He took it and turned it around in his hand to read the label.

"Its apple ginger jelly, your favorite." She beamed. "I made it from Mom's recipe."

"It isn't red."

"I left out the food dye. It won't make a difference in the taste." She took the jar from him and he picked up the remote control. "Don't turn the TV back on Dad," she said. "I'm going to make us an English muffin with some of this light butter and we'll try some of the Jelly."

"Okay, but, I can watch and eat at the same time," he said as he flicked the television back on and the noise resumed.

Helen took a deep breath and turned to the small kitchen where the toaster oven was. She went about making the muffins then unfolded a TV-tray and put it between his chair and hers. "Here, I'll open the jar." She picked it up and loosened the top. "Do you want me to put some on for you?"

"Alright, do you have any tea?" he asked.

"Yes." Helen smiled pleased that she had remembered. "I made some licorice tea, your favorite. Here," She handed him a napkin and then poured some tea for both of them. She took a bite of her muffin. "It tastes pretty good. Mom's recipe was the best." She felt exhausted having to talk over the volume of the television set.

Her father ate the whole muffin in just a few bites then took a sip of his hot tea.

"What did you think, Dad?"

"What?" He yelled without taking his eyes from the picture.

"How did you like the jelly?" she said even louder than before.

"It's not the same if it's not red." He still didn't look away from the television set.

Helen picked up the remote control and pressed the button to mute the sound. "I just can't please you, can I Dad?" she said feeling the tears threatening at the back of her eyes.

He looked at her then and his eyes softened. "I'm sorry if I hurt your feelings, Helen." They looked at each other for a minute. "But you shouldn't try to compete with your mother." He reached for the remote control and turned up the sound.

"I wasn't trying to compete with anyone," she said as she stood and prepared to leave.

*

Matthew was working in the garden when Helen pulled into the driveway and proceeded to the Garage. She pulled the car into the garage and closed the door without coming out to see what he was doing. She'd been very distant lately. The unhappiness she'd expressed toward him had really shaken him up. She was working up to leaving him. He could feel it.

He swallowed a lump in his throat as he stood up from the bed of impatiens he'd been weeding and pulled off his gloves. I can't live without her. He thought. I hope I didn't figure it out too late.

Washing his hands he went into the house and trained his ears to detect what part of the house she was in. There were clear sounds coming from the bar in the living room.

"That bad?" he said from the living room door.

Helen was standing at the bar shaking a pitcher of martinis. "That bad," she said getting down a second martini glass. "Want one? I made a double for me but if you want one you can have it."

"No thanks, it's a little early for me," he said coming to her side. "I don't think I've ever seen you have a drink this early either. Tell me what happened."

"I don't want to talk about it," she said emptying the contents of the pitcher into her glass and taking a sip. She turned to Matthew and smiled coldly. "I left out the food coloring."

"The food coloring?"

"Yes, Mom always died her jelly. Apple ginger was red. Apple mint was green, Apple cinnamon was blue and onion was yellow. I left it out." She went to the couch and sat down, took another sip of her martini and put the glass on the table beside her. "Maybe all that food coloring had something to do with why she died of cancer."

"Maybe," Matthew said sitting down beside her and putting his arm around her shoulders.

"Don't be nice to me, Matt," she said shrugging him off. "I'll crumble."

"You can crumble if you need to," he said putting his arm back on her shoulder. "I'm sorry he hurt you. He just can't see anything but how much he misses your mother."

"I miss her too. I loved her very much. But I still love him without her. He still has a son and a daughter. Why can't he be grateful for that? Do you know what he said to me?" She took another sip of her martini then another.

"Slow down, Helen, you're not used to hard liquor." Matthew took the glass from her hand and put it down on the coffee table. "What did he say to you?"

"You have no right to dictate to me about drinking, Matt." Helen's eyes sparked.

"I'm not dictating to you. You can drink all you want. I just suggest you slow down. What did he say to you?"

Helen leaned forward, retrieved the drink, took another sip and put it on the table beside her. "He said I should never try to compete with my mother." Her hands covered her face and she began to sob.

"I'm sorry, sweetheart." Matthew pulled her across his lap and she curled into a ball against him.

"I wasn't trying to compete with anyone." She sobbed. "I felt small as I left that apartment, a five foot eight woman, Matt. I felt invisible."

"You're not invisible." Matthew soothed. "You're not small."

Helen sobbed in his arms until the tears slowly dried. She became aware of the stiffening of his penis against her leg and pulled slightly away. "I can't have sex with you, Matt. I just couldn't right now."

"I don't expect you to, Helen. Just relax." He pulled her back to his chest and buried his face in her hair savoring the scent of her.

*

"Gwen, could you come in here for a minute." Phillip called from the small room off the kitchen where he had put together a small home office. He did all the household budget and project budgets. He was always working on restoring some car and he was such an accountant he had accounts he used to save money to do it. He was determined not to get to retirement age with a pile of debts to pay.

"What is it, Phil? I'm starting a new mix of bath salts and I need to hide in my workshop for a couple of hours."

"Could you give me a few minutes before you go in?" He turned from the computer. "I have a little problem I need to talk to you about."

"What's wrong, Phil?" she sat on the stool beside his chair. "You're not sick or something, are you?"

"No." He smiled at her and put his hand on her knee. "But thanks for the concern. It's my Mother."

"Oh no, has something happened? Not pneumonia again, I hope." Gwen leaned forward in concern. "I went to see her last week and she seemed fine."

"No, she's doing pretty well. In fact, I've been able to cut out all the sitters except from the hours of midnight to seven am. She still needs help in the night since she has to go to the bathroom seventeen times." They laughed together. "And she needs help with her shower in the morning. But other than that she's pretty self sufficient."

"So what's the problem?"

"Money, she's running out of money." Phillip turned back to the computer. "Let me show you the figures."

"Phil, don't show me figures. I trust your assessment. Just tell me the bottom line."

"She ran through a lot of it right after the stroke. Remember she had to have round the clock sitters." Phillip looked at her. She nodded her agreement and he went on. "Well, at this point, she still has some left, enough to last a couple more years spending at this rate, but I don't want to wish her life away and I don't like the thought of putting her into a Medicare approved nursing home when she's still so vital."

"We won't do that. I love Martha. She and I get along fine. She'll come here."

Phillip smiled and leaned forward to kiss his wife. "I love you, Gwen. What did I ever do to deserve you?"

"So that was what you were hoping I'd say."

"Yes, but I know you said that on the spur of the moment. I want you to think about it. My mother can be very bossy and very critical. It would be an adjustment."

"Well, let's just think about it." Gwen stood and walked over to the window. She looked out at the garden for a minute. "Where will we put her?"

"I was thinking that you and I could move upstairs. There are three bedrooms up there. Roddy still comes home for holidays and summers, but Andrea and Frankie aren't ever going to live here again. Andrea's bedroom has its own bath. Let's go in and redecorate it for us. Make it our bedroom. We can make Frankie's a guest room and Roddy still has his place on the other end of the house from us. We've got our privacy and Mom can have the master bedroom down here on the first floor."

"You've really thought this through. You had a lot of faith in me."

"I did but I still want you to think about it. If it's really too much we'll find another way." He came to the window beside her and put his hand around her waist. "I mean that, Gwen."

"I'm fine with it, sounds like a good change." She looked up at him. "I think changing the kid's rooms might be hard for me, though."

"Me too, but we'll do it together." Phillip kissed her. His throat felt tight. "I love you so much, Gwen. I'm glad we're not going through what Helen and Matt are."

"I'm glad too. I'm worried about that," she said. "So how long do we have to make these changes?"

"Well, first we have to talk to Mom. I hope she's not too attached to that place."

"I don't think she is. All she really does anymore is watch TV. She doesn't use any of the functions they provide at the assisted living place," Gwen said. "…But what about meals? They feed her three times a day."

"Well, you feed me twice a day. I think if we don't have to pay the huge rent on that apartment, we can afford to have someone here at night. With both of us so busy, we can't help her go to the bathroom seventeen times at night." They laughed together again. "And I think we can swing having a sitter for three or four hours during the day, at lunch time, to get her fed and out to the grocery store or anything else she might need."

"You've worked on this."

"I've been thinking about it for a while. I've also looked into a service for transportation to appointments and whatever. It won't all fall on you Gwen." He assured her. "I figure two months. I'll give notice at the assisted living complex."

"Can I go to my workshop then?"

"Go to your workshop."

"I think I'll call Helen and Matt and invite them to dinner first. Is that alright with you?"

"Sounds great," He had already turned back to the computer and was shutting it down. "While you're in your workshop, though, I'll be in the garage with the Healy, okay?"

"Okay."

*

"Helen," She heard the voice from far away, but wasn't sure it was real. "Helen," It was real. It was Matt.

"Hmmm," she said not opening her eyes. Her head ached a little bit but it wasn't too bad. She was afraid to open her eyes. What would light do to her?

"Gwen just called. She wants us to come to dinner tonight," Matthew said. "We don't have to go but we don't have any other plans and as far as I can tell, you haven't eaten anything today but an English muffin."

She opened one eye. Matthew was sitting beside her on the bed looking down at her. She opened the other eye and looked around. They were in the guest room where she'd been sleeping for the last few weeks. She felt for her clothing. She was fully dressed. Good. "What did you tell her?" she asked surprised by the croaking sound of her voice.

"I said I'd check with you and call her back. She's doing corn on the cob again and she has chicken wings and salad. She isn't grilling, though. It's too hot outside."

"I don't think I can eat." Helen pushed herself up in the bed and leaned against the pillows.

"Honey, you went to sleep at just a little past noon and its four thirty," Matt said standing up and going to the door. "If you don't want to go over there, we'll need to go out because you have to eat something."

"Whoa," she said. "I slept all day?"

"You had a double martini before noon. I think sleeping all day was a good idea." Matthew laughed. "What should I tell Gwen?"

"Tell her we'll be there. I'm going to take a shower."

*

"Come in." Phillip ushered them into the kitchen where Gwen was putting together dinner.

"Hey, Matt," Gwen said. "Hey, Helen, anyone want a glass of wine?"

"No thank you," Helen said quickly. Gwen looked at her surprised.

"Helen visited her father this morning," Matthew said. "She had a double martini when she got back."

"...at 11:30 am," Helen added. "Have you got any ginger ale?"

"Yes, I'll put it on ice." Gwen laughed. "Do you need some aspirin?"

"I already took some."

"Come in to the bar, Matt." Phillip laughed. "I'll fix you a martini."

"Wine is fine with me, today, Phil. I'm cutting back."

"Speaking of which, I changed the menu a little, guys," Gwen said. "Chicken wings are just too fat. We're having skinless thighs. I did them in the clay cooker so they wouldn't dry out. I guess we're all trying to get a little healthier."

"Life style changes are hard, though," Matthew said. "I think it would be easier if I'd get some results. I just don't feel like I'm getting anywhere."

"I feel the same way," Gwen said. "I've been on weight watchers for six weeks now and I've only lost seven pounds."

"That's a good weight loss, dear," Phillip said. "And you don't need to lose much. It's about more than losing weight. It's about getting in shape and I personally like your shape."

"Thanks sweetie." Gwen kissed Phillip's cheek as she set a bowl of potato salad and one of Cole slaw on the table.

"You two are disgusting," Helen said.

"I think they're refreshing." Matthew squeezed Gwen's shoulder as she put a plate down in front of him.

"But I want to lose pounds." Gwen continued. "Why don't you think you're getting results, Matt? I can see a real difference in you. You're shaping up." She patted his flattening middle playfully.

"Yeah, I have lost some weight but I'm still tired all the time. I just wish I had some more energy."

"You're still working out regularly, though," Phillip said. "I guess this is a lesson we all have to learn. At our age you have to be patient. Changes happen more slowly."

"I think we're all doing great," Helen sipped her ginger ale.

"What are you talking about, Helen?" Gwen said. "You've never had to lose weight and you stay in shape naturally."

"I may not have a weight problem but I could feel how my muscles had gotten soft before we joined the Gym," she said. "And when we started walking three times a week and cycling I could hardly go any distance at all without getting winded. That reminds me," Helen said getting up to help Gwen set the table. "I was thinking how the four of us haven't gotten away together for a long time. Let's go hiking next weekend. Just one day, we don't have to camp or anything."

"That's a great idea," Phillip said. "I'll look for a trail in my book of Georgia hiking. We'll start with a short one, maybe just two or three miles."

"I'll pack a lunch," Gwen said.

"I hope I don't embarrass myself." Matthew laughed. "But I agree it sounds like a good idea. Maybe that's exactly what I need to refresh me. Some cool mountain air and wilderness. Let's find a trail in the mountains, Phil."

They all sat down to dinner in the bright kitchen alcove.

"I grilled the corn last night. It's just as good cold," Gwen said. "In fact the only thing warm on this table is the chicken. I think this is the hottest it's ever been in the end of June."

"It is hot outside," Helen said. "So Gwen we sign the lease on the shop tomorrow. I can't believe it's already July first."

"Me neither, when can the construction crew come in to get started, Matt?"

"They'll be there on Wednesday, but of course, Thursday is the fourth of July, so we won't get very far this week, but it's a start."

"That's right. Dandy and Greg are moving in on the fourth. So that will be over for our hike on Saturday," Helen said. "Are you still thinking of opening on October first, Gwen?"

"If we possibly can."

"We'll give it our best," Matthew said as he started on his dinner.

*

"Here we are, Gwen."

"I'm nervous."

"About what? We're just signing a lease." Helen sat next to Gwen in the small office of the agent. "We've had the lawyer go over it. We've pretty much gotten everything we wanted. We even managed to get the landlord to pay for the exterminator."

"It's a five year lease, though. I just wish it wasn't so long."

"I'm planning to be here five years, aren't you?"

"Yes, but..."

"No buts. Anyway, here is Mr. Robins."

Mr. Robins came out of the back room just as Matthew and Phillip came through the front door.

"What are you two doing here?" Helen asked.

"Just wanted to add some moral support," Phillip said sitting down beside Gwen.

"We don't need moral support." Helen snapped.

"I do," Gwen said taking Phil's hand. "Did I see Grace outside?" She strained to see out the window.

"Yes. She and Frankie wanted to see the store. They said they'd wait outside."

"It's too hot out there. Tell them to come in." Phillip got up to go after them.

"I'll leave if you want me to, Helen," Matthew said from the door.

"No as long as you're here you might as well stay." Helen felt intruded on. It was her store and so far he was spending more time in it than she was. He'd even be working in it before she would.

"If you're sure," he said sitting down in a chair at the other end of the table from her.

Frankie and Grace came in with Phillip and they all sat down. The lease was signed and they all agreed to go to the store to take a look at it. When they got out the door onto the street Helen and Gwen hugged each other.

"We did it, Helen. We're on our way." Gwen jumped up and down like a child. The whole group moved together down the sidewalk to the store. The new store fronts were impressive. They all stood and admired them. Then Gwen looked at Helen and held out the key to the shop. "You open it, Helen. My hands are shaking."

Helen put a steadying hand on Gwen's. "We'll do it together, Gwen. We're partners." They put the key in the lock and turned it, their hands still joined. The whole group applauded as the door swung open and they went inside.

"Man, look at that HVAC work." Frankie looked up at the ceiling. The false ceiling had been removed for the renovations and everything was exposed. Gwen smiled at her son's enthusiasm.

"He spends most of his time looking at the ceiling these days," Grace said looking at Frankie adoringly.

"I'm glad he enjoys what he does."

"I wonder who did this. I wish I could have worked on it," Frankie said.

"Well, we're going to be here five years, Frankie," Helen said. "You still may get a chance." She went toward the back of the store where the storage room was. "We're taking these walls down, right Gwen?"

"That's right. We're not going to have storage space. Well, besides a small storage closet in the back next to the office. We're going to have all of our merchandise on display. Oh, Helen, I wanted to ask you if it was okay if we called it a gallery instead of a gift shop. That's really what it is. I thought 'Gwen and Helen's Gallery' I know your name was first before, but I didn't want the G's too close."

"I like it. I don't care whose name comes first." Helen laughed. "Will you have to change the sign?"

"No, I haven't put in the order yet. I plan to do that tomorrow. Where is the light switch again Phil?" she said peering in to the back room.

"I'll find it," he said pulling his pen light out and going through the door.

The light came on and they all filed in.

"The office will be in this corner and the closet will be here next to it." Helen said. "There will be a window in the office and another one here." She indicated the back wall of the store. "The owner is encouraging burglar bars but I think a good alarm system should do the trick."

They all looked around the store for a while and discussed their various interests.

"I made reservations at that new Italian restaurant over at the mall," Helen said. "But I only made them for two. I didn't realize we'd have such a group."

"We'll just change the reservations," Gwen said. "Here, I've got my cell." She reached in her purse for the phone.

"You have a cell phone, Mom?" Frankie laughed. "Will wonders never cease?"

*

The phone was ringing. It took Gwen a minute to figure out what was bothering her. She glanced at the clock, 2:00 am. "Oh no!" she said as she looked at the lit caller ID screen. "Phil, it's the hospital. One of the kids... Hello?" she said into the receiver.

"Gwen, this is Helen." Her voice was ominously low. "I'm at the hospital. Matt had a stroke."

Chapter Four

Helen sat in the brightly lit emergency room in a straight back chair. Her hands gripped the metal arms and she stared at the sterile white wall across the room. The television was blasting over her head to the right. She knew it was bothering her but she was afraid to turn it off, afraid of what she would feel if that irritation was gone. Her entire body was humming as if all of her nerve endings were standing up and quivering.

"Helen," Gwen said as she opened the door to the room and peered around the curtain. "Oh Helen," She rushed across the room and pulled her into her arms.

Helen wondered how Gwen had managed to embrace her when she was paralyzed in the chair, clamped to it by hands like steel cuffs. The next thing she knew she had her arms around her best friend and Gwen was whispering something into her hair. She didn't know what but she liked it.

"Where is Matt?" Phillip's voice came from somewhere behind Gwen.

"He's gone to get a CT scan," she said. Her voice sounded muffled. Her face was smashed somewhere in Gwen's middle. Gwen stroked her hair and she felt Phillip's firm hand on her shoulder. She pushed herself back enough to look up at them and Gwen loosened her hold and stepped back. "He's been gone about twenty minutes. I don't know how long these things take."

"What happened?" Phillip asked. "I mean, if you don't want to talk, don't. I just..."

"He said he was tired and went back to his room." She started, sounding dazed. "He and I aren't sharing the same room ... you know ... things haven't been good between us for a while." She met Gwen's eyes sadly.

Gwen nodded and put a hand on Phillip's arm.

Helen had seen the contraction of Phillip's lips and the narrowing of his eyes. She couldn't be mad at him. After all, Matthew was his best friend. "I was just going to put on my p.j. and go back outside for a minute to wind down. It's hot out but I still like to end my day sitting outside for a few minutes. But when I got about half way down the hall, I heard strange noises coming from Matt's room." She paused and rubbed her eyes. "Our room..., it was a strange humming sound." Her voice had become a steady tone and her eyes were focused on the wall on the other side of the room.

"The door was open so I went in without knocking. He was lying across the bed on his back. The strange sound was coming from him. I called his name and he looked at me. His eyes were open but I don't think he was seeing me. His lips started to move and sounds came out but I couldn't understand anything he said."

"Oh Helen, you must have been terrified," Gwen said.

"Terrified isn't exactly the word." Helen spoke quietly. "Horrified works better. Anyway, I said, "Matt, can you move?" Now I think about it that was a stupid question. He obviously couldn't move, although he did turn his head to look at me." She stopped and narrowed her eyes, trying to remember the details.

"So I picked up his right hand and dropped it. It just fell limply to the bed. He kept looking at me but I really don't think he could see me."

"What did you do?" Gwen had seated herself on the floor cross legged and pried Helen's hand off the arm of the chair. She was holding it in both of hers.

"I called 911."

"Has he been able to talk to you at all yet?" Phillip asked. He looked uncomfortable shifting from one foot to the other in front of her.

"I'm sorry I can't offer you a chair," Helen said. "There's only one in the room and I can't seem to get out of it." She took a deep breath. "It seems like he's trying to talk but I can't understand any of it. They haven't told me it's a stroke yet but his father died of a stroke in his mid-fifties. I was there. I know what it looks like."

"He isn't going to die," Phillip said emphatically.

Helen looked up at him for the first time, her eyes widened.

The door opened and two people dressed in scrubs pushed the hospital bed into the room. Matthew lay in the bed looking frightened. A man in a white coat followed them in and looked at Phillip then at Gwen.

"I need to talk to Mr. and Mrs. Riddick," he said. "Alone. Maybe you could wait in the lobby?"

"Of course," Gwen said getting up and reluctantly letting go of Helen's hand. "Come on

Phil." She took his arm and propelled him toward the door.

"Wait." He pulled his arm away from her and went over to the bed where Matthew lay staring wide eyed at the small group of people. He put his hand on Matthew's arm and said, "We're here, Matt. You'll be alright."

Matthew looked up at him frightened and a tear fell out of each eye, one sliding down the side of his face and the other rolling over the bridge of his nose.

"That's right, Matt." Gwen stood beside Phillip. "We love you." She sniffed and taking Phillip's hand urged him out of the room.

*

"She's an unfeeling bitch," Phillip said as he paced the small space in front of Gwen's chair in the tiny corner they'd claimed of the busy ER waiting room. "She told that story without any feeling, not a single tear."

"She's in shock, Phil. Give her a break."

"Come on, Gwen. She didn't even go to his bedside when he came back into the room." He ran his hand through his hair and turned to pace some more. "He can't say anything, obviously, but he knows there's something very wrong and he's scared to death. I could see it in his eyes."

"Me too,"

"Helen just sat there in that chair and stared at the wall."

"Think about what she's been through."

"Gwen," He stopped in front of her chair and went to his knees so that his eyes were level with hers. "I don't care what I'd been through, if it was you, I'd have been by your side with my hand on yours telling you everything was going to be fine."

Gwen looked into his eyes and knew it was true. There were tears swimming behind his lids and his voice broke on every word.

"I'd like to think you'd do the same thing for me?" he pleaded.

"I hope I would." She touched his cheek. "I'm pretty sure I would but Phil, how can any of us know. Experiences like that put us away from ourselves."

He looked down at the floor and took a deep breath. Standing he walked to the window on the wall that Gwen's chair was facing and ran his hand through his hair like he always did when he was upset. "Maybe, but I got the feeling she wished he'd died."

Gwen's resolve not to cry disintegrated. She put her face in her hands.

*

"Gwen?" Helen said. She saw her across the room crying. Phillip was sitting beside her holding her hand in both of his. She took a deep breath and walked across the room to them. "Can you guys take me home? I came in the ambulance."

"Shouldn't you stay with Matt?" Phillip said. His eyes narrowed.

"They're admitting him." She looked at him and gasped at the anger in his eyes. "He's asleep, Phil. They've placed an IV and I think they gave him something to calm him. He's been so agitated the whole time, but he went to sleep so I think they must have given him something."

"They didn't tell you?"

"No."

"You didn't ask?"

"No, Phil, why are you so angry with me?" she asked.

"You just don't seem very upset." He went to the window and stared out at the night.

"I'm numb but screw you then. I'll get a cab."

"Helen, don't do that," Gwen said getting to her feet. "We'll take you home." She went to Helen and hugged her. Helen was stiff. She put her arms around Gwen but they were rigid and she only held her for a second.

"Stop acting like an ass, Phil." Gwen swallowed and looked at him. "We're all upset. If you don't want to drive give me the keys."

Phillip took a deep breath, turned and pulling the keys out of his pocket, tossed them to Gwen and walked out of the building.

Gwen picked the keys up off the floor in front of her where they'd landed and she and Helen walked out behind him. He was nowhere in sight. "Well, let's go." She started toward the parking lot. When they got to the car, Phillip was still nowhere. Gwen unlocked the doors with the keyless remote.

"Where's Phil?" Helen asked. "We can't just leave him."

"Get in Helen. He needs to walk off some pain." She got into the driver's seat and Helen settled in the passenger seat beside her.

"It's," she looked at her watch, "3:30 am. He can't just walk around in the middle of the night."

"We only live a mile and a half from here," Gwen said as she started the car and pulled out of the lot. "He'll be alright."

They moved onto the road and headed toward Helen's house. "Are you sure you don't want to come to our house tonight? You have to be in shock," Gwen said.

"No, I need to go home." Helen yawned. "I want to get a few hours of sleep before I have to get up and start making phone calls."

"That's right. You have some work to do."

"Well, mostly I need to call Matthew's office and tell them what's going on. They need to assign someone new to run the project at the store."

"Helen, don't even think about that right now. It can wait."

"No it can't." She leaned her head back and took a deep breath. "Of course, I'll need to call the kids, well, Dandy anyway. I can't call Danny but she will. Maybe I'll get to see him." She looked out the window into the night. "I'll wait to call Matt's brother until I get the prognosis." She closed her eyes and yawned.

Gwen took a deep breath. Phillip was right. Helen didn't seem to care about what Matthew was going through. She looked at her friend. Her eyes were closed and she could see her heart beating against her ribs. She was surely in shock.

Gwen pulled into Helen's driveway and stopped. Helen opened her eyes and stared at the house. After a minute she seemed to snap out of some trance and reached to the floor of the car to gather her purse.

"Thanks for the ride, Gwen. You and Phil are good friends to rescue me in the middle of the night." She put her arms around Gwen's neck for a quick embrace then got out of the car.

Gwen watched her go to the door and unlock it. She watched until she was inside and the foyer light had been flicked on. "That's what we did," she said out loud as she pulled the car out of the driveway. "We rescued her, but Matt had the stroke."

When she got home, Phillip was already there. "I'm so glad you're home," she said. "I knew you needed to walk but we do live in a big city with a high crime rate." She sat down on the bed where Phillip was leaning back on his pillows with a martini in his hand. "I think I'll get one of those," she said and went into the kitchen to pour herself a glass of wine.

"I'll regret this in a few hours," he said.

"Me too,"

"Gwen, was I wrong or did Helen seem way too removed?"

"You weren't wrong, Phil," she said as she pulled off her clothes. She put on a nightgown and settled herself in the bed against the pillows. "But you know they've been having a hard time. She's probably dealing with some guilt or something." She sipped her wine. "I don't know, but I do know that I love Helen. She's my best friend. I need to give her the benefit of the doubt."

"I guess so." Phillip sipped. "I love her, too, but not as much as I love Matt." He laughed uncomfortably. "That sounded a little strange but he's my best friend and I'll never be able to stop seeing the look of fear in his eyes. And tears, Gwen, he cried." Phillip's voice broke and he took another sip of his drink. "Maybe I should have stayed if she couldn't."

"He was asleep Phil. Helen had been up all night. She had to sleep before she called the kids and his work." She winced remembering that Helen's first concern had been that the shop project not be delayed. It was good that Phillip hadn't heard that.

"I guess so." He drained his glass and put it down on his bedside table. He scooted down in the bed and rolled over. "I think I may be able to sleep now."

"Go ahead and turn out the light," she said sipping her wine. "I'm going to sit up for a little longer."

*

Matthew turned his head toward the door of the hospital room as it opened. Delia came in and hurried to his bed. He could barely see her. For a while he hadn't been able to see anything. He could hear but he couldn't see. Now his vision was clearing a little. It was like looking through thick fog. She was on his left side. Good, he thought as he reached up to her with his left hand. She took it with both of hers and pressed it to her heart. She was crying.

"Daddy, I love you." The words came out on a sob. "Please be alright."

He squeezed her hand and opened his mouth to say something but he couldn't understand the sound he made. He could remember the pain that had shot through his head last night when he'd gone to bed. He remembered lying down and knowing he had to call for help.

But the sounds he'd made were unclear. After that he had drifted in and out of awareness but he was sure that he'd tried to talk. He couldn't understand what he'd said and obviously nobody else could understand it either.

The door to his hospital room opened again and Helen came in. She hurried to the side of the bed where Delia was standing and put her arms around their daughter. He tried to smile but knew his face wasn't working right. It didn't matter. The sight of his wife and daughter together was so nice. Delia was taller than Helen but she looked like a baby crying in her mother's arms.

"Mom, has he said anything?" she asked.

"Not that I could understand." Helen stroked her daughter's long chestnut hair. Matthew smiled again; only to himself he was sure. He was so glad the twins looked more like their mother than they did like him.

"I think he understands me though." Helen looked down at him. Her eyes were cold. He could see the anger in them and he widened his.

She has a right to be mad. He thought. Look what I've done to myself and to her. I wish I'd died. He closed his eyes. He was so tired. All he wanted was to just drift away, never wake up. Oh, he wished that would happen.

*

"Why didn't you call me last night?" Delia said to Helen.

"I don't know, honey. I was just running on instinct." Helen sat down in the chair at the bedside when it was clear that Matthew had gone to sleep.

"I'm a nurse practitioner, Mom. I may have been able to help."

"I got him here fast, Dandy. I've read about how important it is to get emergency treatment fast for a stroke." Helen rubbed her eyes. She looked up in time to see her daughter dash a tear off her cheek and took a deep breath.

The door opened and a man in a white lab coat came in. They both looked at him.

"Hello," he said. "I'm Dr. Jackson. I've been assigned to Matthew's case."

"I'm Helen Riddick, Matt's wife and this is our daughter Delia." Helen stood and shook his hand.

He nodded at Dandy and said. "I've spent the last hour looking over the results of Matthew's tests. I was hoping he was awake so that I could go over them with him."

"Even if he was awake," Helen said stiffly. "I'm not sure he would understand. He hasn't spoken anything we could understand since last night. I'm his durable power of attorney. Tell me about the test results."

"Well," Dr. Jackson said looking at Delia.

"She's our daughter and she's a nurse practitioner. As his power of attorney, I'm telling you that you can talk to her," Helen said firmly. "I have the papers right here." She dug through the bag she'd brought and handed the papers to Dr. Jackson.

He studied them then looked at the bed. Helen and Delia followed his glance. Matthew was awake, his eyes wide. "Oh, you're awake then," Dr. Jackson said. "Good, is it alright if I talk to your wife and daughter?"

Matthew nodded his head.

"Good. I see that you can understand us."

Matthew nodded again, but he closed his eyes. He was so tired. He wasn't sure he could follow a conversation.

Dr. Jackson hesitated for a minute. "Alright." He turned back to Helen. Delia stepped away from the bed to her mother's side. "Matthew has had a stroke. It has affected the left side of the frontal lobe. That's the part of the brain that controls the right side of the body. That's why his right side is weak."

"And it controls speech. That's the reason for the aphasia," Delia said.

"That's right." Dr. Jackson looked at Helen. "Aphasia is the inability to speak." He explained.

"So his right side is paralyzed and he can't talk," Helen said.

"I'm not sure the right side is paralyzed," Dr. Jackson said, picking up Matt's right hand. He tickled the palm and Matt's fingers twitched. "In fact I'm pretty sure it isn't paralyzed. There are two kinds of stroke, ischemic, which is caused by the interruption of the flow of blood to the brain and a hemorrhagic stroke, which is caused by a rupture of blood vessels in the brain. Your husband's..." He paused and looked at Delia.

"...and father's was ischemic. There is no bleeding in the brain. When someone has an ischemic stroke there is swelling that puts pressure on the surrounding parts of the brain making it hard for them to do their job."

"I don't really understand," Helen said.

"When the swelling goes down," Dr. Jackson said. "We may see some improvement in his impairment."

"So are you telling me that things might go back to normal in a couple of days?"

"No." He looked at Delia.

"No, Mom," she said never taking her eyes off the Doctor. "The damage won't ever be repaired."

Helen looked from Dr. Jackson to Delia to Matthew. "So we have to wait a few days to see how bad it is and that's the way he'll be for the rest of his life?"

"Not necessarily," Dr. Jackson said. "You're right about the damage. It will never be repaired, but the brain is an incredible organ. Other parts of it can be trained to do the things the damaged part has always done before. A lot will depend on him, his determination."

They were all silent looking at Matthew for a minute. His eyes were open only a little.

"And his support system," Dr. Jackson said turning back to Helen. "In cases like this we form a therapy team consisting of several types of therapists, nurses and physicians. He'll be evaluated by every part of the team separately then we'll all get together and plot a recovery plan. I think that will be completed by Monday. I'll let you know about the time. Having family and friends get involved in his recovery can make a big difference. One of the problems we have in these cases is depression. If he sinks too deeply into it, he won't do the work he needs to recover."

Dr. Jackson excused himself and left the room. Only seconds after he closed the door behind him, it opened and Daniel Riddick came in holding the hand of a very pregnant young woman.

"Danny," Helen whispered and stood.

He pulled the girl gently but firmly into the room and put his arm around her shoulder as he positioned her beside him. "Hello, Mom," he said stiffly. "This is Sybil, my wife." He released the girls hand and hurried to his father's bedside.

*

"Hello." Gwen picked up the phone on Saturday morning.

"Hey, Gwen, it's me, Helen. I know we can't go to the mountains for a hike like we'd planned but I was hoping you and Phil could meet me at the Chattahoochee River trail, the one over off of Indian Trail Drive." She held her breath and waited for an answer. "It's only about ten minutes away. I could really use a walk in the woods."

"I'm sure you could," Gwen said. She was surprised by Helen's request but she knew it had been a very rough week for her. "I'll get Phil and we'll meet you there." She hung up the phone and went up the stairs to Andrea's old room where Phillip was stripping wall paper.

"Phil, put that stuff away. I told Helen we'd meet her at the trail down by the river. She needs to walk and I'm sure she needs to talk."

"You're kidding." Phillip turned and looked at her narrowing his eyes. "How can she go for a hike when Matt is lying in a hospital room?"

"She's been in there every day this week and to work and to the shop. If she doesn't take a little time for herself, she won't be any good to him," Gwen said. "Now come on, Phil, Helen needs us, too."

They pulled up to the parking lot of the nature trail a half hour later. Helen was leaning against her car dressed in denim shorts and a t-shirt. She had a back pack sitting next to her on the trunk of the car. She smiled and waved at them.

"She doesn't look terribly worn out to me," Phillip said as he pulled into the space beside her.

"Phil, if you can't treat her with respect then just drop me off here. I guess I shouldn't have made you come."

"I'll try." He gave Gwen a meaningful look and got out of the car.

"Thanks for coming, guys." Helen put her arms around both of them at the same time then turned to toss the pack on her back and started toward the trail. "I just really needed some fresh air and to stretch my legs."

They followed behind her in silence for about the first half mile. The trail began at the bottom of a steep hill so they started out climbing. After about half a mile it settled into a series of switch backs with a more gradual uphill path.

"I can't believe we're doing this without Matt." Phillip broke the silence.

"It's probably just as well." Helen called over her shoulder. "He'd have never been able to keep up with us."

"What do you mean just as well?" Phillip said.

Gwen put her hand on his arm and shook her head.

He pulled his arm free of her. "Just as well he had a stroke so he wouldn't slow us down." He stopped and Helen turned around to look at him. "God, Helen, I knew you were having problems but you've been married to him for thirty years."

"Thirty one, Phil, and of course, I didn't mean that." Her voice was angry. "What is your problem with me, Phil? You've been angry with me ever since this happened. I can see it on your face and I can hear it in your voice when we talk on the phone. I didn't do anything to make Matt stroke out. He did that himself."

"Helen!" Phillip's voice rose. "How can you be so cold? The man needs you." He whirled around and started back down the trail. "I've had enough of this. I'm going back. Are you coming with me, Gwen?"

"No, Phil," she said.

He whirled back around and glared at her.

"Phil," she stepped closer to him and put her hand on his arm. "Helen needs me right now. Maybe you should go to the hospital and see Matt." She pleaded with her eyes for his understanding.

"That's right, Phil. You don't have any problem criticizing me for the way I'm dealing with this but I've been in there every day this week. You haven't been there since it happened," Helen said as she turned to start back up the trail.

Phillip took a deep breath. "She's right. I've been avoiding it. I'm afraid of seeing him again."

"That's understandable sweetheart, but I've been there and he's improving, slowly, but he is improving." She stood on her toes and kissed his cheek. "Go and see Matt. Helen needs to talk." She turned and started back up the trail.

"Gwen, you drive home." Phillip called after her. "Don't let her drive."

"We'll be fine," she said over her shoulder as she hurried to catch up with Helen.

"He hates the way I drive," Helen said when she heard Gwen's footsteps behind her.

"He's upset, Helen, now slow down or I'll have a stroke. It's way too hot this time of year to run up a hill."

Helen slowed her pace and stepped to the side of the trail so that Gwen could come up beside her. "I don't really blame Phil for the way he feels about me, though," she said. "I'm so angry. It's got to show."

"Yeah, it does, but I think I can understand it."

"I'm not sure I can," Helen said. "I just wish I could put on a better show for the kids. They're so upset and frightened. They were always so close to him. Matt is an adoring father. Even the whole time Danny's been not speaking to me, he still kept in touch with his Dad." She turned the corner of another switch back and stone stepped across a small stream. On the other side she turned around and extended a hand to Gwen who was not maneuvering the stones quite as well.

"How are things going at home with Danny and Sybil? I guess that was a shock," Gwen said. "How do you feel about your first grandchild?"

"I haven't really had a chance to think about it. Sybil seems sweet. She's been really shy with me. They're staying in the guest room which used to be Dandy's room because there's a double bed in there and there are bunk beds in Danny's room." She laughed.

"That's understandable."

"Yes, but I was sleeping in there. You know Matt and I haven't been sharing a room for a while."

"You mentioned it."

"And, Dandy and Gregg moved into the basement apartment on Thursday as planned," she said. "They had to be out of their apartment. So I had to move back into the master and, honestly, Gwen, I don't want to share that bed with Matt when he's able to come home. God, I'm just so trapped. That's why I'm angry."

"I guess sleeping in the bottom bunk is out of the question."

"I suppose I could," Helen said.

They walked in silence for a while until they came to the wooden observation deck that looked out over the river from the hilltop. Helen walked out to the deck and sat down. She took off the back pack and pulled two bottles of water out, handed one to Gwen and opened the other. Drinking deeply she put the top back on and pulled out a plastic bag full of red grapes.

"I hate him for what he's done to me," she said, pulled a grape off the bunch and popped it into her mouth. "I know what you're thinking. You're thinking. He didn't do anything to you, he did it to himself. I hate him for that, too," Helen said. "I hate him for not taking care of his health. He knew about his family history. His dad died of a stroke in his mid-fifties and his mother was right behind him of a heart attack. I hate him for not learning from that. Do you know, when I looked in his wallet for his insurance card the night he had the stroke, I found his prescription for blood pressure medication. He hadn't filled it and he'd only taken a few of the samples. They were all still in his drawer."

"He was on blood pressure medicine?"

"He was supposed to be but since I didn't make sure he took it, he didn't. I can't believe he's that stupid. And I'm going straight to Hell for feeling that way."

"I don't think you go to Hell for your feelings. I think you go for your actions and you've stood by him and you'll continue to," Gwen said sitting down on the bench across from her and grabbing for a grape. She'd finished half the bottle of water in one move.

"Oh yeah, I'll support him. That's why I'm trapped." She stood, leaned on the rail, looked out over the river and took a deep breath. "I can't quit my job now. With his income reduced to sixty percent while he's on disability, my income becomes a whole lot more important."

"His prognosis is good, though. Didn't you say the doctor was encouraging?"

"Yes, but he'll never be the same." Helen turned around and leaned back against the rail. "He can't even manage to eat on his own or go to the bathroom. How is he going to manage a construction project? Even if he goes back to work, I'm sure his earning potential will be reduced." She sat back down. "And once again, I'm going straight to Hell because I'm so damned mercenary. But I hate selling insurance, Gwen. Sometimes I think it's going to destroy me, just completely destroy me."

"I planned a salary for both of us for the first year of the store. Maybe it'll take off and you'll be able to quit like you planned."

"Not at first. The salary isn't nearly what I make selling insurance. Oh and get this, Danny says that he and Sybil are moving here from Charlotte. I didn't even know he was in Charlotte. He and Sybil are going to live with us until they get a little money put aside to buy a house. So I'm supporting Matt and me, Dandy and Gregg, Sybil and Danny and a baby. With my luck it'll be twins. They run in families, you know."

"Danny just announced that he's moving back in after he hasn't spoken to you for a year?" Gwen said angrily.

"No, he asked very nicely. He even gave me a hug." Her face crumpled and for the first time she cried. Burying her face in her hands, she sobbed weakly. "It felt so good to see him, to hold him. I had to say yes."

Gwen moved across the platform and sat down next to Helen. She put her arms around her friend and said, "Sucks to be you."

Helen laughed and put her arms around Gwen's neck. They held each other like that until Helen's sobs slowed and stopped. She pulled back and dug a tissue out of her pack. "I knew I'd need these." She dried her eyes then dabbed at Gwen's wet shoulder. "Gwen." She sniffed.

"What?"

"Thank you for not reminding me how hard Matt was trying to improve his lifestyle before this happened."

"You didn't need reminding."

*

Phillip stopped outside Matthew's hospital room and took a deep breath. He knocked on the door and waited. What was he waiting for? Did he think Matt was going to tell him to come in? The door opened and Delia stood in front of him.

"Delia," he said and held out his arms. She moved into them and he held her, stroking her hair. "I think you're actually taller than me," he said.

"I'm a giant." She pulled back and wiped the tears from her eyes with the back of her hand. "Come on in." She turned and went back into the room. Pulling a tissue from the box on the bedside table she wiped her eyes.

"I'm sorry, honey. This has to be hard on you," he said looking at the empty spot where the hospital bed should have been. "Has something happened?" he asked in alarm. "Where's your dad?"

"They've taken him to surgery to place a feeding tube. He's developed a mild pneumonia and they've determined that he can't swallow. I guess he must have aspirated something." She blew her nose. "Although I can't imagine what he could have aspirated. He's lost so much weight in just four days, I'm sure he hasn't eaten anything."

"How could he lose a lot of weight in just four days?" Philip was getting nervous again.

"I guess a six foot three man burns a lot of calories just lying in bed."

The door opened and two nurses wheeled the bed back in. Matt lay in the bed but the back of it was raised and he was sitting up. His eyes were clear. He leaned a little to the right side and his right arm lay awkwardly at his side with the palm turned up. The left hand raised in greeting to Phillip.

"Hey, Matt," Phillip went to the left side of the bed and took Matthew's left hand in an awkward embrace. Shaking it gently, he put it back down on the bed. "Where's the tube?" he asked Delia.

"On his abdomen," she said pulling the sheet back to reveal a plastic port. "They inserted it directly into his stomach. He'll need his mouth free for physical therapy."

"You're a lucky man to have two nurses in the family," Phillip said to Matthew. "Daniel's a nurse too, isn't he?" He looked at Delia.

"Yes, he's a psychiatric nurse. I'm sure we won't need that. Daddy isn't going to get depressed, are you?" Delia stood on the right side of his bed

His right hand lifted in her direction for just a second then moved back toward his chest where it settled, fingers twitching awkwardly.

"You moved your right hand." Delia cheered. "Did you see that, Phil? We're making progress."

They both looked at Matthew in time to see him squeeze his eyes shut. Two large tears rolled down his sunken cheeks. Phillip looked across the bed at Delia and reached for her when he saw the look of pain on her face. She took his hand and turned toward the door as it opened and Daniel came in.

"Daniel, look at you?" Phillip exclaimed. "I thought Frankie was tall. What are you now about six foot four." He shook Daniel's hand and slapped his shoulder.

"You've seen me this tall before, Phil." Daniel smiled and returned the embrace. He walked over to the bed next to Delia and put his arm across her shoulders. "How are you today, Dad? The nurse said you've got a mild pneumonia." He spoke to his father easily and Phillip watched Matthew's features relax. "You're not worried about it, are you? These antibiotics will wipe that right out." Daniel tapped the IV line.

Matthew shook his head.

"They placed a feeding tube," Delia said. "He can't eat. Look how thin he is."

As Delia spoke to her brother, Phillip noticed Matthew tense again.

"Phil, would you entertain Dad for a few minutes?" Daniel asked. "I'm going to take Dandy to the cafeteria for a little lunch. I think she forgot to eat again. I can hear her stomach growling." He guided his sister toward the door.

"Sure, no problem," Phillip watched them leave then turned back to Matthew in time to see him brushing at his tears with his left hand. "If you don't cut that out, you'll have me blubbering here in a minute, and you know that's not a pretty sight."

Matthew sniffed and almost smiled. His expression was bland but he pulled his lips to the left side in a lopsided grin. "Tussss..." he said reaching toward the box of tissue on the table.

Phillip handed him one and watched as he awkwardly blotted his eyes and nose. "Now let's do something about that posture," he said. "Did you know you're listing to the right?

Matthew turned his head to the right and hit the bed rail with his nose. "uuhn," he said.

"See what I mean?" Phillip went around the bed to the other side and lowered the rail. Taking Matthew under the arms he lifted him to a sitting position. The effort shook his balance and he sprawled across Matthew's chest. "Oh no," he said looking up at Matthew, their faces only inches apart. "Did I hurt the tube thing?"

Matthew opened his eyes wide and started to shake. He opened his mouth slightly and laughed a low, rolling, easy laugh. It reminded Phillip of the chuckle of a young child before inhibitions set in.

"You're laughing at me, you schmo. I'm trying to help you and you're laughing at me." Phillip resisted the urge to smile and put on a look of disgust instead. He straightened himself up and smoothed his rumpled shirt. "And you may look like you've lost weight but you still weigh at least a ton." He put the bed rail back in place.

"Thend," Matthew said.

"Did you understand what you just said?" Phil straightened the sheets, "Because I didn't." Although, he thought he might have been trying to say friend.

Matthew shook his head.

"Good, it's not just me then."

Matthew laughed again. This time Phillip laughed with him.

*

The next morning Matthew woke up to the sound of someone calling his name.

"Matthew." He heard. It was a voice that he didn't recognize. He tried to ignore it, tried to pretend he was asleep. He really didn't want to talk to another doctor. Talk, that's a laugh. I haven't talked to anyone since this started. I may never talk to anyone again.

"Matthew," the voice insisted. It was a man's voice. He opened his eyes slowly and looked in the direction of the sound. A tall familiar looking man stood at the foot of the bed. "I came as fast as I could get here." The man moved to the side of the bed and took Matthew's left hand. "I had to tie up some loose ends at the office then I flew down. I'd forgotten how hot it is in Georgia at this time of year. I've gotten so used to Maine."

Matthew gently pulled his hand free and looked at the man. This must be his brother. Helen had told him he was coming but he couldn't remember a brother. He hadn't had a problem recognizing people so far but for the life of him he couldn't remember a brother. Did he have parents, too?

"Don't you recognize me? I'm Mark, your younger brother." The man's brows had pulled together in concern.

Matthew shook his head and closed his eyes again.

"His speech is the hardest part of this." Matthew heard Delia's voice as she came into the room. He opened his eyes again, tried to smile at her and stretched out his hand. She walked to the bed and took it. "I'm Delia, his daughter. I guess you're my Uncle Mark."

"I can't believe he doesn't know me," Mark said.

Matthew shrugged and shook his head apologetically.

"Are you sure? Daddy, do you know Mark? He's your brother." She squeezed Matthew's hand.

He opened his eyes and looked at the stranger standing beside him. He studied his face for a minute then shook his head. "Do ... I ... ummm ... mmm." He shook his head and closed his eyes.

"What are you trying to say, Daddy?" Delia asked, her voice breaking on the words.

"You..." He shook his head again and turned his face away. He knew what he wanted to say. He wanted to ask about his parents but he couldn't.

"This hasn't happened before. I hope he hasn't had another stroke." Delia started to cry. "Daddy, you still know me, don't you?"

Matthew opened his eyes again and nodded vigorously. He squeezed his eyes shut as he felt tears threatening.

"What's going on?" Daniel's voice entered the confusion.

"Daddy doesn't recognize Uncle Mark, Danny. He's never had a problem recognizing anyone before. I'm scared."

"Delia, we've talked about this. You need to get hold of yourself." Daniel turned to the bed. "Dad, have you had another stroke?"

Matthew shook his head and pulled his brows together. "Be ... n.n.n ..." He took Delia's hand and frowned at Daniel.

"He's defending you, Dandy. He's alright." Daniel turned to Mark. "Truth is I don't recognize you either." He held out his hand. "I'm Daniel, Matthew's son."

Mark shook his hand. "The twins," he said looked between the two of them. "I remember when you were little. I guess time just got away from me."

"When was the last time you saw Dad?"

"I was here when your grandfather died, then again when your grandmother died a few years later. I guess that's the last time." He looked down at Matthew with his eyes squeezed shut. "We had a kind of falling out."

So my parents are dead and I don't get along with my brother. Matthew thought sadly. My wife hates me and my children can't get along. He sighed. At least I still have Phil and Gwen, but Phil is furious with Helen. He could see it in his face when Helen and Gwen had come yesterday afternoon, and he and Gwen are arguing about it. I've made such a mess of things. Why didn't I just die? Matthew squeezed his eyes against the tears.

"That was twenty some years ago. That's why he doesn't recognize you," Daniel said. "This is a tough time for him. Let's go down to the coffee shop and talk. I think Dad needs a rest. Is that okay with you, Dad?"

Matthew nodded without opening his eyes.

*

"Mark?" Helen opened her front door. "Come in," she said as she stood back and waved him inside. "I didn't realize you were in town. Have you seen Matt?"

"Yeah, I flew in this morning and went to the hospital first."

"Come in to the kitchen. I was just fixing myself some lunch. Can I get you anything?"

"No thanks. I ate at the hospital with the twins. They've grown up to be beautiful, Helen. They're so tall, like their parents," Mark said as he followed her into the kitchen and sat down at the table. "Matthew didn't recognize me." He rubbed his eyes.

"He didn't? He hasn't had a problem recognizing people before. I hope he hasn't had another stroke. The doctor's say he's at risk until we get his arteries cleared out." Helen sat down at the table across from Mark and took a bite of her sandwich.

"Delia was worried about that but Daniel didn't think there was a problem. He was angry with Delia for her concern."

"She's had a hard time with this. She's very close to her father. Her brother is too."

"I just can't believe he didn't know me."

"He's probably blocking. The last time the two of you spoke was not a good experience for him, you know. He loved you a lot. You really hurt him," Helen said. "And now it's been what, about twenty years since you've seen him."

"We've been in touch."

"But you haven't seen each other. You wouldn't tell him what you were doing. You told him not to visit you. He wanted to make things right between you, Mark. You wouldn't let him."

"I know. I know." Mark stood up and walked over to the window. He looked out into the yard and smiled. "He still likes to work in the garden."

"It's his passion."

"Will he ever be able to do that again?"

"We'll have to wait and see. Dr. Jackson seems optimistic."

"Daniel told me. He said there was going to be a meeting tomorrow about his prognosis and therapy plan. He said I should talk to you about attending it." Mark came back to the table and sat down. "Should I be there, Helen?"

"I don't think so, Mark. I don't want to do anything to set him back and if he doesn't recognize you, somewhere deep inside he must not want to. I'll fill you in on what they say. You can see him later and decide what you want to do."

"I want to make things right. I didn't realize how much I loved him until I thought I might lose him." He rubbed his eyes again. "I just hope it isn't too late."

"I hope not, too."

*

"Are you ready to go, Dad?" Daniel said at ten o'clock on Monday morning. He helped Matthew swing his legs over the side of the bed and fastened the safety belt around his waist. Positioning the wheel chair across from him and locking the brakes, he pulled him to a standing position holding fast to the belt. He didn't support him but Matthew felt secure that if he fell Daniel would catch him. With small steps he turned around, put his hands on the arms of the chair and lowered himself into it, still listing to the right.

"You're doing great, Dad. The right side weakness is going to go away fast, I'm sure." Daniel smiled. "Listen, I wanted a minute alone with you before we go into the evaluation room. I wanted to talk to you about Dandy, I mean Delia." Daniel sat down on the bed that Matthew had just left and looked into his father's eyes. "She's having a hard time with all this. I know she upsets you. I've talked to her and I think she'll be able to get hold of herself."

She doesn't have to get hold of herself. Matthew thought but he didn't try to speak.

"You know she's always just worshiped you." Daniel smiled.

Matthew opened his eyes wide, shook his head. I was just as close to you. He though, but he said, "Duurnt."

"I never felt slighted." Daniel smiled and touched his father's shoulder. "But the two of you had a strong attachment. We had one too. I never minded." He stood. "But if her tears upset you, I'll make her stay away until things get better."

Matthew shook his head. "Yes," he said and bit his lip. Why did I say yes? I wanted to say no. He could think it. Why did he say it wrong?

"I know what you mean, Dad. I know you wanted to say no. I just want you to know that I'll do what's best for you." He stood and positioned himself behind the wheelchair. "I just don't know what to think about Mom. She's so distant. I can't read her feelings and she won't talk," he said as he guided the wheel chair down the hall to the conference room. "I guess that's my fault since I've been estranged from her for over a year."

They went through the door into a long room with a conference table in it. There were several people in white lab coats sitting around the table. Delia was there. Helen sat away from the table. She was partly obstructed from his view by Delia. Matthew tried to smile but he knew his expression remained flat.

Daniel maneuvered the chair like a pro. Of course he is a pro, Matthew thought. When he had him arranged at the end of the table he sat down beside him.

The door opened again and Gwen and Phillip came in. "Hey, Matt," Phillip said. "I bet it's nice to be out of that bed for a while, isn't it." He and Gwen sat down at the table with everyone else. Matthew thought maybe the left side of his mouth had smiled when he saw his friends but he wasn't sure.

"I'm glad you could all come," The doctor said from his seat at the end of the table. "I'm Dr. Jackson. I'll be heading up Matthew's rehabilitation team," he said. "We like to involve as many of the friends and family as we can in the rehab. Encouragement and support make a tremendous difference. Matthew has agreed to have you all hear about his treatment, haven't you Matthew." He looked down the length of the table where Matthew sat next to Daniel.

He nodded his head and opened his mouth but didn't say anything.

"Of course, his power of attorney, Helen, has signed the necessary releases, so I think we can get started. What I'm going to do is give you a brief outline of what has happened to Matthew and then the rest of the team will outline their rehabilitation plans." He gestured to the other people wearing white coats in the room. "I'll introduce them first. This is our physical therapist, Jenny Johnson."

She nodded.

"This is our occupational therapist, Gary Hampton and over here is our speech therapist Stan Reeves." They all smiled and nodded.

Matthew looked at Helen. She sat with her hands in her lap and her head bowed. She hadn't looked at him once since he came into the room. Truth is. She hasn't looked at me since this whole thing happened, he thought. She needs to leave me. He sniffed and willed the tears not to escape.

"Matthew has had an ischemic stroke. What that means is that a clot, probably from a blockage in one of his carotid arteries, broke off and traveled to the brain where it lodged blocking blood flow to a portion of his brain.

"Aren't the carotid arteries the ones that provide blood to the brain?" Gwen asked. "If they're blocked, "Why isn't there more damage?"

"They aren't completely blocked." Dr. Jackson answered her question. "We ultra sounded them and discovered plaque buildup in both of them, but only 60% and 40% in the right and left respectively. Also there are alternative routes of blood flow."

"So some of the plaque broke off and went to his brain," Phillip said. "Could more break off? Could this happen again?"

"Yes, but we have him on a blood thinner in an attempt to stop this from happening and hopefully he well reduce the plaque buildup with the proper diet and exercise, and you're not going to smoke anymore cigarettes I hope, Matthew." Dr. Jackson looked at him.

Matthew's eyes widened and he shook his head vehemently.

"Good," Dr. Jackson smiled. "We'll outline a diet for you and Jenny will get you started on a workout that will first build strength and coordination in your weakened right side and then build conditioning in your entire body." He spoke directly to Matthew.

"We've been working out together for several months," Phillip said. "Will we be able to continue that?"

"Absolutely, I hope you will continue it. We project that he will stay here in the critical care unit for about another week. We'll start his therapy while he's here then move him to the rehabilitation unit where he will get more intense therapy in preparation of leaving the hospital. We anticipate about two weeks there and then he should be able to go home. I'll want him to come back here to our outpatient facility for about a month then he can move on to his private Gym. I know a number of physical therapists that work on their off hours as personal trainers. I'll see if I can line one up to work with him at your gym." He looked at Matthew. "Does that sound like a good plan?" he asked. Matthew nodded.

"Are there any other questions so far?" Dr. Jackson paused and looked around the room. "Gary, our occupational therapist will coach you on the everyday things you do that have become hard for you since your stroke, Matthew, brushing your hair, brushing your teeth, going to the bathroom, getting dressed, all those things. Do you have anything to add, Gary?"

"No, that about says it." The young man smiled. "Except that we'll do some fun things too, arts and crafts. We'll even work in the garden."

"Daddy loves to garden," Delia said smiling across the table at her father.

"Stan, I'm going to let you talk about the speech issue," Dr. Jackson said then addressed the room again. "This is going to be our greatest challenge."

"You have a type of aphasia called Broca's aphasia." The young speech therapist began. "That means it has affected the part of the brain that coordinates language output. I guess you've noticed, Matthew that you can pretty much understand what people are saying?"

Matthew nodded his head.

"You also know what you want to say back but it doesn't come out the way you planned, right?"

He nodded again.

"I know that's really frustrating. Your nods and shakes seem to be right though, back and forth for no, up and down for yes."

Matthew nodded.

"That's good. Some people with this type of aphasia can't do that either. But if you say yes or no it sometimes gets backwards doesn't it?"

Matthew nodded and said, "No." He grinned on his left side and laughed. They all laughed with him.

"I'm glad to see you've retained your sense of humor. This can be very frustrating for you and for the people around you as well." He looked around the room. "That's why you have to make him do it right. It'll be tempting to let it go but if you make him do it eventually it'll get easier for him." Stan smiled. "If he just can't find a word, he needs to learn to find another way to say what he's trying to say."

"This part of the brain also controls swallowing." He went on. "That's where we'll start. I've been working with Matthew for the past several days and he's improving fast. I'm hoping we'll have that feeding tube removed by the end of the week. The faster we get that out the faster we can move to the Rehab unit where you'll be with other people who are going through the same thing."

"Support is the most important thing we can give him." Stan addressed the rest of the room. "The more of you who can be involved in his therapy, the better. Be assured that you are welcome to attend all of his sessions. We've made up a schedule of his therapies. If there are any changes, we'll let you know." He pulled papers out of a folder and passed them around the room.

"Stan," Helen said quietly from the back of the room.

"Yes." Everyone looked at her.

"Can he write what he's thinking?"

"No. Writing is the same as talking. It's the expression of his ideas."

"Will he ever be able to?"

"I think so. The extent of his impairment remains to be seen but with the proper training and support he will be able to express himself."

Helen looked at Matthew. He'd begun to lean heavily to the right. "Matt, honey," she said surprising herself with the endearment. "You're tired." She rose and went to the back of the wheel chair. "I'll take him back to his room. I need a few minutes alone with him anyway." She heard the murmur of conversation begin as she went through the door and pushed the chair down the hall.

When they got back to the room she helped Matthew stand, turn around and sit down on the bed. He pulled his feet up onto the bed and leaned back on the pillow. Helen sat down beside him.

"Matt," she said. "You had a room full of people who love you and are going to help you through this."

"Nun..." he put his left hand on hers. The right hand raised and hovered above his chest for a minute then settled on his abdomen.

"No." She bit her lip. "I have to leave."

I know you do, he thought. He wished he could tell her that. He opened his mouth, closed it again then said, "y.y.y ... go."

Helen looked quickly into his eyes. They were saying something. She wasn't sure what. "Are you telling me it's alright?"

He nodded his head, gulping at the lump in his throat.

"You swallowed." Helen smiled as tears rolled over her lower lids and splashed on their clasped hands. "You'll be over this in no time." She took a deep breath. "One of my colleagues at work is going to Europe for three months. She's actually doing some training over there for the company. She has a dog and she wants someone to stay in her apartment to take care of the dog. I wouldn't have to pay anything and by the time the three months are up ... well ... maybe I'll know what to do next."

"Nun ... dogs." He squeezed her hand.

"I know. I don't like dogs. Well, that's about to change." She stood and laid his hand with the other one on his belly. "I won't just be gone, Matt. I'll make sure you have everything you need."

He smiled at her on the left side of his mouth. I won't have you, he thought.

"Thank you for helping me with this." She swallowed the lump in her throat. "I couldn't go if you asked me to stay and I need to go." She turned and left the room.

He had to let her go. Letting her go was his only chance to get her back. Matthew laid his head back on his pillow. He was so tired. Being in that room of energetic people making plans for his recovery was exhausting. When would this all go away? He closed his eyes and released the straining tears.

Chapter Five

"That's an interesting basket, Gwen. Where did you get it?" Phillip asked as he opened the door to his mother's assisted living complex and followed Gwen inside.

"At the Sandy Springs festival, isn't it cute. It's made of Kudzu. You know those vines that grow all over the place and kill trees." Gwen laughed.

"You're kidding."

"No, there was a booth with a little old woman and her two granddaughters, who were grown women, and a great granddaughter in her teens. They were selling them. She paints them all different colors and patterns. She's going to have a display in the Gallery."

"That's great. So you really haven't had to buy much merchandise since you're going with the commission idea."

"Yeah, each artist gives us a start up fee for the space in the shop and then they pay us 30% commission on everything they sell. I'm hoping that'll keep us going. If not I may have to do some buying." They stopped at the door of the apartment and Phillip knocked.

"I'm really impressed, honey. I'm proud of you."

"Thanks, Phil," Gwen beamed as she entered the apartment. "Hello, Martha." She leaned down to embrace her mother-in-law in the chair where she sat.

"Hello, Gwen, what a pretty basket." Martha took it from her. "…And it's full of all kinds of goodies." She riffled through the loaded basket and tipped her cheek up for Phillip to kiss. "Hello, Phillip, what a nice surprise."

They settled into the cozy living room and Phillip cleared his throat.

"Uh-oh, what's wrong? You always clear your throat when you have bad news," Martha said.

"It isn't really bad news, Mom. It's just that we need to cut expenses. You've done well since the stroke and I want your money to last you for as long as you need it."

"I only have the sitters late at night and for a few hours during the day, Phillip. I really need them. I don't want to cut back any more." Martha lifted her chin.

"We weren't thinking of cutting the sitters. We were thinking of eliminating the tremendous rent you pay here by moving you into our house."

"With you?" Martha looked horrified.

"Of course with us, Mom, we aren't planning to move out." Phillip could hear the irritation in his voice. Don't let her get to you, Phil. He coached himself.

"That's not fair, Phillip. What have I done to deserve that?"

Gwen laughed. "You make it sound like prison."

"It's not that, dear, but we'll drive each other crazy and I can't climb all those stairs."

"I don't think we'll drive each other crazy, Mom," Phillip said. His voice had calmed now. "And we thought we'd put you in the downstairs master bedroom. Gwen and I will move up to Andrea's old room. She won't need it anymore."

"We've already started painting it, the room upstairs, I mean," Gwen said enthusiastically. "We'll let you choose the colors for your room. You know there's a little sitting area off that bedroom and I thought we could build in a little kitchen with a microwave and refrigerator like you have here. That way you could join us in the main part of the house when you want to or close yourself up in your room if you want to be alone."

"Well you've really thought this out." Martha looked concerned. "What about all the activities they have here? What will I do all day at your house?"

"The church on the corner has Bingo every Tuesday night and there are all sorts of elder activities at the club house," Phillip said.

"I hate Bingo."

"Well, what activities do you like here?" Gwen said.

"I never participate in anything but stretch and flex but I could if I wanted to."

"Well, I guess you might have to work a little harder at it then, but Mom, I really think this is the answer. You're not ready for a nursing home and Medicare won't pay for anything else."

"What does your sister think about this?"

"I haven't talked to her about it yet."

"Well, you'd better. She'll get all worried that you plan to pass me off to her when you get tired of me."

"We won't get tired of you, Martha," Gwen said and looked at her watch. "I need to run. I have to meet Helen for lunch then go to check on construction at the gallery."

"When do you want to move me out of here?" Martha looked resigned.

"We'll have the renovations to your suite and the bedroom upstairs finished by September. I thought we'd give your thirty day notice then and try to have you in by the end of the month, in time for Gwen's grand opening." Phillip stood. "I need to get back to work, too. I'll walk out with you Gwen." He leaned down to kiss his mother on the cheek. "Don't worry about a thing, Mom. We'll do all the work and you can keep your sitters. Everything will be fine. I promise."

*

"Helen, over here," Gwen waived from her seat in the corner of the café. "Helen waved and then wound her way through the chairs and tables to the booth where Gwen waited.

"You're here early. I thought you had an errand to run."

"I got done faster than I thought. I had to pick up some paint samples for Martha to look at for her room." She spread the samples out on the table.

"They're all purple."

"She loves purple. If she had her way she'd have one of those dark psychedelic purple colors but I'm only going to give her the paler shades to choose from." Gwen smiled wickedly and put the samples back in her purse.

"I can't believe you're going to live with your mother-in-law. I mean I loved Matt's mother but there is no way I'd have lived with her."

"It'll have its challenges I'm sure," Gwen said. "But I don't really mind. With us going upstairs there'll be plenty of privacy. Matt's doing well," she changed the subject. "I'm scheduled to go over there on Thursday for his speech therapy. I'm really enjoying that. It's fun to watch his progress."

"I haven't been in on the therapy. I don't think I can do him much good right now."

"You're still pretty angry?"

"Yeah, I'm keeping my distance. I checked with Dr. Jackson this morning and he says that Matt will be moved to the rehab unit tomorrow. I'll let you know what his new room number is." The waitress came and took their orders. "I'm going over to Melissa's house this afternoon to meet her dog. Tell me how to treat it so Melissa will think I like dogs."

"Is it a girl dog or a boy dog?" Gwen asked.

"Its name is Tiffany so I'm guessing it's a girl. It's a Shit Zu. Sounds nasty doesn't it?"

"To start with call the dog her, not it. Melissa will pick up on it real fast if you refer to her baby as it."

"Really? Okay."

"Stoop down so you're not towering over her. Extend your hand to the dog with your palm up and let her sniff you. If she wags her tail then pet her on the neck. Don't go for the top of the head first. That may be threatening to her." Gwen coached. "And talk to her. Say, "Hello, Tiffany, we're going to get along just fine, aren't we." Gwen's voice raised an octave.

"You're kidding."

"No, I'm not. Helen, you had a cat for years. Didn't you talk to the cat?"

"Well, I guess so, but Rocky was really Matt's cat, and the kids'."

"Well, if you want Melissa to trust you with her baby, you'd better talk to her. Oh and Shee tzoo's are not nasty, at least most of them aren't," she said, exaggerating the pronunciation. "They're cute fluffy little dogs. I can't wait to visit you so I can play with her. I miss having a dog," Gwen said as she started on her sandwich.

"You don't think I'm terrible for moving out of the house?"

"Of course I don't, Helen. You have to take care of yourself. I have to admit. I hope you and Matt get back together some day. I'll miss being a foursome."

"Me too, but I just don't think that's going to happen. Right now, though, I'm just taking one step at a time." Helen picked up her sandwich and took a bite.

"How do the kids feel about it?" Gwen started on her salad.

"Dandy called me a selfish bitch and hasn't spoken to me since. Danny didn't say much. He never says much to me."

*

There was a car parked at the street when Gwen pulled into the driveway that evening. She didn't recognize it and there wasn't anyone in it. She pulled around to the back of the house and into the garage. Climbing the steps, she listened. There were sounds coming from the kitchen, a voice, Andrea's voice. She breathed easy and opened the door.

A stout toddler trudged over with his fleshy arms raised. "Mraama"

"Trevor." Gwen swung him into her arms. "What a nice surprise." She kissed his soft cheek and smoothed a hand over his wispy blond curls. "Andrea, honey," she put her arm around her daughters shoulders and kissed her cheek then pulled back to look at her. She was fat. She'd never been fat before but her shoulders were soft and dimpled and her face was full and round with a small second chin beneath it.

"Mom, I've left Tom." Andrea wrapped her arms around Gwen's neck and sobbed.

Gwen eased her over to a chair, struggling not to drop the baby. She sat down next to her daughter and balanced the squirming toddler on her lap. "What happened, honey?"

"I wanted to have another baby so I told my doctor we were planning one and he said I should lose weight before I got pregnant again. Can you believe he said that to me?" She stood and went to the sink to splash water on her face.

Gwen bounced Trevor then stood him on the floor and went to the counter. The doctor was just doing his job, but Gwen could feel how angry she'd have been. She said, "I'm sure that was insulting to you but why did you leave Tom?"

"When I told him about it, he agreed. He can't love me very much if my weight is that important to him," she said picking up a cookie from a plate and taking a bite. She handed the rest of it to Trevor and he toddled toward the den, sat down on the rug and started dusting cookie crumbs around him in a circle.

"Trevor, honey, come here and eat your cookie in the kitchen." Gwen called.

"No!' He squealed.

"That's his favorite word these days," Andrea said. "Mom, why is my room torn up?"

"Dad and I are moving into it." Gwen went into the den and picked up the toddler. He started to scream and kick his legs crumbling the now soggy cookie into pieces and flinging it all over the rug.

"Mom, we don't put restrictions on where he can eat," Andrea said taking the screaming baby from her mother and putting his head soothingly on her shoulder.

"When he's here he'll eat in the kitchen, just like you did." Gwen pulled the small vacuum off the wall and cleaned up the crumbs. She replaced the device and stretched her arms out to the baby. "Now come back to Gramma and I'll explain the rules to you. Then you'll understand."

Trevor smiled from his place on his mother's soft shoulder then turned his head away being shy.

"Come see Gramma, Trevor." Gwen persisted. He turned back and stretched his arms out to her. She carried him over to the sink and dampened a cloth to wipe his face and hands.

"Why are you moving into my room? Where will I live?" Andrea sat down at the kitchen table.

"I guess you'll have to use Frankie's room. How long do you think you'll be staying?"

"Well, I'll need to find a job and I'll need to save enough money for first and last month's rent on an apartment."

"Honey, are you really planning to leave Tom for good. Don't you think the relationship is worth saving?" Gwen put the toddler back down on the floor and handed him a cracker. "Stay in the kitchen with that, Trevor." He walked toward the den then stopped and turned around grinning devilishly at her. She smiled and took a tentative step toward him.

He squealed with childish laughter and sat down hard on the tile floor.

"Good boy," Gwen said and reaching down tickled his bare tummy.

"It's over, Mom. I think he's having an affair."

"Oh no, Andrea, really?" Gwen looked at her daughter. "Why do you think that? Is there any evidence?"

"He just doesn't have any time for me anymore. He's traveling a lot and when he comes home he's always working on something. We can't even do anything fun on the weekends anymore."

"Well, honey, he's starting a career. When your Dad and I were first married he was like that."

"It's worse than that. I'm telling you, Mom." Andrea scooped Trevor up off the floor and headed toward the stairs. "I guess I'll just have to move into Frankie's room. Lord knows he won't be using it. Not with the lady doctor keeping him happy. By the way, Mom," she stopped on the second stair and turned. "Where's Sandy?"

"Oh, honey," Gwen said. "I guess I should have called you. Sandy died."

"When?"

"Oh it's been a couple of months. I can't believe I didn't tell you."

Andrea's face had crumpled again and tears were rolling down her cheeks. "I can't believe you didn't either. God, Mom, don't you even care about your family anymore." She turned and ran up the stairs.

Gwen could hear her sobs as they faded down the hall then she heard the door to Frankie's room close. "Of course, I care about my family." She went over to the phone stand and picked up the receiver. She punched in Rodney's cell phone number and listened as it rang. He picked up on the third ring.

"Hello?"

"Hey, Roddy, this is your Mom," she said. "I'm glad I didn't get you during class."

"I would have had the phone turned off."

"Good. It was good to see you when you visited a few weeks ago even though I couldn't see your handsome face behind that beard."

"I'm not shaving it off, Mom."

"I figured." They laughed together. "Roddy, did I tell you that Sandy died?"

"Yeah, you told me while I was there. Remember, I missed her. Why?"

"Apparently I forgot to tell Andrea and she came down today and discovered it. She's mad at me now; accusing me of not caring about the family."

"Same old Andy, drama queen."

"I guess so, well anyway, I thought it would be nice if you came to dinner on Saturday night. You could bring Amber, she seemed nice. I liked her very much. We'll eat early so it won't interfere with your plans if you have a party to go to or something. I'm going to invite Frankie and Grace, too."

"That would be nice, Mom, the whole family together. I'll check with Amber. We'll come early so we can visit with Andy and Tom and the little monster then we'll leave right after dinner."

"Tom's not here. Maybe he will be by then, though. I'll see you." She hung up the phone and turned to greet Phillip as he came through the door from the garage.

"Is that Andrea's car out front?" he asked as he came through the door.

"Yes. She's upstairs. Apparently she and Tom have had a fight. She says she's leaving him. She's crying right now. I guess I forgot to tell her about Sandy. I didn't know she cared about Sandy that much." Gwen turned to the refrigerator and looked inside. It was full of bottles and small jars of baby food. "I was thinking of a cold chicken salad for dinner. I don't suppose babies eat that, though."

"I'm sure Andrea will take care of feeding Trevor." Phillip started for the stairs. "Is she upset about her room?" he asked as he started up.

"I guess so. Maybe we should have talked to her about that, too," Gwen said as she started slicing vegetables.

Phillip walked up the stairs slowly listening to the sounds coming from Frankie's room. Andrea was crying softly and Trevor was chattering happily. He knocked on the door and called. "Andrea, it's Dad, can I come in?" She opened the door and threw herself against his chest. He put his arms around her and stroked her curly red hair. He'd always wondered where the red came from. He couldn't remember anyone in his family having red hair. Gwen said she'd had a red headed cousin but he'd never met her.

"I'm sorry, baby," he whispered. "What happened? I thought you were so happy with Tom. You seemed to be so in love with him and he seems to be such a good man."

"I think he's having an affair."

"I'll kill that son-of-a-bitch!" Phillip stiffened and held her away to look at her face.

She looked down and laughed. "I thought you just said he was a good man."

"Well, not if he's cheating on my little girl."

Andrea looked up at him and he met her eyes. They were swollen from crying. She sniffed and blotted her nose with a well used wadded up tissue. He reached for another from the box on the night stand and handed it to her.

"Well, I'm not sure of anything but he just doesn't seem to be very interested in me lately. He works all the time and..." She sat down on the bed and took the toy that Trevor extended to her from the floor and distractedly passed it from hand to hand. "And he called me fat."

"That was stupid." Phillip sat down on the bed beside her.

"You don't think I'm fat?" She looked up at him. "Mom does, I could tell."

"You look the way you're supposed to look during the childbearing years. You should have seen your mother. She was such a little tub."

Andrea laughed, picked Trevor up and settled him in her lap. "Better not let her hear you say that." She smiled at him. "And you should appreciate the fact that I'm not mad that you just called me a tub by comparison."

"I was hoping you wouldn't notice." He laughed, squeezed her shoulder and touched Trevor's nose. The baby giggled and grabbed at his Grampa's finger. "Really, honey, I think you're lovely and I'll kill Tom for you if you want me too."

"I love you, Dad."

"I love you, too, now tell me what's really going on."

"Well, I want to have another baby," she said and looked at him. "It was nice having a brother so close to me in age. Was it hard for you and Mom?"

"I don't know. Yes. It was hard but how can you complain about babies?" Phillip laughed. "Truth is I don't remember thinking about it. When Rodney came along five years later I thought about it and made sure it didn't happen again," he squeezed her shoulder. "Not that I regret Rodney. He's a great kid." He heard the phone ring and heard Gwen pick it up and say hello downstairs in the kitchen. "Maybe we need to do some sound proofing while we're renovating up here."

"Tom doesn't want any more kids. He's adamant. He even wants to have a vasectomy."

"I'm starting to have a little trouble with this conversation, Andy," Phillip said as he tried to tune his ears to the conversation Gwen was having on the phone a floor below them.

*

"Hello," Gwen said into the receiver of the phone. She'd read the caller ID and knew it was Tom.

"Gwen?" he said. "This is Tom Bullard."

"I know that, honey, I have caller ID. I was wondering when we'd hear from you."

"I know my wife is there. She left me a note."

"She's upstairs talking to her father. Do you want to tell me your side of this, Tom?"

"I'm hoping you trust me more than to believe I'm having an affair," Tom said sounding hopeful.

"That's my inclination," Gwen said. "But, I can't be sure and if you are, of course, you know I'll never forgive you. Andrea is my child."

"I'm not. I just don't ever want to go through what I went through when Trevor was born. I didn't know she'd suffer so much and we have Trevor. Why do we need to go through that again?"

"So you don't just think she's too fat?"

"She is fat. We're both fat and if the doctor says that isn't safe then that's another reason not to have another baby." Tom took a deep breath. "Can I speak to her?"

"I'll call her." Gwen put the phone down and went to the stairs. She felt warm inside. Tom still loved Andrea. She could hear it in his voice. "Andrea," she called. "Tom's on the phone. What should I tell him?"

"Tell him I'm not here."

"I can't. I already told him you were." Gwen called back.

"You can't just walk away from a marriage without talking," Phillip said, pulling Trevor out of her arms, "You can't walk away from a family," he said bouncing the baby a little when he started to fuss. "I'm taking Trev down to the garage. I think it's time he got acquainted with automotive tools."

"He's just a baby, Dad." She called as she picked up the phone on the bedside table. "Don't let him get oily or anything."

Phillip left the room with the baby and headed down the steps. He heard Andrea's voice say, "Hello." Then she started talking quietly. He couldn't hear what she said.

"We're going down to the garage. I've only got a few more things to tighten up on that motor. Then I can start working on the interior. Maybe Trevor and I will make a trip to the junk yard this weekend," Phillip said as he hurried through the kitchen to the bedroom.

"I'll hold him while you change your clothes," Gwen said following her husband and grandson into the bedroom.

"You don't have to. I was planning to let him play in my box of shoe polish," Phillip said. "That should entertain him."

"Very funny," Gwen picked up the baby and kissed his cheek. "So what do you think?"
"I think they'll patch it up."
"I hope so."

*

"I'm going to the store this morning, honey," Gwen said to Andrea on Thursday morning when she came down with Trevor. They'd been there for two days and Tom had called every day but there was no indication that Andrea and Trevor would be leaving soon.

"Why don't you stop by around lunch time? You can see the gallery and then we can have lunch." Gwen looked at the back of her daughter as she put Trevor into the high chair and leaned forward to buckle him in. She wore low slung pants and the straps of her thong underwear wound their way out of her pants, through deep troughs in the fat on her hips and disappeared around the front of her where, Gwen imagined, they plunged back under the waist band of her low slung jeans. God, that's a horrible style. She thought.

"Not today, Mom. I'm going to take Trev to visit Nana." She turned around. "What?" she asked. Apparently, Gwen's expression gave away her thoughts.

"Nothing ... I mean ... I wish you'd make a little time to come by the gallery. I'd love to show it to you." Gwen turned around and straightened her face as she poured coffee into her travel mug and gathered her purse. "But I guess it's good that you're going to see Nana." She turned back around smiling.

"Maybe I could come by the gallery this afternoon. I was going to go to lunch with Dandy. I can't wait to show Trevor off to her." Andrea looked proudly at her son who was smearing scrambled eggs all over the tray of his high chair.

"Are you going to change your clothes before you go to lunch?" Gwen bit her lip. Why did I say that?

"Mom, get off my back. Maybe you don't like the way I dress but I don't like the way you dress either." Andrea dished herself up a plateful of the scrambled eggs Phillip had made before he left for work. "Is there any toast?" she asked.

"In the oven," Gwen said. "I'm going now. Come by later if you can." She picked up her purse and hurried down the stairs to the garage.

Pulling into the small alley lot behind the strip of stores, Gwen was surprised to see Helen's car in her designated spot. She got out and went to the back door of the shop. It was locked. She put her key in the lock and opened the door. The sounds of construction greeted her and she entered and locked the door behind her.

"I didn't expect to find you here," she said to Helen as she opened the door to the office.

"I only have a minute, but I wanted to make sure the computer had been set up right. I knew you had picked it up yesterday." Helen sat at the desk. The computer screen was set on the table so that she could see out the window while looking at the computer.

"Phil set it up for me. I may be a techno-dolt but he isn't."

"I'm not questioning your abilities, Gwen. I just want to be involved," Helen said getting up and coming around the desk. "The construction is going well. That new project manager is doing a fine job, don't you think?"

"Fine," Gwen said as the two of them walked out to the front of the store.

"Mitzi's coming by today, right?" Helen asked. "...to drop off tile samples and paint swatches?"

"That's right."

"Is something bothering you, Gwen. You're not your enthusiastic self this morning."

"Oh, I'm just being a critical mother again," Gwen said looking at the construction activity around her.

"You were never a critical mother," Helen said. "Well, no more critical than any mother. Isn't that what mother's are supposed to do?"

"Not to twenty eight year old children."

"Things aren't going well with Andrea?"

"Well, it's just that she still dresses in that horrible style. You know how the kids dress, low slung jeans with the thong underwear sliding up out of the butt cleavage, and the midriff tops." Gwen grimaced.

"Dandy still dresses like that, too, when she's not wearing hospital scrubs. I don't like it, but I've gotten used to it," Helen said. "I guess this will be the candy counter." She looked at the counter going up in an L shape on the back corner of the shop across from the office.

"That's right and the dipping machines will go in over here." Gwen indicated the spot behind the long part of the counter. "That way people can watch you dip the fruit."

"I don't think I'll be doing that for a while," Helen said sounding resigned. "I'll have to teach you, or whoever we hire."

"Anyway, I never liked that fashion but now that she's fat it's even worse. Of course, I can't say anything but it's hard not to."

"Andrea's fat? I can't imagine." Helen looked at Gwen startled.

"Well, yeah, she is. Well, not obese, just chubby."

Helen looked down at the floor and picked up a nail. She walked over to the window and looked out. "Here comes Mitzi and she has a young woman with her and a baby."

"That must be Linda." Gwen hurried over to look out the window. "I know she has a child about Trevor's age. She's heavy too, isn't she, Helen?" Gwen looked at her friend. "But she looks nice, matronly, motherly. It's because of the way she's dressed. I wish Andrea would let me advise her."

"Do you remember how you looked when you were having your kids, Gwen?" Helen asked.

"Well, yeah, I put on weight. I mean everyone does, for the extra insulation and nourishment and stuff, but I didn't show my butt." She watched as Mitzi helped her daughter put the child into the stroller and strap him in.

"I put on weight, too," Helen said.

"Oh, shut up. You've never put on weight in your life."

"Okay, I've never had a real problem," Helen said. "But that was the heaviest I've ever

been. One day when I went to visit my parents my mom said, "Helen, everyone gains weight when they're having babies but you have to dress differently. What you're wearing makes you look like a beer keg."
"You're kidding. I can't imagine your mother saying that to you."
"Well, she did. I didn't speak to her for a week." They watched quietly as Mitzi and Linda walked down the sidewalk toward the store. "Did your mother ever comment on the way you dressed when you were fat after your babies?"
"She always hated the way I dressed but you know what? She was right. When I look back at pictures of myself, I realize those styles were unflattering. It's the same with Andrea. I wish I could make her see it."
"Well, you can't. Not anymore than your mom could make you see it."
"That sucks."

*

"Hello, Gwen. Amm ... glad ... you..." Matthew stammered when Gwen came into the room.
"What did you want to say, Matthew?" Stan, the speech therapist, said as Gwen made herself comfortable at the table in the conference room where Matthew was having his speech therapy session.
"I ... glad ... she ..."
"Did you mean to say I'm glad you came?" Stan prompted.
Matthew nodded.

"Alright, I'll say it first. Then Gwen will say it. Okay with you, Gwen?" The therapist looked at her. She nodded.

"I'm glad you came," Stan said

"I'm glad you came," Gwen said

"I..."

"I'm..." Stan said

"I'm ... glad ... she..."

"...you..." Stan corrected.

"I know what he means," Gwen said.

The therapist looked at her seriously

"He's right, Matt." Gwen laughed and squeezed Matthew's hand. "Say it right."

"I'm ... glad ... you ... see."

"Came," Stan said.

Matthew scowled and rolled his lips between his teeth.

He's angry. Gwen thought. I know he understands what's going on. "Why can't we just learn to understand him?" she said to Stan. "I mean he's trying, as time goes on..."

"I know it's hard," Stan said. "But he's not that pitiful."

"Ahmm ... piful," Matthew said. He laughed, shook his head and continued. "Ah unnerstan ... you. Your ... prolem."

Stan laughed. Gwen laughed and hugged Matthew. "You're something else, Matt. Now say it right. I'm glad you came."

*

"We practiced it, but he just couldn't get it right." Gwen told Phillip and Andrea at dinner that night. "Then he said, I'm ... glad to ... see you. Stan said if he can find another way to say something, it's just as good as saying the words he meant to say in the first place. He's still there."

"I know he is," Phillip said.

*

Helen looked around the room she had shared with Matthew for twenty five years. They had lived in an apartment for the first few years of their marriage. Then they'd bought a townhouse when the twins were born. But after only a couple of years there, they'd bought this house and had lived here ever since. The kids had grown up here. She opened the closet to look at the marks she'd made on the back of the door of their heights as they'd grown.

She shut the door and picked up the two suitcases she'd packed with her clothes and personal items. It was Saturday morning and today was her first day of dog sitting. She looked around one more time for anything she may have forgotten. It's not like I can't come back if I remember something, she reminded herself and carried the bags out of the bedroom and into the kitchen. She took the bags out to the garage, put them in the trunk of the car and went back in to get the box of candy making supplies she had packed up that morning.

"I guess you're all packed," Sybil said as she came into the room and lowered herself awkwardly into a chair at the kitchen table.

"Yes, I'm all packed." Helen turned to look at her. "I hope you don't think I'm leaving because of you, honey. I can see how much Danny loves you. I appreciate that." Helen went to the table and sat down across from Sybil.

"No, I understand." She looked at her bulging middle shyly. "I am a little disappointed, though. I was hoping you'd teach me about making candy. I was kind of hoping I might be able to help out in the store some." She looked up quickly. "I mean not that you'd need to hire me but it might be kind of fun."

"I'm glad you're interested," Helen said. "Why didn't you mention it before?"

"I wasn't sure how you'd feel about it."

"Sybil, are you a nurse, too?" Helen felt bad that she hadn't taken the time to find out more about her new daughter-in-law.

"No. I was a secretary at the Hospital in Charlotte where Daniel worked," she said. "I don't really have any skills of any kind."

"You must have secretarial skills if you were employed as one."

"Yeah, I do but I don't like it very much. I don't know what I'll do after the baby comes. I guess I'll need to work but I don't want to work in an office anymore." She stood with difficulty and went to the refrigerator to pour herself a glass of water.

"Are you carrying twins?" Helen asked. "You're awfully big for..." She hesitated, realizing that she didn't even know when her grandchild was due. I've really been distracted. "When are you due, Sybil?"

"November, it's only one baby, but the doctor says he's big, probably already about five pounds."

"It's a boy?" Helen asked. "I'm sorry I haven't been more welcoming to you, honey. I'm ashamed."

"Oh no, don't be." Sybil sat down across from her again. "You've been through a lot."

"Have you been to a doctor since you've been here?"

"Oh yes, Daniel, had that all lined up before we left Charlotte. He's a wonderful man." Sybil's face lit up.

Helen felt a stab of some emotion. Was it pain? Was she jealous? If so what did she envy? She looked back to the pretty girl across from her. Her hair was very blond and if she wasn't mistaken it was that way all the way down to the roots. It was curly, too and her eyes were brown, but not really brown, more honey colored.

"I'll be happy to teach you how to make candy. We'll need help in the store and I think we actually have budgeted to hire a couple of clerks. Do you think you'd like to do that?" Helen reached across the table and put her hand on Sybil's.

"Yes, I think I would." She looked down at her bulging middle. "I guess you wouldn't want me doing much looking like this, though."

"You look wonderful, that won't be a problem, but the grand opening isn't until October first. That's six weeks off. If you're still feeling up to it by then we'd love to have you help out in the store. "In the meantime, you can come over to my apartment for candy making lessons. You know we're going to have dipping machines in the shop. Would you like to learn how to use those?"

"Yes, I would." The girl's eyes were bright with excitement.

"Good. I'll give you directions to my apartment." She paused. "I mean the one I'm staying in. Are you alright with dogs?"

"I love dogs."

"Really? I wish I did." Helen laughed. "Do you have a car?"

"Yes, but I rode down with Daniel. He went up to Charlotte on a bus this morning to get my car."

"Oh." Helen stood. "Well, I'll call you when I get settled and we can arrange a time to get together." She walked around the table and kissed Sybil on the cheek. "Welcome to the family, honey. I'm sorry it's such a rocky time."

"I'm sorry, too," Sybil said. "I mean for all of you."

Helen went into the garage, raised the door and backed out. Delia was standing in the yard with a garden hose watering one of Matthew's favorite shrubs. Helen stopped the car, put it in park and got out. *I hope she doesn't hose me down.* She thought as she approached her daughter.

"Dandy, I'm leaving now." Delia didn't turn around. "I know you're mad at me but I need to do this, for myself."

"And that's all that really counts, right Mom? You, yourself."

"No, my family counts, too."

"And Dad's not part of your family?" Delia still hadn't looked at her.

Helen put her hand on her daughters shoulder. Delia shook it off, released the handle turning off the water and turned to look at her. Helen stepped back from the anger in her eyes. "Oh, Dandy ..." She took a deep breath. "I care about your dad. I'm not good for him right now. I'm too angry. I need to sort out my feelings before I make any decisions about him, about us. Please try to understand."

"What are you angry about, Mom? Are you mad at him because he's sick?" She turned back around and pressed the handle on the nozzle. "I understand. Just go on, okay! Oh, and Mom, my name is Delia!"

Helen made her way back across the yard to her car. She wondered if the rift between Delia and herself would ever mend. Daniel hadn't talked to her about her leaving. How did he feel about it? Did he hate her too? She swallowed the lump in her throat, got into the car and pulled out of the driveway.

*

"You don't have to ring the bell, Tom," Gwen said as she swung the front door open. It was mid-day on Saturday and she was mixing up potato salad and preparing the bean casserole to go into the oven for her family dinner that night. "You're family, you just come right in." She accepted his one armed embrace and stood on her tip toes to kiss his cheek.

"I wasn't sure, what with my wife leaving me and slinging all sorts of accusations around. Is she here? I didn't see her car up front." He held a gift wrapped box under his arm and a vase of flowers in his hand. "I'm bearing gifts," he laughed

"I see that." Gwen smiled. She loved her son-in-law. He was so obviously in love with Andrea and he had such a lively sense of humor. She took a good look at him. "My goodness, you have gotten fat." She laughed. "I'm sorry. I would have been furious if you'd said that to me."

"You haven't gotten fat, though," Tom laughed. "In fact, I think you've trimmed down. Not that you needed to, of course."

"Of course," Gwen took the flowers from him and went into the kitchen to top off the vase with water. "Andrea and Phil went to visit Matt. Did Andrea tell you what happened to Matt?"

"Yes she did. How's he doing?"

"Really very well"

"Good, I'm glad to hear it. You know what? I've figured out what happened with me and Andy." Tom followed her into the kitchen and sat down at the table. "It's that cookbook my mom gave her for Christmas."

"A cookbook?" Gwen said putting the vase on the table. "Can I get you something, a soft drink, or a beer?" She offered.

"No thanks, I just drank a bottle of water. I'm sloshing." He patted his bulging belly. "I guess I had mentioned to her at one time that Andrea doesn't cook." He looked sheepish. "Not that I mind. I'm a pretty good cook and I enjoy it. Anyway, Mom gave her a cookbook for Christmas. Well, guess what? Now she cooks."

"She does! I can't imagine. The boys used to make me label anything she made so they wouldn't accidently eat it." They both laughed.

"Now she's an excellent cook. That's a good cookbook but all the recipes feed six to eight people." He stretched his legs out and rubbed his belly again. "There are only two of us and the food is so good, it's hard to stop. That's why I bought her this." He leaned forward and picked up the gift. "It's a cookbook, *Gourmet Cooking for Two.*"

"Great idea," Gwen said. She cocked her head to listen. "I think they're home." She heard the front door swing open then slam closed.

"What are you doing here?" Andrea demanded as she stormed angrily into the room.

"Andy, give me a chance to apologize." Tom stood. "Hello, Phil." He held out his hand to his father-in-law.

"I'm glad you didn't say you wanted me to kill him, Andy," Phillip said taking Tom's hand. "He's huge!"

"That's the second fat remark I've gotten since I've been here," Tom said, but he was smiling.

"See how it feels?" Andrea said.

"I didn't call you fat. Listen, baby, let's go upstairs and talk about it. Your parents don't want to hear this. Where's Trevor?" He looked around at Gwen.

"He's asleep in the den. I'll watch him." She looked in the direction of the den where a cooing sound had started up. "In fact he's awake now. You two go on up before he sees you. Dad and I will take care of him."

"That's right," Phillip said starting toward the room where the baby was calling. "Anyway, he needs to help me. That kid has become an A-1 mechanic's assistant. We've finished with the engine on the Healy, now we're starting on the interior."

"You're kidding?" Tom said.

"He's not kidding!" Gwen said ushering the two of them toward the stairs.

*

"Is the coast clear?" Phillip said as he peered through the door from the garage an hour later.

"Coast is clear." Gwen laughed. "They've gone out to get Tom a toothbrush. Apparently he forgot his. They were smiling when they left."

"Were there any fireworks after Trev and I left, screaming or furniture being tossed around?"

"I didn't hear any." Gwen laughed and took the happy baby from his Grampa's arms. "I think Trevor really likes being with you down there. I hope you're being careful."

"Oh yeah, he stays in his play pen most of the time. I give him the toy tools, you know, the ones I got him the other day when he and I made that emergency trip to the toy store."

Gwen laughed.

"I just talk to him the whole time I'm working," Phil said. "When I scrape paint, he scrapes paint. When I pull fabric, he pulls fabric."

"What fabric does he pull?"

"His blanket, his shirt, his diaper..."

"And he's happy in the play pen?" Gwen put the baby in the high chair and fastened the tray in front of him.

"He's okay most of the time. When he gets cranky in there, I put him in the driver's seat. I swear this kid already knows what a sports car is." Phillip sat down beside the baby.

"Mom, we're here." Rodney's voice sounded from the front door. They heard the door shut behind him and their youngest son came into the room. "Trev, my man, good to see you," he held his hand out to the baby and took the small fat fist in his. Turning he hugged his mother and put an arm affectionately across his Dad's shoulders.

"Good to see you, son," Phillip said, standing to receive the embrace. "Hello, Amber." He gave the girl that accompanied his son a quick hug.

Gwen looked at her bearded son and smiled. He had such a handsome face, too bad he covered it up, but she wouldn't say anything. He wasn't as tall as Frankie, but he was taller than his dad. The last time he'd let her measure him, he was six feet tall. She really didn't think he'd grown any since then. His dark hair was long and curled around his shoulders.

"I'm so glad you could come." She hugged Amber. The girl was almost as tall as Rodney and her hair was just as dark but it hung perfectly straight to her waist. Gwen couldn't help but wonder if their children would have straight hair or curly. She shook her head. That was premature. "Won't this be nice, having the whole family together?" she said.

"Is Nana coming?" Rodney asked.

"Yeah, the sitter is bringing her," Phillip said. "That way if she decides to leave in the middle of the meal it won't interrupt anyone."

"Except Sally," Gwen said.

"Sally is Nana's sitter," Rodney explained to Amber.

"We're back," Andrea came into the room with Tom behind her. Frankie and Grace followed them into the suddenly crowded kitchen. "And look who we found on the doorstep."

"Hey, Mom," Frankie gave her a hug. Grace stepped forward and extended her arms for a hug. Gwen felt warm inside. It was so wonderful having her whole family together.

"I brought you a present, Mom." Frankie pulled a netted bag off his shoulder. It had zippers on the top and front. "Look inside," he said pushing it toward her.

Gwen pulled the zipper on the top open and looked into the huge green eyes of a solid black kitten. "Oh." She breathed. Reaching inside the bag she gently pulled the frightened looking kitten out. It was definitely afraid but it didn't fight her.

"Frankie," Phillip said. "She said she didn't want any more pets."

"She was mistaken," Frankie said confidently.

"I was." Gwen pressed the tiny creature to her face and felt a tear escape her lower lid and roll down her cheek.

Chapter Six

"His name is Cole," Gwen said to Helen at lunch the following Wednesday. "It's perfect. I love the name for a man and with him being so black. I thought about spelling it C-o-a-l but I like C-o-l-e better."

"I thought you didn't want to deal with the grief at the end," Helen said.

"I didn't. But I guess I will. That won't be for a long time, though, so I'm not going to think about it." She looked at her menu. "I think I'll splurge and have a cheeseburger and fries."

"Not me," Helen said. The waitress came to their table and she ordered a veggie burger and cole slaw. "I'm keeping my arteries clear."

"A veggie burger and slaw for me, too." Gwen pouted. "You're such a party pooper, Helen."

"You didn't have to order the same thing."

"Actually, I'd probably have had heart burn and regretted eating a burger and fries." She laughed. "So how are things going with Tiffany?"

"Okay, I think. She's really sweet. She likes to curl up with me on the couch in the evening. Melissa left me two pages of instructions about how to feed her and when to walk her. She has to be kept in a cage at night and during the day while I'm gone. I feel bad about that."

"Does she seem to mind?" Gwen said biting into her burger.

"No." Helen chewed and swallowed looking thoughtful. "When I say kennel up, that's what Melissa told me to say, she just goes to the kennel and gets inside. She lies down on her bed, crosses her little paws and puts her chin down on them. But those big brown eyes look sad."

"She's playing you. Dogs are good at that."

"Oh come on, Gwen, dogs don't think like that," she swallowed. "Do they?"

"I've always thought so but how can you really know." Gwen sipped her water. "Have you ever let her out of her cage because of the way she looks at you?"

"No."

"Has she stopped looking at you that way?"

"No."

"Then maybe you're right, Helen," Gwen said. "Maybe she isn't playing you. I guess I just give in too fast. Cole is sleeping in the bed with us already," she laughed.

"I don't think I'd want to sleep with a dog. We let Rocky sleep on our bed with us but he wasn't interested in me. He was Matt's cat he slept on Matt's pillow." Helen pushed her slaw around on her plate. "Matt is going home on Monday, did you hear?"

"Yeah, they're having some kind of graduation ceremony for him at the rehab," Gwen said. "Phil and I are going. Daniel and Delia are going too, and Frankie."

"Frankie?"

"Yes, Frankie, Daniel and Phil have been working with Matt on the physical therapy. I do the speech therapy, Delia comes when she can. I think she helps him with the occupational therapy.

She's having a hard time with it," Gwen said, taking her wallet out of her purse and extracting a credit card. "I'll get lunch. I know you're struggling to support your whole family."

"No way, split it down the middle," Helen said to the waitress.

Gwen shrugged and handed her card to the waitress. "You should have heard Phil tell the story of the first time Matt used his walker." She laughed.

"What happened?" Helen's voice was low.

Gwen looked at her closely. "I'm sorry. Maybe I shouldn't talk about this."

"No ... tell me."

"Well, they got him up on his feet and showed him how to hold onto the walker. They put a belt around his waist in case he started to fall, they'd have something to grab."

"Go ahead."

"Then they started down the hall." Gwen started to laugh. "I wish you could have heard Phil tell this story. I hope I can do it justice. Apparently Matt started down the hall. The therapist was right behind him holding onto the belt. Daniel fell in behind the therapist and without even thinking Frankie and Phil fell in, single file, behind him and Mark was behind them, all single file. They walked all the way down the hall to the end and then instead of them all turning around and coming back they followed Matt around a U turn, still single file, and started back down the hall." Gwen was giggling at the image in her mind. "Well about half way back Matt sings out "Choooo ... Choooo...," he says, "Alll ... aboard." She looked up laughing, but stopped immediately. Helen sat stone still, her eyes staring blankly at the table.

"Are you alright, Helen?" She reached across the table and put her hand on Helen's folded ones.

"I'm fine. I guess that means he remembered who Mark is."

"Yes, Mark is flying back from Maine to go to the graduation. I think they've mended some fences."

"Good," Helen shook her head slightly and smiled at Gwen. "He's got his sense of humor back, too. I'm so glad."

"He never lost it, Helen." Gwen removed her hand from Helen's and took the card and check the waitress had put on the table. They both turned their attention to adding a tip and signing their names. "Are you going to his graduation? I think it would mean a lot to him."

"He called me and asked me to. I could barely understand what he said."

"His speech is improving a lot. He told me about the call. You make him nervous."

"Maybe I shouldn't go then." Helen stood up clutching her purse to her middle defensively.

"I think you should go. Helen, you have to do what's right for you, I know, but I still think you should go."

*

"Tiffany!" Helen called as she came into the apartment. "Helen's home." She laughed at herself. "I'm talking to a dog." She laughed again. "Now I'm talking to myself."

She put her keys and purse down on the table in the foyer and went into the kitchen where the little dog stood at the door of the crate wagging her tale. Helen opened the door and the dog bounded out yapping happily and running around her in circles.

"You know, I love this little greeting I get from you every day when I come home. I'm beginning to see why people like dogs." She picked up the leash from the top of the crate and snapped it onto the little dog's collar. "We'd better get you outside pretty fast, though. I know you're about to pop."

She picked the little dog up and carried her to the elevator. The apartment was on the fifth floor. They waited for the doors to open then got in and rode down. The complex had a nice size park around it. It was well tended with paths and benches. There were picnic areas with grills that the residents could use. At this point, Helen hadn't seen many people using them. It was late August and Georgia was still very hot, too hot to barbecue.

She took one of the plastic bags that the complex supplied to dog walkers and followed Tiffany around the pathways until she had completed her toilet needs. Then she went over to the bench she had decided was her favorite and sat down. There was a large shade tree behind her and it was the coolest spot in the yard. Tiffany had an extendable leash and she played happily in the grass with bugs or whatever bounced around for her to chase.

Helen took a deep breath. She was starting to unwind from the day at the insurance company.

It was nice taking a walk after work. Why had she never done it before? You don't have to have a dog to take a walk. She thought as she looked across the expanse of lawn. She could imagine children playing with balls or Frisbees when the weather cooled off. She waved to the man across the lawn from her. She'd seen him there before. In fact, he was there almost every afternoon when she got home.

"He's obviously an artist," she said to Tiffany. He had a kind of board that he held in his right hand. He held something in his left hand. It could have been a pencil but he kept lowering it to something on the bench beside him. She thought it must be a paint pallet so it must be a brush he held in his hand. "I wonder what he's painting," she said.

He waved back without putting the brush down.

"Let's go meet a neighbor, Tif." Helen stood and started across the lawn. When she drew near to him, he looked up and smiled. His smile was warm and Helen felt something tingle in her throat. He was handsome in a rugged way and young. Certainly no more than forty years old. Stop ogling young men, Helen. She scolded herself. You're not that pathetic.

"Hello, Tiffany," he said putting his board down carefully beside him and reaching for the little dog. He picked her up and let her lick his face.

"You know each other," Helen said smiling and holding out her hand. "I'm Helen Riddick. I'm taking care of Tiffany while Melissa is in Europe."

"It's nice to meet you. Melissa told me about you. I was going to come over and introduce myself, eventually," he said blushing slightly and looking down.

He's shy, Helen thought. "I see you out here every day. I hope we're not in the way of what you're painting." She looked across the lawn at the bench under the spreading tree.

"No." He smiled and picked up his board showing it to her. "You are what I'm painting."

"Oh gosh," Helen said. The picture was of her and Tiffany. Her skirt was spread out on either side of her on the bench and she smiled down at the little dog where she sat in the grass.

"The likeness is good. Can you see us that well from this distance?"

"It's not that far away. I'm Victor Crain." He held out his hand and when she put her hand into his he lifted it and pressed it to his lips.

Helen laughed and Victor blushed again. "Don't you have to get my permission to paint me?"

"No, do you mind? I'll give it to you."

"I don't know." She looked at the picture. "I just feel a little strange that you've been looking at us close enough to paint a picture and I didn't even know it. That's not the suit I'm wearing today," she said.

"That's the one you wore the first day. It sort of stuck in my mind." He took the board back from her. "I hope I haven't offended you."

"No. Now that I'm getting used to the idea I don't mind it so much. But you can't give your paintings away. How will you make a living?"

"I don't make a living on my paintings," he said. "I work for a living like everyone else."

"But with this kind of talent, you could make a living. You could paint portraits. Don't you like to paint portraits?"

"Yes I do. That's what I really like to paint. I love capturing the essence of people. I like portraits of animals too. They're all different, you know. Sometimes the differences are subtle, but they're there. It's a real challenge to capture that."

He looked intense as he spoke. Helen was hesitant to say anything.

"I'm sorry." Victor laughed. "I get very passionate about my art."

"What do you do for a living?"

"I'm a doctor."

"You're a doctor!" Helen laughed. "I didn't expect that."

"I'm passionate about that work, too." He laughed with her. "The only place I've actually sold any of my art is to text book companies. I draw illustrations of anatomy."

"What a great idea." Helen stood up and leaned over to pick up Tiffany who was lying on her back in the grass with her legs straight up. "I guess I should take her back upstairs and feed her. I got home a little late tonight."

"Yeah, I was just about to give up on you when you came out." He stood and gathered up his art supplies. "I'm glad you came over to talk."

"I guess I'll see you tomorrow?"

"I guess so." He smiled at her and she felt that tingle again.

*

"Daddy, that's beautiful!" Delia said as she came into the occupational therapy room.

Matthew looked up at her and smiled. "Not ... beautiful ... as ... you," he said, reaching for her hand. His little girl truly was beautiful. She looked just like her mother, only taller.

"Thank you, Daddy. That's a nice thing to say." She sat down at the table next to him. "Did they have these pots and potting soil here already or did you have to ask them to get some for you?"

"They ... were ... here." Matthew was working on a potted plant. It was some kind of dwarf tree. He was twisting a wire around one of its many trunks and bending the trunk into a curve. "I ... asked ... wire."

He lifted his right hand toward the branch he was holding in his left hand. It seemed to go too far and knocked the branch over almost breaking it. "Damn!" He swore.

"Still having a little trouble controlling that right hand?" Delia took his hand in hers and guided it to the plant.

"It's ... stronger ... but ... still stupid."

"It isn't stupid and neither are you. You'll get control of it," she said. "Your speech is coming along really well. Do you ever have trouble understanding?"

"Yes ... too many people ... conversion," he said putting his hand into a bag of some kind of seeds and sprinkling them on the soil in the pot around the tree. Some of them spilled onto the table and he concentrated on picking them up with his right hand.

"Conversion ...? I'm not sure what you mean."

"Talking to ... each ... other." Matthew smoothed the seeds over the surface of the soil, picked up a spray bottle with his left hand and soaked them with water. "Left hand ... getting smarter." He laughed.

"Oh, conversation ... you have a hard time following a conversation," Delia said. "What kind of seeds are those?"

"Grass seeds."

"What a great idea. Your little bonsai will look like a miniature field." She kissed his cheek. "You are really so artistic, Daddy."

"Love to garden," he said, "even small ... garden."

"I love to garden," Daniel said coming into the room with Frankie right behind him. "Even in a small garden. Dandy, you shouldn't let him get away with not saying things right." He scolded. "How are you today, Dad?"

"I'm ... doing ... very ... well, thank you, son." He laughed. "It takes ... too ... long to ... s.say all ... the ... w,w.words."

"... all of the words." Daniel smiled.

"Jeez, Danny, you're a slave driver," Frankie said.

"I am not. I'm doing what's right."

"Danny, slow down, Daddy, has a hard time following a conversation."

"I bet you just love it when she talks about you like you weren't here, don't you, Dad?" Daniel laughed and made a dodging motion at his sister's frosty look.

"I ... love ... everything ... she does." Matthew pushed his chair back and stood up. He reached for his walker where it was parked up against the wall. He really only used it for balance anymore. His right leg was getting stronger now and he hoped he wouldn't have to use the walker much longer. "Time for ... physcal ... therpy?"

"That's right," Daniel said falling in beside him. "Are you coming with us today, Dandy?"

"No, I was just taking a break. I'm on the third floor today. I need to go back." She stopped Matthew at the door. "Don't let him work you too hard, Daddy." She kissed his cheek again. "See ya later, Frankie."

"She's a sweet ... girl." Matthew smiled then looked at Frankie. "How ... are you, Frank? Still ... married to ... a doctor?"

"I never was married to a doctor." Frankie feigned irritation. "Everyone sure is in a hurry to get me married off. Why is that?"

"Just hoping ... you ... know a good ... op ... op ..."

"... opportunity ..." Daniel supplied.

"Yeah," Matthew moved down the hall at a comfortable clip.

"Say it, Dad."

"... chance." He could feel his smile stretching across his face. Those muscles were coming back, too. *I guess those ridiculous exercises the speech therapist makes me do are paying off,* he thought.

"Well, I do know a good, chance, opportunity when I see one," Frankie said. "I plan to marry her but I'll do it in my own time."

"Good for you," Matthew said. "How's ... Sybil, Dan. She was in ... yesterday. Are ... twins?"

"No, just one baby, a boy, he's pretty big. I'm getting a little worried." Daniel guided them all into the physical therapy room. "What do you want to start with, Dad, the exercise bike?"

"Sounds ... good, then ... extra weight ... training on ... right ... side."

"I thought Jenny said not to do that. Didn't she want the right side to catch up slowly?" Daniel asked.

"He's made me see the error of my ways," The physical therapist said from behind Daniel.

"Oh hey, Jenny, what's going on?" Daniel turned to look at her.

"Your Dad's been coming in here by himself and working that right side. I was surprised he was making such excellent progress," she smiled at Matthew. "I guess he taught me a new strategy. We'll just watch the blood pressure and go gentle with those movements. We don't want any broken vessels or anything while he's on the blood thinner. He's promised me he'll bring someone with him from now on, too."

"... gentle ..." Matthew said as he took his position on the bicycle and started to work out.

*

Helen put the key in the lock and turned it to open the front door of the shop. It was dusk, but the street lights were on. She had been at the park with Tiffany and just wanted to stop by the store to check on the construction. She hadn't had much time to check in lately.

She pushed the door open and reached for the light, but before her hand made contact with the switch the lights came on. "Aahhhh," she screamed.

The little dog pulled the leash out of her hand and ran across the room growling and barking. She leapt at the man standing just outside the office door and latched onto his leg with her teeth.

"Ouch!" He yelled. "Get this creature off me, Helen!"

Registering the fact that he knew her name, Helen focused on Phillip's face. "What are you doing here?" she asked hurrying across the room to gently extract the little dog from his ankle. "It's okay, Tiffany. This is Phil, our friend." The little dog growled at him from her arms.

"I'm bleeding here, Helen! That damn dog is vicious!"

"She was protecting me." Helen smiled at the furry ball of protection in her arms and stroked her head.

"I wasn't attacking you." Phillip frowned and sat down in a rolling stool behind the candy counter. The counter was the first thing on the display floor outside of the office.

"Well, you startled me. What were you doing in here in the dark, waiting for someone to come in so you could scare them to death?"

"Of course not, I came in the back door. I need to install some software on the computer." Phillip was rolling up his pants leg to expose the bite wound. There were four distinct bite marks in his leg. One was torn and bleeding. The others were only oozing small drops of blood.

"She really did bite you, I'm sorry. I guess she takes her protection job seriously." Helen put the little dog down on the floor and Tiffany circled Phillip warily.

"Don't turn her loose again. I'm not safe."

"I think she knows you're okay now." Helen knelt in front of him to study the wound. "We'd better clean that up, though, there's a first aid kit in the closet, the first thing Gwen bought. She's so practical." She stood and turned to open the closet.

"She's done a good job on opening this shop," Phillip said watching as Helen knelt in front of him with the first aid kit and pulled out the squirt bottle of alcohol. "It's amazing what she can do that I didn't know about."

"Gwen does have a lot of talent." She wiped off the blood on his leg with a gauze sponge and applied pressure to the wounds to stop the bleeding.

"Ouch, be careful, Helen, that hurts." He sucked in his breath as she squirted the alcohol into each puncture wound. "Hey, stop that!"

"Don't be such a baby, Phil. I have to clean the wounds. You don't want to get an infection do you?" She put adhesive bandages over all of the wounds and started packing up the kit. "You'll want to take those off once the bleeding stops. The wounds need air to heel."

"Thanks, Doc." Phillip smiled at her as she stood up and looked at him.

"You know, I've missed you, Phil. Have you forgiven me for being so angry with Matt?"

Phillip sobered. "No, I really don't understand it. It's not like he had a stroke on purpose to bother you."

"No, I guess you haven't forgiven me." Helen put the box back in the closet and went into the office. "I'm not going to talk about it, Phil. It's obvious that you wouldn't understand."

He picked up a box of disks off the counter and followed her into the office. She was sitting at the desk watching the computer screen as it started up. "I hope you don't plan to stay long," he said angrily. "I need to install this accounting program."

"You know, Phil, it is my shop. My name is on that loan with Gwen's," she said. "You're just working for us."

"God, you have become a nasty bitch."

Helen leaned back and took a deep breath. "I'm sorry. I shouldn't have said that." She stood and motioned for Phillip to take the chair behind the computer. "This is another thing that I'm mad at Matt about. He deprived me of my friendship with you."

Phillip sat down at the computer deliberately ignoring her and opened a box to extract the disk.

"So you aren't going to talk to me now?" Helen said.

Slipping the disk into the computer he turned and looked at her. His eyes were cold. "The only reason we were ever friends, Helen, was because you were married to my best friend," he said turning back to the computer. "You're hurting him now. I can't be your friend anymore."

Helen sat down in the chair in front of the desk and rubbed her eyes with her hands. "What you just said was mean. I didn't know you were mean," she said. "But still, I don't believe that's true. I think you and I have a friendship that doesn't depend on Matt, or Gwen. You're just mad at me right now."

Phillip was silent as he watched the computer monitor.

"I hope you can get over it before it ruins our relationship completely, because that would be a shame. We all need friends."

"Helen," a man's voice called from the front of the shop.

"In here, Victor," she called. "I guess I didn't lock the front door," she said turning back to Phillip. She gasped at his expression.

"Who's that?" he demanded.

"A friend, I'm allowed to have friends," she said. "He wanted to see the shop then we'll run Tiffany home and go to dinner together." She stood angrily as Victor stuck his head through the office door.

"Oh, you're not alone. Good," Victor said. "I was going to say I didn't think it was safe to leave the front door open like that with you back here in the office."

"Victor, I'd like you to meet my partner's husband, Phillip," she said, "Phil, my neighbor, Victor Crane."

Phillip extended his hand reluctantly then turned back to the computer.

"I'm trying to talk Victor into taking a space in the Gallery." Helen continued. "He paints."

"Good luck to you," Phillip said without turning around.

"Show me the shop, Helen," Victor said scooping up the little dog so that she could lick his face and pat his chest with her wagging tail.

"That dog seems to like you," Phillip grumbled.

"Tiffany likes everybody," Victor said.

"Not everybody." Helen guided him out of the office. "Let me show you my candy counter."

*

"Matt's doing so well," Phillip said that night at dinner. "I got there late. Frankie and Danny were already there and they were all three working out on the free weights. I swear he's in better shape than I am. I need to start going back to the gym. I haven't gone since Matt got sick."

They were having dinner alone. The kids had all gone back to their own lives. Andrea and Tom had apparently patched things up.

"You'd better start going to the gym again then. Before you know it, Matt, will be ready to run again. How far were you going, two miles?"

"Yeah, two miles," he said pushing away from the table. "I miss him."

"You miss him?" Gwen looked up at the seriousness of his voice.

"Yeah, do you think he'll ever be the same?"

'No, but he'll still be Matt."

"It's the speech that makes it hard. We used to have such good conversations." Phillip looked reflective. "We had all sorts of philosophies and theories. I really miss that."

"I can be philosophical, talk to me."

"It's not the same." Phillip stood up and took his half empty plate to the sink. "I ran into Helen at the shop. Did you know she's seeing another man?"

"No, really? I wonder why she didn't tell me." Gwen followed him to the sink.

"His name is Victor Crain. Sounds like something out of a ghost story." He rinsed his plate and put it into the dish washer.

"...The painter? I knew about him but Helen said he was a friend. I didn't think they were seeing each other romantically."

"There's no such thing as just friends between a man and a woman, Gwen, don't be stupid."

"Hey, don't call me stupid and you're the one that's being stupid."

Phillip took a deep breath. He didn't want to fight with Gwen. "I'm sorry I shouldn't have said that."

"Phil, you and Helen are friends. Why couldn't she be friends with another man?"

"I don't want to talk about this anymore." Phillip dried his hands on a towel and left the room.

Gwen followed him into the living room. "Well maybe that's why we don't have philosophical conversations, because you don't want to talk about it."

"I don't want to argue anymore today, Gwen."

"You and Helen argued?"

"Yes."

"About what?"

"I don't want to talk about it."

*

Gwen pulled into the parking lot at the hospital. It was Monday morning and she had come to see Matthew graduate. He was going home and the kids had planned a little welcoming party. The twins had both taken the day off. Frankie could only get the morning and Grace couldn't take time off from medical school, but she and Phillip would be there.

She waved to Phillip who was pulling into a space a few cars down from hers then waved to Daniel as he pulled into the lot with Sybil in the passenger seat and Helen in the back. He had told Helen he was going to pick her up so that she wouldn't be tempted not to come.

"Are you ready?" Phillip asked as he approached her.

"Let's wait for Helen and the kids." Gwen started to walk toward the spot where Daniel had parked the car.

Sybil struggled to get out of the passenger seat with her bulging belly and Phillip who had hung back at first leapt forward to help her.

"Would you take Sybil in?" Daniel said as he opened the door for Helen. "I need a few minutes with Mom."

"Sure," Phillip took Sybil's arm and guided her toward the elevators of the parking deck.

"I can take myself in," she protested shyly.

"But we'll enjoy your company," Phillip said.

"What's he going to talk to her about?" Gwen asked hurrying after them. "If he's going to hurt her maybe I should stay. This is a very emotional time for them both."

"He isn't going to hurt her," Sybil said. "He's going to explain to her why he thinks it's important for her to be here. Then he's going to let her decide what to do."

"Maybe he should have done that before he brought her all the way here," Gwen said.

"He's reducing his risks." Sybil laughed and they stepped into the elevator.

*

"Danny, Daniel," Helen said. "Please don't preach me a sermon. I know you're mad at me…"

"I'm not mad at you, Mom." Daniel was guiding her over to the door to the stairs of the parking deck. "There's a nice little garden at the bottom of the steps. We have a few minutes before we have to be in there and I'd like to talk to you."

"You're not mad at me for leaving?" She followed him down the steps. He was skipping down them at a fast trot, but she didn't have any trouble keeping up.

Daniel guided her to a gardened fountain area and sat down on the bench indicating with his hand that she should sit beside him. "Dad's been here. I recognize his gardening style." He laughed.

Helen looked around her. It did look like Matthew. He always made is gardens look so natural. She smiled.

"That's occupational therapy." Daniel continued. "Mom, I wanted to tell you that I understand why you left."

"You do?" Helen looked at her son. He was looking at her so intently, actually making eye contact. He was beautiful. Matthew had always said the twins looked like her and they did have her coloring, but she could see Matthew in this tall hansom son of theirs. She could see the Matthew she'd fallen in love with. The one she'd loved for so many years. "Well, maybe you can explain it to me then. I don't understand. I just know I had to leave." She looked down at her folded hands.

"I don't know if I can explain it. I'm not sure it can be put into words, but I'm sure it's a lot like why I left." Daniel reached over and put his large hand on her folded ones. "I'm sorry if I hurt you, Mom, but I had to go."

Helen jumped at the contact. He hadn't touched her in years, except for a stiff hug when he'd first come back. She looked up into his eyes and sniffed. "You don't hate me?"

"No," he said moving his hand and standing up. He walked around the small garden examining the plants. "I did for a while. At least, I thought I did. I can't even remember the reasons I had for it." He turned back to look at her. "I felt like I didn't know where you ended and I began."

"That's a good way to put it, honey." Helen wiped a tear that had escaped her lower lid. "That's exactly it."

"And it made me furious with you." He continued, "Even though it wasn't your fault."

"It probably was to some degree. I love your sister, but you and I had some kind of special bond." She sniffed again and took a deep breath. "At least, that's the way it felt to me."

"That's the way it felt to me, too." He sat back down beside her and turned her to face him. "I felt like if I didn't learn how to break that bond, get away from it, I'd never be able to live without you. I'd never be able to have a life of my own. I felt like I was trapped, like you were trapping me."

"I'm sorry." Helen sniffed and wiped at a new stream of tears.

Daniel pulled a tissue out of his pocket and handed it to her. "I didn't tell you that to make you sorry. I told you that to make you understand."

"That's pretty much what I'm doing now with your father, but does it mean we'll never be close again." She blew her nose. "I'm not sure your dad and I ever will be."

"Well, that's really not any of my business but I think you and I can work things out. You may have noticed. I have a life of my own now, and a family." He smiled. "But the one thing I regret is that I couldn't have explained this to you before I went away."

"You couldn't explain it to yourself."

"No. But I was important to you and I hurt you. I regret that."

"Yes, you did hurt me." Helen tucked the used tissue into her bag.

"That's why I wanted you to come here today."

"I don't follow," she smiled stiffly.

"Whether or not you and Dad ever get back together again or even become friends, you have a family together. You'll always share children and grandchildren." He smiled. "You'll always care about him."

"Yeah, if I can ever forgive him for messing things up this way." She stood up and Daniel stood up with her.

"Mom," He put his hands on her shoulders and turned her to look at him. "This graduation might not seem like much to you, but it's the whole world to Dad. It matters a lot. One day you'll know how much it mattered to him for you to be here. I don't want you to regret hurting him."

"Oh shit!" She dug in her bag for the tissue she had just put away. Daniel put his arms around her and she buried her face in his shirt enjoying the familiar scent of him. "How did you get to be so smart?" she said as she gave in to her tears.

*

Gwen watched as Daniel and Helen came into the room. Helen had obviously been crying. "Maybe I should have stayed with them," she whispered to Phillip.

"They don't look mad at each other to me." Phillip snarled.

"No they don't," she said as Daniel seated his mother in one of the folding chairs that had been set up for this occasion. Turning to Phillip she said, "You be civil to Helen, Phil. If you can't do it for her sake, do it for Matt's."

"I will."

"We're here today to graduate Matthew Riddick to the real world." Jenny, the physical therapist said at the front of the room. "He's accomplished a lot in the past month. I know none of you can even imagine having to relearn as much as he has in that amount of time."

Gwen looked around, the room. Daniel sat next to Helen with Sybil on his other side. Delia was across the aisle from them with her husband, Greg. Frankie was beside them. She and Phillip were behind them. There were a couple of other patients across the aisle. The doctor and therapists and a couple of nurses stood at the front of the room.

"In fact," Jenny continued, "Matt has accomplished all the goals we set for him and exceeded most of them, Ladies and Gents," she smiled, "Matthew Riddick."

Matthew entered the room from the back and started up the isle with his walker. He beamed with pride as he picked the walker up off the floor and took several steps without it. Everyone leaned toward him as he lowered it quickly to the floor when his balance wavered. Then there was a rumble of laughter when they all settled back in their chairs.

Matthew walked up to the lectern where Jenny had spoken. He parked his walker on the right of it and stood behind it holding the sides for balance.

Gwen saw him look at each of the people that were there and then focus on Helen. He smiled and his face lit up. "I ... want ... to ... thank each of you," he took a breath. "But ... we don't ... have ... all ... day." He laughed and the group laughed too.

"We have all the time in the world, Dad," Daniel said.

"Maybe ... you ... do ... but ... I've got places ... to ... go and people ... to ... see."

Everyone laughed again then the room quieted as Matthew held up his right hand. It wavered in the air for a few minutes then slapped back down on the lectern.

"Gravity," Matthew said looking at his wayward hand. This brought another round of laughter then everyone quieted again. "You're all ... wonderful and I want to thank ... my beautiful wife." The room was silent as Matthew looked directly at Helen. "Thank you, Helen ... you ... make me ... want ... to live."

Gwen burst into tears as the blur of Helen's navy blue suite moved toward the lectern. Phillip pulled her into his arms. She could hear other sniffles and sobs as the rest of the audience succumbed to their feelings. "Is Helen holding Matthew?" she whispered to Phillip and blinked at her tears.

"No, Matthew is holding Helen."

*

"Delia and I'll get Dad checked out," Daniel said to her after they had been served cookies and juice. Matthew had gone back to his room to get his belongings. "Sybil can run you back to your apartment."

"You'll come to our welcome home party, wont you?" Delia said. Her eyes were frosty as she glared at Helen.

"No, honey, I need to go home now."

"So that was all just an act."

"Dandy, leave it alone okay," Daniel said. "Go on with Sybil, Mom."

"Thank you, Danny," Helen said to her son then turned to her daughter. "I need some time to myself right now, Delia, but no, it wasn't an act. I care about your father and I'm glad to see him doing so well."

"But you need some time to yourself," Delia said. "It's all about what you need isn't it?"

"It's not all about that, no, but my reasons for leaving haven't changed."

"Of course not, you're still a selfish bitch." Delia turned and left the room.

"Sorry, Mom," Daniel said. "I've got no influence over her."

"I don't expect you to and she has a right to her feelings. I'm just not used to her being so mad at me," she said as she looked in the direction of her daughters exit. "Thanks for everything, Danny, I love you." She kissed his cheek. "Are you ready to go, Sybil?"

"Yes, you know, maybe you could show me a little of your candy making stuff. I'm sure it'll take a good hour to get him out of here, maybe more."

"Sure, that would be great."

"I'll see you at home, Dan." Sybil kissed her husband and Helen noticed the happy look on both of their faces. She felt that discomfort again.

I wish I could understand it, she thought as she and Sybil made their way to the parking deck.

*

"Thanks for doing this with me," Helen said to Gwen when she let her into the apartment on the Saturday after Matthew's graduation. They were going hiking. She had looked up Georgia hiking trails and found one north of Atlanta that would only be about an hour's drive and was only moderately strenuous.

"No need to thank me. I just wish Phil had come along." Gwen's brow was wrinkled in concern.

"I'm sorry, Gwen. I swear I'm not trying to make him mad."

"I know you aren't. He's just so angry with you. I can't seem to make him understand how hard all this is on you." Gwen looked around the apartment. "Where's Tiffany?"

"Tiff," Helen called. "Mama Gwen's here."

"Mama Gwen? I suppose you're Mama Helen."

"Of course," Helen laughed as the little dog bounded into the room. She scooped her up and let her lick her face.

"You've changed, Helen." Gwen reached for Tiffany and let her lick her face, too.

"I sure have. Dogs are the most wonderful creatures. In fact, when Melissa gets back I plan to get one of my own." Helen was packing water bottles and sandwiches into her pack.

"Really?"

"Really, I thought I might try to talk Melissa into giving me my little Tiff, but I don't think that's likely." She put a dog bowl into her pack.

"I wouldn't think so. Is Tiffany coming with us, Helen? Didn't you say she's an old dog? Can she hike a mountain trail?" Gwen asked, concerned.

"She's twelve years old and in excellent shape," Helen said putting her back pack on the chair next to the door. "And she only weighs nine pounds. If she gets tired I'll carry her. Would you like a cup of coffee while we wait for Victor?"

"Victor's coming?"

"Yes, you don't mind do you?" Helen looked at Gwen. "Didn't you like him when I brought him to the shop the other day?"

"I only met him for a minute. What's not to like." Gwen swallowed. "Good thing Phil isn't here," she said quietly.

"That's true," Helen said putting steaming cups of coffee down on the table and sitting down across from where Gwen sat holding Tiffany. "Phil doesn't think I should have any friends. I guess he and Dandy, Delia, both think I'm a selfish bitch."

"Well, I don't know," Gwen said blowing on her coffee. "He doesn't want to talk about it. He seems to think you're seeing Victor romantically," she said. "Are you?"

"Not at this point," Helen said picking up her mug to sip cautiously at the hot beverage.

"But you might?"

"If he's interested, he's a lot younger than me, you know." The doorbell rang and Helen looked up. "That's him."

"You don't have to buzz him up?" Gwen asked.

"He's coming from the floor above us." Helen went to the door and opened it for Victor. "Ready to go?" She beamed at him and Gwen thought she hadn't seen Helen so relaxed in years.

"Ready," Victor said and waved at Gwen.

"Good, here's the pack. You carry it." Helen tossed the backpack at Victor and picked up Tiffany who was dancing around Victor's feet.

"Why do I have to carry it?" Victor protested. "It's heavy as led. What do you have in here?"

"You'll be glad we have it when we stop for lunch on the trail," Helen said gathering her keys and purse and ushering everyone out the door. "And you have to carry it because you're the man." She laughed at Victor's shocked expression.

"You're a male chauvinist!" he said as they got into the elevator.

"Damn right!"

"So does the man have to carry the pack even if the woman is bigger than he is?" Victor said.

"I'm not bigger than you." Helen punched his arm playfully.

"Yes you are. Isn't she, Gwen."

"Well let's see," Gwen said as they walked off the elevator onto the parking deck. "Stand back to back."

Helen and Victor stood back to back, heads touching and Gwen stepped back a couple of feet to study them. "Sorry guys, you're exactly the same height."

"Well, if we're equal, why does the man have to carry the pack?" Victor said as he put the pack into the trunk of Helen's car.

"You weigh more," Helen laughed and slammed the trunk shut. "And don't even ask how much I weigh. I'm just sure you weigh more. Now, Victor can you ride in the back or do you get car sick?"

"I don't get car sick, why?"

"Because, if Gwen sits in the back seat, she'll vomit."

"What would you have said if I told you I get car sick?"

"We'd all three have to ride in the front," Helen said opening the driver's side door.

"Oh, well, in that case, I get car sick," Victor said. "Gwen can sit on my lap."

They all finally piled into the car. Victor sat in the back and Gwen sat shotgun. Helen couldn't believe how much fun the friendly banter had been. She hadn't felt so relaxed in years.

"Now watch for signs to Panther Creek Trail. It has to be along here on the right somewhere," Helen said as they neared their destination. They'd driven about an hour and a half north. Everyone had fallen quiet for about the last half hour. Before that they'd joked with each other about all kinds of silly things. And Tiffany had moved from one lap to the other always straining to see out the window.

"There it is," Gwen pointed to a National Forest sign.

"Good. There should be a parking area on the right just up ahead. Here it is," Helen said as she pulled onto the gravel parking space and stopped the car.

They all got out of the car and Helen hauled the pack out of the trunk. "I'll carry it," she said and slipped her arms into the straps.

"We'll take turns." Victor smiled and tapped her on the shoulder.

"Not me," Gwen laughed. "You're both definitely bigger than me."

"So, Helen, how long did you say this trail was?" Victor asked after they'd been walking for a while.

"Are you already getting tired?" Helen laughed. "You're not even carrying the pack."

"You didn't answer my question, and it is my turn to carry the pack," he said, stopping her to pull the straps off her shoulders. "I was just wondering because I'm getting hungry. What time is it?" He glanced at his watch. "One o'clock, no wonder I'm hungry. Let's eat."

"No," Helen said. "There's a picnic table at the end and it overlooks a pool beneath a waterfall. I've researched this trail. It's the perfect place to have lunch. Come on, the trail's only five miles long. We must be almost there."

"Five miles!" Gwen said. "Helen, I have to be home by dinner time."

"No, you don't. Besides, at five miles an hour it's only an hour's walk. I've got it all figured out." Tiffany took a deep breath and sat down. "Are you tired, honey?" Helen scooped the little dog up and started back up the path.

"Are we going five miles an hour?" Gwen mumbled. "No wonder I'm tired."

"We're going about that fast. Here we are." Helen called. She'd rounded a turn in the trail and come to an opening in front of a pool of water. The waterfall was in two layers. It fell from high above them into what looked like a rock basin then over the edge into the pool at their feet. "Over there," she pointed to a picnic table. It was across the stream that flowed from the falls.

"How do we get over there?" Gwen asked. "I don't see a bridge."

"We stone step," Helen said as she started across the stream going from stone to stone. She stopped about half way across. There was a long stretch between stones and the water was rapid between them. "We'll have to help Gwen here, Victor." She turned smiling to see both of her friends standing on the bank. The small dog in her arms molded to her torso and started to shake. "What are you waiting for?"

Gwen took a deep breath and tapped Victor on the arm. "Better go on, and you will have to help me over there. But she's determined so just don't let me fall into the river."

"Come on, Gwen," Helen said when they had settled at the picnic table and she was taking the food out of the backpack. "You have to admit this spot is perfect."

"Yes, it is. I just wish my shoes weren't wet."

"Your feet are warm, though, aren't they?" Helen laughed.

Chapter Six / 173

"Yes, I can't believe you packed bedroom slippers."

"I know you that well. Victor, I have cucumber sandwiches, pimento cheese, and turkey and Swiss. What would you like?"

"I'll give you one guess," he said. "Gwen, I'm sorry I let you fall in the river."

"It wasn't your fault." Gwen laughed. "My legs are just too short. At least only my feet got wet. I hope my shoes and socks will dry out before we start hiking home, though. The sun is hot." She had put her soaked footwear in a sunny spot to dry after sliding off the rock on the far edge of the stream into the water.

"If not, you can hike back in the slippers. You've done that before." Helen handed her a cucumber sandwich.

"That's true." She took a bite then looked up at Victor. "We have a history."

"I can see that," he smiled. "Listen, I'm having a great day. What would the two of you think about coming down to Little Cumberland Island with me for a long weekend? I have a house down there. It's a great spot." He bit into his turkey and Swiss and looked across at the waterfall.

"What?" Gwen said.

"You have a house on Little Cumberland Island?" Helen said. "Matt and I went down there with friends once. I always wanted to get a place there, but Matt didn't think we could afford it."

"Would that invitation include Phil?" Gwen asked cautiously.

"Of course," Victor looked at her. "The house has three bedrooms. We can all have our own space."

"Wow," Gwen sighed. "What a great offer. I'll have to ask Phil, but I should tell you now that I don't think he'll be agreeable."

"Why not, would it help if I talked to him?" Victor asked.

"Well, I don't care what Phil says." Helen interrupted. "I say yes."

"Even if it's just the three of us?" Victor asked.

"Just the two of you," Gwen looked back and forth between them. Their eyes were holding each other. "If Phil doesn't go, I won't."

"Even then," Helen said without breaking eye contact with Victor. "Let's take a little walk, Victor." Helen stood and took his arm. "You don't mind do you, Gwen, you could come along, but your feet are wet."

"My feet are dry. My shoes are wet," she said. "But no, you two go ahead, just don't forget I'm here. I don't want to hike home alone."

*

"I hate to say it, Phil, but I think you're right. Helen and Victor were just so comfortable with each other today." Gwen and Phillip were having dinner that same night. He was waiting with a meal for her when she got home.

"She's cheating," Phillip said.

"Well, I don't know about that. I mean, they weren't making out or anything." She rolled the wine around in her glass. "Anyway, she and Matt are separated."

"Yes, but they're still married." Phillip flipped the burgers on the grill and slammed the lid shut. "The bitch is cheating on my best friend. I can't believe you're still friends with her."

"You really need to get hold of yourself, Phil," Gwen said. "Helen is your friend too. If she needs to move on we have to let her. Matt seems to understand that." They fell silent for a while then Gwen said, "But it's really going to be an adjustment. I just can't imagine socializing with Helen separately than Matt." The phone rang and she went inside to answer it. "Oh no, it's the hospital again." She carried the cordless phone out the door. "I hope nothing's happened to Matt. Hello," she said into the receiver.

"Gwen," Helen's voice shook.

"It's not Matt again?"

"No, it's my Dad. He fell and broke his hip. I'm in the emergency room." Helen sniffed. "I just need someone to go over to the apartment and walk Tiffany in a couple of hours. Could you do that? I can't reach Victor. He's probably outside painting."

"Of course,"

"You'll have to come by here first and get the key. I'm sorry to put this on you, but Danny and Dandy are both here. I don't know who else to ask."

"I don't mind. I'll be there in about an hour. Are you alright?"

"No," Helen said and hung up the phone.

Chapter Seven

"The phone was ringing when I got to the door of the apartment. It was Danny calling from the hospital," Helen said to Gwen the next morning over the phone. "I got home about three in the morning. I stayed until Dad was admitted and made sure he was comfortable in his room. They gave him something to ease the pain and help him sleep."

"Did the kids stay with you?"

"No, I insisted they go home at about midnight. They have families of their own." She took a deep breath. "They're good kids, Gwen. Dandy, Delia still barely speaks to me, but she was good with Dad, and Danny's really come around. He even seems to care how I feel."

"How do you feel, Helen?" Gwen said.

"I feel like if anybody else needs me to take care of them, they'd better just tell me now. I don't think I can stand any more surprises." She paused and took a deep breath. "And I'm going straight to hell for feeling that way, straight to hell."

*

Monday morning Gwen walked through the open door to the shop and stopped to look around at the progress of the construction. "You guys are working hard, I know," she said to the construction crew. "But we need all the paneled shelves finished in two weeks. It's just three weeks to our grand opening."

"We're doing our best, but we're shorthanded, Gwen." The foreman of the crew said, "It seems like we lost a lot of good people all at once."

"I suppose I could extend the opening," she said looking toward the open door. There was a strange rattling sound coming down the sidewalk toward the shop. She recognized it, but couldn't place it. "Why is the door open?" She turned back to the foreman.

"With the weather cooling off a little, we just thought some fresh air would be nice." He backed away from the wall frame he was working on. "But it's getting a little warm in here." He moved toward the door to close it.

"Wait a minute." Gwen stopped him. "What's that sound?"

"Mr. Riddick!" the foreman said as he reached the open door and looked out. "What are you doing here, sir?" He went outside and took Matthew under the arm as he guided his walker into the shop door.

"Came ... to ... check out the project."

"Matt." Gwen hurried over to him. "Who brought you here?" She looked out the door expecting to see Daniel or Delia.

"Me."

Gwen tilted her head and looked at him. "You walked all the way here from your house with your walker?"

"Only two miles." He grinned as he turned to sit on the seat of the walker.

"Matt, I'm not sure that was wise." Gwen folded her arms. "I know the weather has cooled off, but in September in Georgia it's still hot."

"Stores are cool ..." he grinned. "And I have a ... f.fancy ... walker. It ... has a ... s.s.s... place to sit."

"So you're telling me that you stopped to cool off in stores along the way?" Gwen laughed. "You're so smart. How did the store keepers feel about that?"

"Made some friends." Matthew stood and looked around the shop. "Can ... I ... s... see ... the ... p.plans, Leo?" He looked at the foreman.

"They're over here Mr. Riddick."

The foreman guided Matthew over to the candy counter where the plans were stretched out. Matthew studied them. Gwen watched as his face first registered confusion then slowly his brows relaxed into lines of comprehension. He put his finger on the plans and moved it around as if tracing the outline of something then he looked at the front of the counter below.

"Helen will have ... pan ... pan..." He frowned in frustration. "Display ... sh.sh.sh, damn," he said.

"Helen will have paneled display shelves around her counter," Gwen said.

"That's it."

"Say it Matt, you know I won't let you get away with that."

"Paneled display shelves ... here." He smiled at Gwen and pointed at the sides of the counter. "Okay, okay, Helen will have paneled ... dis ... dis ... shelves around ... her ... c.c.c.c ... work sur...face." He laughed and turned in the direction of the temporary tool shelves that the crew had set up. He walked over to them and started looking through the supplies.

"Mr. Riddick, shouldn't you keep your walker with you?" The foreman started to push the device toward Matthew.

"Only need it for long trips," he said as he selected a pair of safety glasses and some gloves.

"What are you doing, Matt?" Gwen asked as she watched him put on his safety gear.

"I'm ... building ... Helen's shelves."

*

"I just don't know what to do, Phil," Gwen said at dinner that night. "We've got three weeks to the opening. I'm not sure the work will be done in time."

"Well, if it isn't ready it'll just be a little longer before you open. You'll still be in time for the holiday season."

"I know, but I need to get the flyer printed and out two weeks before the opening. The layout designer I hired emailed me the proofs today and they're beautiful. I'm really pleased. I've got all the artists represented in it." She sighed. "I really want to open on the first. Should I risk it?"

"Yes, I think you should. Besides, you said Matt was helping now. I can't believe that guy." Phillip smiled. "Talk about determined."

"That's true." She studied her plate for a minute. "And if we're not quite finished at opening, we'll just clean up and finish slowly after hours. You know Matt almost completed Helen's display shelves today, and his work is beautiful. I hate to say it, but it's better than the crew. He smashed his thumb with the hammer twice, but he didn't seem to mind."

"I'm not surprised. It's interesting that he started with Helen's shelves." Phillip scowled as he took another bite of potatoes. "He's still so much in love with her. I wonder if he knows she's running around with other men."

"Phil, you're starting to really bother me with this hatred of Helen. She's going through hell. If she can find a little relief by making a new friend, she has every right to." Gwen leaned back in her chair and looked at him. "Don't you have any feelings for her? You've been friends for thirty some years, and that wasn't just because of Matt. I saw the way you and Helen teased each other all the time. You enjoyed her sense of humor."

Phillip took a deep breath. "Yeah, I did." He pushed himself back from the table. "And to tell you the truth, I miss her sometimes. Used to be that when I'd get way too caught up in something, you know, blowing things out of proportion, she could tease me back down to earth." He stood, cleared his dishes and carried them to the sink. "But I just can't get past what she's doing to Matt. I'm sorry, Gwen, I just can't."

Gwen stood and gathered her dishes. She carried them to the sink and took Phillip's place to rinse them and put them in the dishwasher. "Let Matthew defend himself, Phil, maybe he's alright with it. Has it ever dawned on you that Matt may feel the same way she does?"

"He hasn't put up a fight, has he? But why would he insist on putting in her shelves then?"

"I don't know, maybe he just wanted to feel useful or maybe he wanted to prove to himself that he could still be useful." They worked together in silence then went into the living room to settle down for the evening.

"Then it's settled." Phillip broke the silence. "You'll send your flyer to the printer. Have you arranged for distribution?"

"Yep, got it lined up with the local newspaper. I'm also sending invitations to all the new politicians in Sandy Springs and the leading businesses." Gwen stretched her legs out in front of her and yawned. "We'll have an open house by invitation only on the afternoon of October first with wine and cheese, then open to the public the next day. We're almost there." She grinned then covered her face with her hands. "God I hope this works."

*

Gwen turned on the light in the kitchen and went to the stove to put on the kettle. She'd gotten in the habit of having a cup of peppermint tea in the morning. She was trying to cut down on caffeine. She wasn't going overboard, a little chocolate here and there, an occasional cup of coffee, but she didn't want to be dependent on it anymore. She didn't want any more headaches if she missed her morning cup.

"I guess I'll just make enough coffee for me," Phillip said yawning. He went to the coffee maker and started setting it up for his morning cup.

"I wish you'd cut down on caffeine, too," she said.

"I have," he said scratching his butt through his bathrobe. "You've got me on this half caff stuff." He pointed to the can.

"That's true." Gwen lifted the steaming kettle from the burner and poured hot water into her tea cup. She dropped the tea bag into it and set the kettle on the cool back burner.

"Good morning," Phillip's mother said as she pushed her walker into the room and over to the stove.

"Good morning, Mom." He leaned down to kiss her cheek as she put the kettle back on the front burner and turned on the stove.

"That kettle just has boiled, Martha," Gwen said.

"I know, dear, but I want it to boil properly."

Gwen looked sharply at Phillip. He smiled sheepishly.

"I brought my own tea bag too." Martha lifted the bag to demonstrate. "I don't care for that new age stuff."

*

Gwen let herself into the store and put the cat carrier on the floor. She'd been bringing Cole to work with her for the past few weeks. She didn't like leaving him at home. The construction crew had been thoroughly educated on keeping him inside and so far he'd preferred to play in the office anyway so there hadn't been a problem.

The crew hadn't arrived yet so she switched on the lights and unlocked the office door. Mornings were nice in the shop when she got there early. It was peaceful. She'd taken to sitting in front of the computer and typing out her plans for the day. Sometimes she found herself getting poetic in her writing. It was fun. She'd just never thought about writing. Maybe I'll start keeping a journal, she thought.

She switched on the light and turned on the computer. The screen lit up promptly and Gwen smiled, they'd bought top of the line. Of course, it would be outdated in a handful of years, but hopefully by then they'd be able to afford to upgrade.

The playful kitten spotted the light of the screen and jumped up on the desk. He lay down in front of it and gently touched the screen where the mouse was moving.

"That's not the kind of mouse I brought you in here to catch." Gwen laughed and buried her nose in his soft fur.

Pulling a memory stick out of her purse, she slipped it into the USB port and started up the program. She opened a new file and named it Gwen's journal, saved it on the memory stick, and started to type.

September 20

Things are coming together here at the shop. It's almost what I planned, but something isn't right. I thought I would love the work, the challenge, but I have this uneasy feeling. I wish I could identify it.

I can't talk to Phil about it. After all, I pretty much defied him in starting this project. He's been very supportive, but I just don't feel comfortable telling him I'm not happy.

Well, I guess not happy isn't the way to describe it. I don't know. Something is missing. I keep going over all the plans and covering all the bases. I've done everything I'm supposed to.

Maybe the problem isn't with the shop. Maybe it's with me.

*

"Mornin, Gwen." Matthew stood at the door to the office. "Did I interrupt?"

"No, no, come on in." She saved the file and removed the memory stick from the computer. She slipped it into her purse. "I'm starting a journal. I know most people use one of those nice little journal books, but the arthritis in my hands makes it hard for me to write longhand." She laughed and massaged her right hand with her left.

"I have that too." Matthew laughed and sat down in the chair across the desk. Cole leaped off the desk, hit the floor and bounced up into Matthew's lap. The small cat arched his back as he rubbed against his chest and purred. "Cole is growing."

"Yes he is. I was hoping he'd help keep the mice out of here, but so far all he's chased is the computer mouse."

"Smart cat."

Gwen loved the way Matthew said what he wanted to in only a few words. "Did you walk again?" she asked. He'd walked to the shop everyday that week. It was Friday. He was tired the day before and she had hoped he would take the day off.

"No, Daniel dropped me ... on his way." He leaned forward to look closely at Gwen. "Something bothering ...?"

"No, I'm fine!" she said quickly and turned to the computer screen to open her email.

Matthew put his hand on her arm. "You protest ... too much."

She looked at him and smiled. "Are you quoting Shakespeare, now?" She laughed.

"Now you're de ... de...."

"Deflecting."

"Right."

"Say it."

"defecting ... whatever ..." Matthew waved her protest away. "Talk, Gwen."

She leaned back in her chair and took a deep breath. "I don't know what to say, Matt. Something is missing. I should be so happy right now. I thought I would be, but ..."

"Things okay at home ... Martha ...?"

"She's fine. Well, she does get kind of critical." She laughed. "Apparently I don't know how to boil water."

"You're a great cook."

"Oh, so far, she's okay with my cooking. It's just the boiling water she doesn't like," Gwen laughed. "And the new age tea. No, it's not Martha. I can adjust to her criticism. It's me, Matt."

He looked at her as she paused and she took a deep breath. "I thought this would make me so happy." She looked around the office. "I was hoping it would take away this uneasy feeling I have. I feel like I've forgotten to do something. When I look at my children, I think. There was something I was supposed to do as their mother, but I forgot to do it."

"That sounds so stupid, but I have the same feeling about the shop, Matt, like there is something really important I was supposed to do, but I forgot." She took a deep breath and picked up the kitten that was playing at her feet now. Pulling him close to her face she inhaled the sweet scent of him. "You know, on my death bed, my last words will probably be: *What did I forget to do?*"

She looked at Matthew sitting across from her. He looked back at her sincerely, but didn't say anything. "No comment?" she asked.

"I've felt that way," he said.

"Did you ever figure out what you forgot?"

"Not yet ... still working on it."

"Well, thanks for listening. I think I'll take a walk in the park. Will you make sure the crew remembers to keep Cole inside?" She rose and put the cat down in Matthew's lap.

"Sure ... Gwen." He took her hand as she passed him. "I..."

"It's okay. You don't know what to say. Like I said, I don't know what to say. I'll only be an hour or so. Will you be here when I get back?"

"Yes," he rose and followed her out into the store. "I'll be here till noon. Going to lunch with Delia. Working out this afternoon with Phil. Busy man."

"At the Gym? Are you ready for that?"

"Been working out ... physical therapy."

*

Gwen pulled into a parking space and got out of the car. She started down the paved walkway. It was a beautiful fall day. Atlanta was still warm in September, but not hot and there was a gentle breeze. She took a deep breath and looked around her. A woman passed her with a golden retriever and the dog pulled toward her in greeting. Gwen stretched out a hand to pet it, but the woman pulled the dog back and scolded it with a command.

Gwen shrugged and continued. I guess they have to have some discipline, but I'd have loved to pet the dog. She continued down the path. After she'd walked for about a mile she broke into a run, stopping after a minute when her feet reminded her that she wasn't wearing running shoes.

Spotting a bench at the top of a hill looking over a small pond, she sat down and took off her loafers to massage her feet. A very small poodle on an extendable leash approached her and sniffed around under the bench.

"Hello," she reached down to pet the little dog. It sprang into her lap surprising a laugh from her. She turned her head as the little dog lapped at her face.

"I'm so sorry. I hope you like dogs," she said, as she pulled the dog away from her.

"I do. She's a friendly little thing." Gwen wiped the dog slobber off her face. "What's her name?" she asked the young woman who sat down beside her.

"Isabella, and mine is Alison."

"It's nice to meet you, Alison," Gwen said reaching for Isabella. "May I hold her for a minute?"

"Sure."

"That's an awfully long name for such a little thing." Gwen stroked the dogs head.

"She has a small body, but a big personality." They sat quietly looking at the pond for a minute.

"There are turtles in there. Have you seen them?" Allison asked.

"No. Are you sure you're not just seeing round rocks?" Gwen strained to look at the pond.

"Look down there by that log. Some of them are snappers. One day we were walking along here and there was a big one right on the path. Isabella was jumping around it and getting nose to nose with it. I didn't know any better," Allison said. "Luckily, a man came along and warned me to get Isa back. He said that thing could take off her whole head."

Gwen looked at the young woman. She was animated when she talked. She smiled and looked back as if they'd known each other all their lives. "Look, there goes one." She pointed at the opposite shore of the pond.

A large round turtle crawled toward the pond and plunged awkwardly into the water.

"Come down closer, you won't believe how graceful they are in the water." Allison hurried toward the pond with Isabella. Gwen followed more sedately and watched as the turtle glided gracefully through the murky water of the pond then surfaced, legs spread, to hang in the water with just it's head above the surface.

Gwen didn't know if she was more amused by the turtle or by Allison's fascination with it. Was I ever that fascinated by life? She wondered, or ever that observant?

"It's hard to believe something that awkward on land is that graceful in the water, isn't it?" Allison smiled at Gwen and she smiled back despite her morning gloom. She felt better.

"What did you say your name was?"

"I don't think I said. It's Gwen."

"It's nice to meet you, Gwen." They fell in beside each other and walked along the path to Gwen's car.

*

Back in the small office of the gallery, Gwen studied the layout of the magazine. It would go to the printer on Monday and just like with everything else, she felt like she was forgetting something.

All of the advertisements looked beautiful. They had donated an ad to a Greyhound rescue group. They were going to put a display in the gallery. Charity is good for business and this was a good cause. It was Frankie's idea. Gwen looked at the majestic looking dogs in the picture. "Maybe I should get a greyhound," she said out loud to herself.

"No ... they eat cats," Matt said coming into the room.

"Do they?" She looked up at him.

"Some do. How's ... the magazine?" He sat down in the chair he'd been in that morning.

"I've forgotten something." She laughed.

"... and you don't know what." They enjoyed a good laugh together. "How was the walk, you look ... re ... better."

"I am. I met the nicest girl, well young woman. I would guess she was about thirty. She was refreshingly thrilled with life. We were down by the pond over at the park and she saw a turtle. She became so animated about how awkward it was on land and so graceful in the water."

"I love things like that." Matthew grinned. "I was working in the yard once ... there was a box tor ... tor ..."

"Turtle."

"Yeah ... it was startled by me and it started to run. Have you ever seen a box ... turrrrtle ... run?" He laughed, "funny ... funny."

"No, I haven't," Gwen said, thoughtfully. "And if I had I probably wouldn't have noticed."

"Maybe that's what's missing, Gwen."

"What?"

"Your partisp ... shit." Matthew frowned.

"My participation, but Matt, I've done a lot of the work on this gallery and I'm selling soap. I raised my kids, how is that not participating. I found the layout designer and graphic artist for the magazine, and the printer. I even found someone to write an article." She looked at the computer screen.

"Letter from ... the editor," Matthew said.

"Who's the editor?"

"You are. It's your ... magazine."

Gwen looked thoughtfully at the screen. "Nobody ever reads the letter from the editor."

"Call it ... *Gwen's Journal* ..." he said thoughtfully. "Everyone wants to read a journal."

*

Editor's Journal
by Gwen Desmond
September edition

There is a pond at the park full of water turtles. Have you ever watched a water turtle swim. They glide gracefully dipping and surfacing in a dance so perfectly choreographed that it must be divine.

Put them on land though and they lumber awkwardly around. It's a good thing for their shell and for some, a strong set of jaws, because they could never run from predators.

The pond lies on the north end of the park where the trail divides. I've never walked that way before, but I did recently and was rewarded by the peaceful essence of a shady park bench where I sat and watched turtles, Canada geese, some wild ducks a sprinkling of colorful birds and of course the magnificence of the natural flora.

Next week I'll take the other fork in the trail. I've probably been that way before, but I can't remember. I'll tell you about that in October.

There is a wealth of exploration to be done here in our new city. Watch for a new spot each month in my journal.

"Now you have to have a picture of yourself taken," Phillip said as he read the article. "I love your writing, honey, it's nice and short. Gives you the facts you need, but doesn't keep you reading too long."

"I'm not putting a picture of myself in the magazine. It's an ad magazine," she said. "Besides, I'm not photogenic."

"We'll go to a real studio and have a pro take it. You have to Gwen. All editors have their picture in their magazine."

"I'm not an editor. I make soap."

"Where did you get this idea, anyway? I thought it was just an add magazine."

"It seems to be evolving." She pulled her bedroom slippers on and started for the kitchen. "I'm going to get a glass of wine. Do you want one?"

"Sure." When she returned to the bedroom where Phillip was sitting up with his computer on his lap he said, "Do you have time to get the article into this edition? I thought it went to the printer on Monday. Doesn't it have to be designed into the layout or whatever you call it?"

"Yes but I got in touch with Brad late this afternoon and he's agreed to work on it over the weekend. He does this stuff on a freelance basis, you know. He's putting himself through the Art Institute. You know, I'm meeting and working with a number of young people. It's kind of refreshing."

"A nice change from us old people," Phillip sipped his wine.

"I don't think I meant that. Matt is refreshing lately, too. You know his stroke has pulled us all together in a way."

"Everyone except Helen," he frowned.

"That's true. Have you talked to her lately? I don't think I saw her all week. How's her dad?"

"Gwen, she and I are not speaking. You know that."

"I can't believe I haven't called her, some friend. I talked to her in the middle of the week but it's been a couple of days. I'll call her in the morning." Gwen looked sad.

"You're a good friend, honey."

"Did I tell you about Allison?"

"Yes, the girl you met in the park. Have you seen her again?"

"No, but we did exchange names and numbers. Maybe I'll call her and set up lunch or something. Maybe Helen would join us, you know, to get away from it all for a little while." She stroked the black kitten that had curled into her lap. "I think I want to get a dog again, something small, maybe a toy poodle this time."

"I figured you couldn't go long without a bunch of pets."

"I think I'll look into a small dog rescue group."

*

The phone was ringing. Gwen looked at the clock. It was 4:00 am, her mouth was dry and her head ached. Regretting the bedtime glass of wine, she reached for the phone. "Poor Helen," she said. "What now?"

"This is a collect call from a correctional institution. Will you accept charges from ..." the automated message paused. "... Rodney ..." his voice sounded in the pause.

"Yes!" Gwen felt her heart start to pound in her chest. "Phil, wake up. It's Rodney. He's in jail."

Phillip sat up in bed, "Give me the phone," he said, reaching for it.

"No," Gwen moved away from him "Rodney, are you alright?"

"I'm not hurt or anything, but I'm in jail. I need you to bail me out."

"What happened? Why were you arrested?"

"I don't want to talk about it right now, just come and get me."

Phillip pulled the phone out of her grasp. She released it easily. The anger in Rodney's voice and his refusal to talk to her made her feel like she couldn't breathe.

"What the hell is going on, Rodney?" She heard Phillip's angry demand. "Well, I guess if you want me to get out of bed and come down there to bail your ass out, you'd better start talking anyway. What did you do?"

Gwen looked blankly at Phillip as he frowned into the phone. Her ears were ringing and the headache had turned to nausea. She got up and went to the bathroom, but she didn't vomit. She wished she would, maybe she'd feel better.

"He got a DUI," Phillip said as he came into the bathroom. "Are you alright?" he asked concerned at her pallor.

"No, I have a hangover," she splashed water on her face, wiped it off with a towel, and pulled her toothbrush out of the holder.

"You wouldn't if you'd been allowed a full night's sleep."

"Maybe I would have. Sometimes I do, they don't last long but sometimes I do." she rinsed her mouth. "Is Rodney alright, was he hurt? Did he have an accident?"

"No, apparently he got pulled over for swerving. What the hell was he doing out driving around drunk in the middle of the night." He stormed back into the bedroom and pulled on his jeans. "I guess I'd better go get him. I should let him spend the night in jail."

"I don't think I could stand that," Gwen said as she pulled on her jeans and went into the closet for a t-shirt. "Are you sober enough to drive?" she asked Phillip. "You just finished a glass of wine a few hours ago."

"Plenty of time to metabolize Gwen, don't nag, I'm really not in the mood." He tied his shoes and stood to collect his wallet. "You don't have to go with me."

"I won't be comfortable until I see him," she said. "Her ears were still ringing and she felt a little off balance, but strangely devoid of any emotion. Still, there was a vague anxiety, something she couldn't quite name. "Let's go. I want to get a coke on the way out."

"Do you know where the jail is?" Gwen asked when they were on the road. "I don't. I've never needed to before."

"Well, I do know, not that I've needed to, but I just do." He snapped.

"Don't snap at me. I'm not the one in jail," she looked straight ahead. It was dark and the city streets were deserted. "This isn't a very good part of town. I hope you know where you're going. I wouldn't want to stop to ask for directions."

"We're not stopping for directions. I'm pretty sure it's around here somewhere," Phillip said looking for street signs and building labels.

"So we're just going to drive around downtown Atlanta in the middle of the night and hope we bump into the jail." Gwen could hear hysterics in her voice.

"That's right, so shut up okay."

"Don't tell me to shut up, you ass..."

"Here it is. Pull yourself together unless you want to wait in the car."

Gwen looked around the deserted parking lot of the Atlanta jail. The street corners were crawling with shadows and there was a fringe of dark forest surrounding it. "I'm not staying out here by myself." She scrambled out of the car and hurried after Phillip.

They approached the desk in the lobby of the jail. "I've come to get my son. He was arrested on a DUI charge about an hour ago." Phillip told the receptionist.

"He's not here yet," she said belligerently. "And if he was, I wouldn't give him to you. I can smell alcohol on your breath."

"It's none of your business what I consume. I'm fifty five years old. It's legal. Now I know my son is here because I got a collect call from him. If you don't want to help me I want to talk to your supervisor."

"Did you drive here? That's not legal." The clerk was a small round woman with a big fat attitude.

Phillip stepped back and took a deep breath.

"Look, lady," Gwen stepped up anger bubbling to the surface. "It's none of your damn business ..."

"Gwen," Phillip put his arm on her shoulder and pulled her around to look at him. "Don't swear. It won't get us anywhere." He turned back to the clerk. "My wife is understandably upset. Our son is in jail and this is our first experience with this." His voice was low and controlled, but Gwen could hear the suppressed anger. "If you want to breathalyze me or something, that's fine. But if you don't want to help me find my son, then let me speak to your supervisor."

The clerk looked around cautiously to the window behind her where the office staff was busily at work. There was a glass office in the corner with an official looking uniformed man working at a computer. The clerk looked as if she was contemplating what to do then she got up and went through the door.

Phillip guided Gwen to a chair in the waiting area and sat down beside her. They watched as the surly clerk talked to a couple of people and one uniformed man disappeared through a doorway in the back of the room.

The clerk came back through the door and said, "I've sent someone to look for your son. He is here, got here a couple of hours ago. I've got someone checking on the paperwork."

They sat in the waiting area for another hour. Gwen went to the desk and asked the clerk what was taking so long. The woman gave her a short and unsatisfying answer. Gwen returned to her seat. An hour later, she had paced the room several times. Phillip was dozing in the metal chair looking uncomfortable. The surly clerk stood and went back into the glass room. Gwen watched as she pulled her purse out of a drawer and then exited the back of the room.

"I think her shift is over," she said to Phillip. "Maybe we'll get somewhere now."

"Excuse me, sir." The uniformed man they'd seen working in the office at the computer was standing at the desk calling to Phillip. "You've been here a long time. Is there a problem?"

"We're here to get our son. He came in about three am. We've paid his bail, but he hasn't come out yet." Gwen explained to the officer.

"What's his name? I'll check on it."

Gwen told him and turned to the window of the parking lot when the officer went through the door. The clerk was standing next to a car talking to the man she'd sent back to check on Rodney hours ago. They were both laughing. "I wonder what's so funny?" she said irritably to Phillip.

"I wonder."

"Your son should be out in a minute." The officer appeared at the desk. "We're right at shift change and the attendant is late. I'm sorry for the mix up."

"But we've been here for hours," Gwen said. "I asked that clerk several times about Rodney. Why would there have been a mix up?"

The side door opened and Rodney came through it looking tired and dirty.

"Rodney!" Gwen hurried over to embrace him.

He pushed her away and walked toward Phillip. "Don't give me any shit about this, Dad," he said. "The guard told me at 5:00 am this morning that you'd paid my bail, but they wouldn't let me go home with you because you were drunk."

"That bitch!" Gwen turned to the door to the parking lot. "I'll kill her!" she said as the clerk got into the driver's seat and started her car.

Phillip grabbed Gwen by the arm restraining her. "Gwen calm down. It doesn't matter." He turned to Rodney. "We weren't drunk, Rodney, now just get in the car and wait for me." Rodney took the keys that Phillip handed him and went through the door.

"Did you hear what he said?" Gwen turned to the officer at the desk. "Why would she want to undermine a family like that? At least Rodney has parents who will come and get him out of jail in the middle of the night. How many of the kids in there don't?" She was panting with anger. "And we weren't drunk."

"Gwen calm down and let's go." Phillip had her around the waist and was pulling her to the door.

"I'm sorry for the inconvenience, ma'am." The officer yawned. "I'll check into the matter. They shouldn't have told him that."

"Inconvenience?" Gwen took a deep breath and walked to the car. "That's putting it a little mildly, more like a year off my life. Phil, I'm so angry. Why would she do that?"

"Just malicious, let it go." They got into the car.

"Rodney, we weren't drunk," she said and turned around to look at her son. He sat in the corner of the seat looking childlike.

"I know and it wouldn't matter if you were. Why should you expect to have to come and bail me out of jail in the middle of the night?" His face crumpled. He buried it in his hands and began to cry.

"Oh baby," Gwen reached between the seats and touched his arm. "It'll be alright. We'll get through this."

*

"I need to get my car out of impound," Rodney said coming into the kitchen that afternoon.

They had brought him to the house and all three of them had fallen into bed exhausted. Gwen and Phillip had been up for about an hour when Rodney finally got up.

"Then I'll need to go to my apartment." He sat down at the table and took the cup that Gwen offered him. "Yuck!" he pushed the cup away after sipping from it. "What is that?"

"It's licorice tea. It's supposed to give you energy."

"Is there any coffee?"

Gwen poured him a cup from the coffee maker and sat down at the table with him. "What happened, Roddy, why were you driving around in the middle of the night drunk?"

"I don't want to talk about it," he said. "And you might as well know, I'm going to have to move back home for a while. I lost my job."

"You lost your job?" Phillip said as he came through the door from the garage. "What happened?"

"I don't want to talk about it."

"You're going to move home so that we can support you, but you don't want to talk about it. Rodney, that's not fair. We have a right to know what's going on." Phillip sat down at the table with them.

"Well then you have a right to know that I didn't enroll in school this semester, which is just as well since they'll expel me as soon as they get wind of this," he said, getting up and starting for the stairs. "I'm going to take a shower and get dressed. Then someone will have to take me to get my car. They charge by the day at those impound lots."

"Sounds like he has experience with this," Gwen said as they watched him go up the stairs.

*

"That has to be about the worst experience I've ever had." Gwen told Helen. They were having lunch together the following week. Alison couldn't make it this time, but they'd made a date for the three of them to have lunch the first week of October.

"So has he moved back home yet."

"Yeah, he's been sleeping at the house and moving his stuff in gradually. I guess he has until the end of the month to get out of his apartment. His roommates have found a replacement. You know Phil and I would have paid his rent if he'd asked us to."

"Why do you suppose he suddenly quit school? I thought he was doing so well."

"I did too, but he won't talk to us about it."

"He won't talk to you about it? Don't you think he owes you an explanation? I mean you're paying his tuition." Helen sipped her tea and looked at the menu.

"Well, yeah, but I don't know how to handle this. He's awfully demanding for someone who doesn't want to talk about it, but I can't force him to tell me."

"Of course you can. He's living in your house. You're paying his bills. You have a right." She leaned forward. "Gwen if he won't talk to you then you should throw him out."

"Yeah, like you throw your kids out when they don't do what you want."

Helen leaned back and laughed. "You're right. I just moved out instead. Maybe you should move in with me."

"I don't think Phil and I would fit in your apartment, but we could get a bigger place."

"Yeah, just abandon the houses to the kids and get a parent's apartment." They were both laughing now. They ordered their lunch when the waitress came and handed her their menus.

"Speaking of parents, how's your Dad?" Gwen leaned back. "He looked pretty sad when I went by to see him last week."

"It's a real problem." Helen sighed. "On a younger healthier person, they'd do surgery on his hip, but he has some health problems that make them reluctant. They're going to try some alternative treatments, but if they don't work. I guess we'll have to look at surgery."

"That's scary, but what's really scary is his attitude. He just seemed really depressed to me."

"He is, but I'm used to it. He has been since Mom died." Helen looked at the plate that the waitress put down in front of her. "You know, Gwen, I just don't have any feelings anymore. I think I'm dead inside. I used to try to make Dad happy. I don't try anymore. I don't even really mind that Dandy hates me. I thought I'd be really happy if Danny ever spoke to me again, but he's really pretty nice to me now. Big woop." She picked up her fork and started to push the food around on her plate.

"How do you feel about the gallery? Isn't that exciting to you anymore?" Gwen said as she took a bite of her salad.

"Why should it be? It's not my project. It's yours...and Matt's. I don't have time to get excited about it. I have to make the living that supports the house that everyone else lives in." She put her fork down and pushed the plate away. "I don't even care about food anymore."

"You should, you're getting thinner and you didn't have weight to lose. I wish that was my problem." Gwen looked at Helen. "Are you going to the island with Victor?"

"Yep."

"Even without Phil and me?"

"Yep."

"Are you having an affair with him?" Gwen put down her fork. "Not that it's any of my business."

"It isn't your business, but no. I'm not having an affair with him at the moment. In fact, I think he has a thing going with Melissa. I've found some pictures of the two of them around the house and they seem close." She took a deep breath. "But, I have to admit, the only time I feel alive at all is when I'm with him, and Tiffany. I never would have thought I could enjoy the company of a dog so much."

"You said you aren't having an affair at the moment. Does that mean you may in the future?"

"Anything is possible and we will be alone together on that island."

"Does Matthew know you're going?"

"Only if you've told him," Helen pulled her wallet out of her purse. "I've got to get back to work," she said as she put her card down on the check.

"Don't you think Matt has a right to know? You are still married to him."

"That doesn't give him a right to know everything. Besides I don't know how long I'll be married to him. We're separated, you know."

Chapter Eight

Phillip pulled into the parking space and got out of the car. He walked over to a park bench and sat down to adjust his shoe laces. I really need to run. He thought as he stood and stretched.

"Hey, Phil."

He looked up at the sound of Matthew's voice. "Hey Matt, I called to see if you wanted to run with me, but Delia said you weren't home."

"We think…the same." Matthew pushed his walker ahead of him to where Phillip stood stretching his legs. "Can I… p… p... put my walker in… your car. I think… I'm ready to try …without it."

"Maybe you should bring it along just in case you need it."

"No… just one mile …I've already done one with it."

"Alright," Phillip unlocked the car and watched as Matthew folded the walker and put it in the back seat. "But don't expect me to carry you back. You're way too big for me."

Matthew laughed and started down the trail at a jog.

"Hey, wait for me." Phillip hurried to catch up to him.

"I thought … you may … need to be alone," Matthew said as they jogged side by side.

"You mean because of what's going on with Rodney."

"Yeah, I'm sorry about what happened. H.has he talked yet?" Matthew swerved and bumped into Phillip

"No and it's really irritating. I thought he was doing so well. Finally I thought one of my kids would do something in the conventional way. You know go to college, have a career."

"Andrea did that."

"I guess so, but she got married and didn't use her education."

"She uses it every day... I'm sure."

They ran in silence for a few minutes.

"The truth is I feel a little guilty. I've been so busy with helping Gwen with the shop and work and all. I didn't even notice that I hadn't paid tuition for Rodney this fall."

"You're only... human."

"Yeah, but I think maybe that's Rodney's problem. You know, he was kind of an afterthought. Gwen and I weren't expecting another baby when he came along. Maybe that's the way he grew up, with nobody really paying attention."

"You paid attention, Phil." Matthew swerved again and Phillip put his hand out to steady him.

"You okay?"

"Balance problem, sorry." Matthew laughed. "I'm... w... working on it." They slowed to a walk and Matthew turned around. "...half mile marker." He pointed to a sign on the path.

Phillip turned around and fell in beside him. They started to jog again. "Anyway," he continued. "Rodney was such an easy kid. I thought everything was going fine, but maybe he was just being easy because he didn't think anyone cared enough to help him out if he needed it."

"I'm sure he... knew ...you cared."

"Maybe." They ran in silence for a minute. The trail curved and Matthew had to slow to a walk to make the turn. Phillip put out his hand just as Matthew's balance wavered and caught him taking his full weight and staggering. "Hey, I told you I couldn't carry you." They laughed as they staggered together to a bench on the side of the trail.

"Sorry," Matthew laughed as he sat down hard and rubbed his face with his hands. "I was doing... s...so well, too."

"Yeah, you were. You'll get your balance back. You've definitely got your strength back." Phillip rubbed his arm. "And even though you look thin as a rail, you weigh a ton."

"Muscle... is... heavy." They laughed.

"I hope I can be as strong as you are. I mean with this challenge I'm facing." He took a deep breath. "I really love that kid, but I'm pissed off at him right now."

"You have a right. What will you do now?" Matthew stood and started up the trail at a slow jog in the direction of Phillip's car.

"Well, with the gallery opening next week. We'll have a distraction," Phillip said as he caught up with him. "I think that's kind of good. Gwen asked Rodney to help her set up the displays." They slowed to a walk as they approached the car. "I guess we'll give him a chance to settle in a little then he's going to have to talk about it. I mean he at least has to have a plan of some kind."

"Can I give you a lift somewhere?" Phillip asked as he unlocked the door.

"No," Matthew took the walker out of the back seat and unfolded it. "Daniel is picking me up at the corner. We're going to the con... vales... cent home to visit Helen's Dad then ...meeting my occupation... therapist for a... driving lesson."

"A driving lesson, are you ready for that?"

"I'm ready." Matthew slapped him on the back and started down the path. "Go for a real run now." He called over his shoulder.

*

Phillip opened the door to the gallery and went in. Helen was standing behind the candy counter with Sybil. She looked up and smiled. "Hello Phil, what are you doing here on a Saturday?"

"I just came by to do a couple of things in the office," he said stiffly. "I won't get in your way." He headed for the back of the shop. "How are you feeling, Sybil?" he asked as he passed the candy counter.

"I'm fine, Mr. Desmond."

"Call me Phil, how long before the baby comes?

"Well, they keep changing my due date, but it looks like about six weeks." The girl put her hand on her swollen belly proudly and smiled. "My new date is November 17th.

"Well, you look like you're about to pop."

"Phil, what a stupid thing to say to a pregnant woman," Helen laughed.

"It's alright." Sybil smiled. "I feel like I'm about to pop."

Phillip frowned at Helen and started for the office.

"Anyway, I'm glad it's the middle of November," Helen said. "I'm going down to Cumberland Island in the middle of October. I definitely want to be back when my first grandchild comes."

Phillip stopped and scowled at her. "So you're definitely going down there, even without us."

"Definitely."

He turned and went into the office closing the door soundly behind him. He sat down behind the desk and started up the computer. The door opened and Helen came into the room closing the door again and sitting down across the desk from him.

"Don't you knock?" Phillip demanded.

"This is my office as much as it is yours. I don't have to knock."

"What if I'd been adjusting my underwear or something?"

Helen laughed. "I'd have loved to see that." She leaned forward in the chair. "Phil, when are you going to get over this problem you have with me? Shouldn't we call a truce? I mean with all of us working here, we need to get along."

"Do you get along with Matt?"

"Of course I do, when I see him. Our schedules don't coincide very much, that's all."

"Does he know you're going away with another man?"

"I'm going away with a friend. Why is there anything wrong with that?"

"Don't play stupid, Helen. Men and women are never just friends."

"You and I are just friends."

Phillip widened his eyes. He looked at her startled, but said nothing.

She took a deep breath and stood up. "Look, when you want to talk to me about our relationship in a reasonable way. Let me know. As far as my personal life goes, I'd appreciate it if you would just stay out of it. It's really none of your business."

"Fine." He looked back at the computer dismissing her. She slammed the door as she left the room.

*

"Oh shit!" Gwen sat up in bed. "I'm out of my flipping mind."

"It isn't going to matter." Phillip patted her on the leg and snored slightly. "I'm sure those numbers will come together just fine." He rolled over and snored again.

"Why did you let me do this!" she slapped him on the back.

He sat up and turned to look at her. "What are you doing, Gwen. I was asleep. What did I do?" He looked disoriented as he rubbed his eyes.

"I've spent so much money. There's no way this is going to work. What was I thinking?" She buried her face in her hands. "I don't do things like this." Standing, she walked to the end of the bed and started to pace back and forth.

"This was all your idea, Helen. I should never have agreed. Our life was just fine. You were the one that was restless." She walked over to Phillip's side of the bed and looked straight at him. "You idiot, why didn't you stop me? Now we'll fall over the side."

"Fall over the side?" Phillip looked at his wife. It was dark, but he could see the contours of her face. Her eyes were glazed. "Gwen, are you sleep walking? You're having a dream."

"We'll fall over the side!" she repeated and started to shake.

"Gwen, honey," he touched her gently on the arm. She'd walked and talked in her sleep before and he knew that she startled easily when this happened. "You're dreaming. Everything is alright, wake up."

"We'll fall over the side." Her voice was weak now and it caught on the words. She started to cry.

Phillip put his hands on her elbows and gently pulled her toward him. "Here, sit down on the bed." He guided her to sit beside him and gently started to rub her shoulder. "It was just a dream."

"A dream!" she buried her face in her hands again. "It's a nightmare and now that I'm awake it's even worse." She nudged herself away from him with her elbows and tried to get out of the bed.

"Damn it, Gwen!" Phillip took a deep breath and held tight as she tried to struggle away. "It's two o'clock in the morning. Tomorrow is our opening day. Shut up and go to sleep."

"I was asleep. If you'd left me alone maybe everything would have worked out."

"How could I leave you alone? You attacked me."

"And besides, it's not opening day. It's only the wine and cheese party. We don't open until the next day." She walked back around to her side of the bed and crawled under the covers. "Phil, what if nobody comes to the party, what if nobody comes on opening day?"

"We'll have to drink all the wine ourselves." He lay back down and moved toward her in the bed. "Damn cat," he said as he maneuvered Cole out from between them and pulled her into his arms. He kissed her temple and felt her begin to relax.

"I've decided we'll have wine spritzers and lemonade." Gwen took a deep breath. "Phil, do you think we drink too much?"

"Maybe, but we don't have anything to be ashamed of. We're responsible drinkers."

"But maybe we didn't set a good example for our kids."

"My parents drank more than I do." Phillip relaxed and lay back on his pillow.

"Mine didn't, but they drank as much. My mom still does," Gwen said. "Does your mom drink now?"

"She can't. Remember? It makes her have weak spells." Phillip yawned and rolled over facing away from her.

"Phil, I'm not going to be able to sleep," she said and rolled over behind him. She put her hand over his waist and nuzzled his neck. "Maybe if we had sex I could." She felt his back stiffen.

Chapter Eight

"I need to go to sleep, Gwen. I have to work in the morning then we have the wine and cheese party at the gallery. Who did you invite anyway?"

"The new mayor, and all of the police force, and all of the major business owners of Sandy Springs, but forget that." She nuzzled his ear. "I need to sleep, too, and you're the only one who can help me do that."

"Gwen, I'm not a lamp. You can't just flick a switch and turn me on."

She ran her hand down his chest to his navel, circled it with her finger and slid down to his genitals. Feeling his penis harden in her hand, she said, "Are you sure?"

*

"Matt, how are we going to cover this unfinished shelf? I really don't want the place to look unfinished tonight." Gwen and Matt were getting the gallery set up for the party. They'd worked all day in silence. But Gwen was getting a hysterical note in her voice. It was an hour before people were supposed to arrive.

"I've got that... covered." Matt laughed and pulled a black velveteen rubber backed mat out of his bag. It was fitted perfectly to the shelf. He put it down and smoothed it out.

"You think of everything. I don't know what I would have done without you on this whole project." She stood on tip toes and kissed his cheek.

"Hey, what's going on here?" Phillip said as he came through the door.

"Your wife is... coming on... to... you," Matt said then grinned childishly.

"You mean you."

"I said... you." The three of them laughed. "Anyway, I was just about to... suggggest... celery tea."

"Celery tea?" Gwen grimaced.

"Camera tea." Matthew knit his brows together in concentration. "I hate this aphasia."

"You said that just fine."

"Of all the things this stroke did to me, I hate that one the worst."

"You're getting better, Matt," Phillip said. "You didn't hesitate at all on that sentence."

"Chamomile tea," Gwen said pulling the box and the electric kettle out from behind the candy counter. That was where they had set up the bar. It was the most suited to it.

"That's what I meant." Matthew sat down on his walker. "I think the aphasia gets worse when I know I'm going to see Helen. I get... tongue... tied, like a boy with... first crush."

"That's the first time you've said anything about that," Gwen said as she and Phillip exchanged a look. "I thought you were alright with what was going on between you and Helen."

"I... hate... it." Matthew swallowed and turned around but not before Gwen saw his eyes cloud up. "I thought she'd come back by now, if I gave her some s.s.space," he said as he gathered his tools and put them in his toolbox.

"Have you talked to her about this?" Phillip asked.

"Can't..." Matthew looked back at them. "... afraid to... and now she's going away... with another man."

"You know about that?" Phillip said.

"Danny told me."

"Victor is just a friend," Gwen said, weakly.

Matthew looked at her skeptically. "Well, here's Daniel. He's taking me home for... shower... change. I'll see you in... hour." He hurried out the front door to where Daniel had pulled to the curb outside the shop.

"That's the first time he's talked about that since Helen left," Phillip said.

"Yeah, I see how you feel now. When you see the pain in his eyes, it makes you mad at Helen."

"Hey guys," Helen said as she swept into the gallery from the back door, tall, thin and dressed to kill. "The place looks great! Why aren't you dressed and ready?"

"Because I've been working all day getting the place ready for tonight, with no help from you I might add," Gwen snapped. "I'm going home to change, be back in an hour." She turned, picked up her purse and stormed out the back door.

"What did I do?" Helen said to Phillip.

"Nothing, you look great, Helen." Phillip headed toward the office. "I think I'll get some work done while you put the finishing touches on your candy counter. The artists will arrive in an hour to put their finishing touches on. I'll let you greet them."

Helen stood staring after Phillip for a minute after he disappeared into the office. "I wonder what that was about," she said as she turned to her candy display.

*

It was warm outside. Fall in Atlanta started late, but the evenings were cooling off and Gwen could feel the difference in the air when the door opened for her first guest. It was the newly elected mayor of Sandy Springs.

"Welcome to Local Talent," Gwen said and cleared her throat. Did her voice sound hoarse? "I'm honored that you would come and help celebrate our opening."

"Thank you for inviting me," The mayor said. "What a wonderful idea. Our city is full of talented people."

Gwen guided her around the room. Each artist stood with the individual display. They were all dressed nicely and were smiling their welcome. She heard the door open and close behind her and turned to see several of the other guests come in. Phillip greeted them and gestured with his hand at the different displays.

Rodney stood behind the candy counter offering spritzers and lemonade to the different guests. Gwen frowned. That was not the best place to put your child when he'd just been arrested for DUI.

Matthew came in from the office looking fine in his suite and Helen stood at the front door talking to newly arrived guests. Soon the room was buzzing with conversation.

"Well, Mom, you did it," Andrea said from behind her.

"Andy, honey, I didn't know you were coming." Gwen turned and hugged her daughter.

"I wouldn't miss your opening night for anything in the world."

Gwen looked around the room again. "It seems to be pretty successful. At least the opening party is. Hopefully the shop will be too."

"There's my girl," Phillip said crossing the room to hug her. "I didn't tell her. It was hard, but I didn't." He looked at Gwen. "She wanted to surprise you."

"She did surprise me and what a nice surprise." Gwen tried not to look at the inch of flesh showing between her daughters blouse and pants. "You look wonderful, honey," she said.

"I've lost five pounds," Andrea said proudly.

"I thought you looked like you'd lost weight," Gwen said. "Is Tom here?" She looked around the room.

"No. He stayed home with Trevor. I wanted a little time to myself." Andrea looked around the room. "I'm going to say hello to Sybil and Danny," she said as she hurried off to talk to her friends.

The sound of the door opening again and another gust of cool air caught Gwen's attention and she looked toward the front of the shop. "Oh no," she said. "What's she doing here? You didn't keep that a secret, too did you?" she looked at Phillip angrily.

"Hell no. If I'd known your mother was coming I'd have prepared you." Phillip squared his shoulders and said, "Hello Gail. What a wonderful surprise."

Gail Saunders stood an inch taller than Phillip. She was a big woman, not fat, just big, tall, broad shouldered. Her arms were long and her legs were longer. She just seemed to fill a room. Gwen swore she felt herself shrink as her mother wrapped her in a swinging embrace. "I wouldn't have missed your opening for anything in the world." She put Gwen back on the ground and held her by the shoulders. "Stand up straight now, honey." She looked critically at her. "I'd forgotten you were so small. What in the world have you done with your hair?" She looked around the room "Well, I'm off to find those grandchildren of mine."

"Gwen, are you alright?" Phillip asked cautiously.

"I think I need some celery tea."

*

Helen watched as Matthew approached the display where she and Victor stood relaxing as the party wound down. Her heart had started beating uncomfortably when she'd made eye contact with him across the room and he started her way. She hated to admit she'd been admiring the way he looked. He'd dressed in a suit for the party. She didn't recognize the suit. It must be new, because it fit him perfectly and he had lost a lot of weight. His shoulders were wide and square, and his waist was trim. She had admired him from the back at first then he had turned and looked directly into her eyes. His face was lean and his features were sharp. He smiled and started her way.

"It was… a… good… party," he said when he reached her. Why did his speech get worse when he talked to her? He took a deep breath. "Winding down now."

"Yes, which is good since we need to be well rested for opening day tomorrow," Helen said. "Have you met Victor, Matt?"

"I don't think…" Matthew held out his hand. "Matthew Riddick." The two men shook hands. "Your work is good. Why… all… prints?"

"I don't want to sell the originals," Victor said. "Helen tried to get me to sell some of them." He smiled at her. "This is the compromise we came to."

Matthew stiffened at the easy smile that Helen and Victor exchanged. "I… want this… original," he said pointing to the painting of Helen with the little dog.

"It's not for sale," Victor said firmly looking up into Matthew's eyes. "Like I said, I won't sell the originals."

"I'll… buy… print, then."

"Matt, you don't have to do that. We're supposed to be selling to the public, not each other." Helen interrupted. "Anyway, we're not selling anything tonight. Tomorrow is the grand opening."

Matthew turned and smiled at her. "Will you be here?"

"Yes, I've taken the day off at the insurance company."

"Good… tomorrow."

*

"I can't believe I'm so nervous," Gwen said as she pulled on the suit she had bought for her grand opening the next morning. "I should have been more nervous last night."

"You were. At least I didn't wake up bruised this morning." Phillip laughed.

"I didn't bruise you. I wish you could be there. Couldn't you have taken the day off? Helen did."

"So Helen will be there. You don't need me." Phillip tied his shoe laces and stood up. "I really need to tie up some things at the office today. I'll come by after work. I think I'll probably be coming by every day after work. That's been the hardest adjustment for me, you not being home in the afternoon when I get off work."

"You'll get used to it. Anyway, I don't see why it matters. All you ever do is go down to the garage and work on the Healy."

"I know, but it's just nice knowing you're there. Anyway the Healy's almost finished. I put on the last coat of paint two days ago." He kissed her cheek and picked up his keys. "You know what I was thinking?" he said as they walked down the stairs and stopped in the kitchen. "Maybe I'll take a picture of it and advertise for it in the gallery. I could be one of your artists."

"That would be good," Gwen said. She sat down at the table looking distracted. "Phil, what if nobody comes in?"

"No such luck, sweetheart. I know that your mother and your daughter will be in. Take heart."

"Oh, Man!" Gwen put her face in her hands. Phillip kissed her on the top of the head and went down the steps to the garage.

She arrived at the store at 9:30 am, half an hour before they opened. She let herself in through the back door and turned on the lights in the shop to look around. They had cleaned up from the party the night before and everything looked ready to go.

"Good morning, Gwen. Are you as excited as I am?" Helen came out of the office looking elegant in a pink suit very similar to the one Gwen was wearing. "It looks like we have the same taste in clothes." She laughed.

"You look better in yours than I do in mine," Gwen said sadly.

"Your mother's visit is getting to you, Gwen. You look beautiful. I've never understood why you let her get to you so much," Helen said. "Come on into the office and sit down. I found this wonderful tea in here. It's called chamomile and it has a calming effect."

Gwen followed Helen into the office and sat down in the chair across from the desk. "That's Matt's tea."

"Really?" Helen looked up from the tea pot she was about to pour from. "He doesn't drink strong black coffee anymore?"

"Of course not, Helen, he's a health nut now, remember."

"No. I didn't know that. Well, I wonder how long that will last. Here have a cup. It's really very good." Helen sat down in the desk chair and sipped her tea. "So what did your mother say to you last night that made you look so hurt?"

"Did I look hurt?"

"Very."

"She didn't say anything except the usual. Why are you so small? What have you done with your hair? You know what though. I felt guilty, because I'd just bitten my lip not to tell Andrea to pull up her pants and change her blouse. I also wanted to demand that Rodney shave off that awful beard."

"Oh really, I like his beard."

"Well, I don't! He has a handsome face. He shouldn't hide it." Gwen sipped her tea and sighed. "I don't know Helen. My mother always makes me feel so... so..."

"You sound like Matt."

Gwen smiled. "I don't think I'm going to be able to find the word for it. She's just so successful and so happy and so overwhelming. Why do I bother to even try? I can't measure up to her."

"You don't have to measure up to her. You aren't in competition with her," Helen said. "And if you were, you'd have to agree that you're a better mother. You certainly don't make your children feel... whatever it is."

"No, but I make alcoholics out of them."

Helen leaned back and took another sip. "I'm not even going to respond to that. All three of your kids were there last night and I don't think any of them had a drink. You had a spritzer and your mother demanded loudly that Rodney not water down perfectly good wine." Helen stood. "It's time to open the store. Gwen," she put her hand on Gwen's shoulder. "Whatever is happening with Rodney is not caused by the alcohol. I talked to him a little last night."

"Did he open up to you?" Gwen stood and the two of them went out into the store.

"Not really, it wasn't the time or place, but he gave me an idea that he might. I asked him to come to the apartment to help me move some plants in off the balcony. I offered to pay him, of course. He said he would. Maybe he'll talk to me then. Rodney and I have always been close."

"Yes. You have. Thanks, Helen."

"So did your mother stay with you last night?"

"No, we really didn't have the room with Andrea here and Rodney. Of course, you know Martha is with us and Mom can't stand Martha."

"Oh, that's right. Martha looked wonderful last night. Even with the walker she's a striking woman."

"She is. She's nice to me too, critical sometimes. Maybe that's just the way mothers are. After all, I criticize my kids all the time."

"But you tell me about it, not them." Helen opened the blinds and turned the open sign around. She unlocked the door and went over to her candy counter. Gwen sat down on the chair next the computer on the checkout counter.

"I don't say it directly, but I think it comes out in other ways. I always seem to have my foot in my mouth with Andrea. Maybe it would be better if I just said. Your clothes are all wrong. It would have the same affect."

"She'd be mad at you, but she wouldn't change her clothes."

"That's right."

"At least you have relationships with your kids," Helen said as she busied herself setting up the chocolate dipping machines.

"I thought you said Daniel was nice to you now."

"When he sees me, but mostly he just doesn't see me. I'm getting along great with Sybil. I guess I should be grateful for that." The bells on the front door jingled as it opened. "Here she comes now. Hello Sybil. I told you to come at noon. This is a little early for someone this close to delivery."

"Not really. If I keep busy, I don't concentrate on my heartburn and swollen feet." The pretty girl laughed.

"Well, I insist that you stay off of those swollen feet." Helen pushed the stool over to her and Sybil sat on it. She was so small that she had to put her hands on the counter to pull herself up. "Don't you dare fall off that stool. Danny wouldn't speak to me for the rest of my life."

"I won't. I'm taking care of little Gabriel."

"Gabriel? Is that his name?" Helen said. Her tone was startled.

"Yes. Don't you like it?"

"Well, I guess so. It sounds so biblical. Isn't that an angel?"

"Yes, that's what this baby is, an angel." Sybil rested her hand on her belly and smiled.

"Well, don't be so sure about that." Helen laughed. "But you know what? I like it. Gabriel, people will call him Gabe."

"I know. I like that, too."

Anyway, what's the matter with biblical names, Helen?" Gwen said. "Daniel is one, so is Matthew."

"You're right. It's a beautiful name."

The bell jingled again and they all looked toward the door. "Hello." A pretty young woman came into the store.

"Allison." Gwen hurried over to her and hugged her. "Helen, this is my friend. Remember, the one I told you about. Allison, this is Helen, we're having lunch with her next week and this is her daughter in law, and our junior candy expert, Sybil."

"It's nice to meet you both," Allison said. "I just couldn't wait to see the gallery." She started to walk around.

After an hour, Gwen sat down behind the computer and put her chin in her hands. "No one has come in at all."

"Hey, I'm someone," Allison said. "And your mom was here and your daughter, too."

"I mean no one but friends and family. I can't run a business on friends and family."

"No, we can't," Helen said. "Maybe I should have gone to work today."

"Stop it, you two," Sybil said. "It takes a while for a business to get going. Nobody knows about us yet. We don't have a reputation."

"Okay, you're right. I won't give up." Gwen stood and straightened her shoulders.

"Me neither," Helen said, busying herself with dipping strawberries in chocolate.

*

Phillip pulled into the empty parking lot of the small strip of stores. There were a couple other cars, but they seemed to all be at the other end of the lot. He parked toward the road, not wanting to take up customer parking and went inside. Gwen was tidying a shelf and Helen was showing Sybil how to mold cordial filled truffles. They all looked up when the bells jingled.

Helen shrugged. "Hello, Phil, come on in."

He looked at Gwen. She was smiling unnaturally, her eyes were overly bright, and her cheeks were pink. "Hey, Phil, how was your day?"

"How was my day? It was the same as always. Tell me what happened here. How was our grand opening?"

"It will also be our grand closing," Gwen said and ran into the office.

"No one came?" Phillip looked at Helen and Sybil.

"No!" Helen said and followed Gwen out of the room.

Phillip looked at Sybil and raised a brow in question.

"People came," she said. "I think Helen and Gwen were expecting crowds."

"But there were no crowds."

"No. No crowds." Sybil laughed. "Friends and family came by early and bought stuff. We had a little flurry of activity at about 1:00 o'clock. I think we sold a couple hundred dollars worth of merchandise, but no crowds. Then at about 3:00 o'clock, I suggested that I take some of Helen's chocolate dipped strawberries out on a tray and offer samples. That's right about the time all of the team mom's are running out to get Gatorade for baseball and soccer practice and we got some interest then. It may have had something to do with this." She laughed and pointed to her swollen belly. "People kept telling me to sit down. We sold all of Helen's strawberries, no boxed candies, though. No one bought soap, except Allison."

"It doesn't sound bad for the first day."

"It isn't bad, but I think they were hoping for instant fame and fortune."

Phillip laughed. "You've got a great attitude, Sybil. I see why Danny loves you so much."

"Thanks. I just know that it takes a little more work to sell things than the artist thinks it should. I mean, you have to market yourself."

"Have you ever had to market yourself?" Phillip sat down on a stool at the candy counter across from Sybil.

"Nothing to market," she said, and busied herself wiping down the counter. "Matthew didn't come in today." She changed the subject. "He didn't want to crowd Helen. I wonder if that was the wrong thing to do. He's so upbeat, you know. Maybe he could have lifted some spirits."

"He's upbeat," Phillip repeated. "Sybil, do you think you can watch things out here for a minute while I go in there and mop up the tears."

"Sure. I'll scream if I need you." She smiled.

Phillip noticed for the first time that she had dimples, not in her cheeks, like most dimples, but next to her mouth. She's lovely, he thought. He stood, went to the office door and knocked softly.

"Phil, you don't have to knock," Helen said as she yanked the door open. "I'll just join Sybil out here while you put Gwen back together." She tried to push past him.

"So is Sybil supposed to put you back together?"

"I don't need putting back together. I'm fine."

"Helen," Phillip put his hand on her arm as she tried to push past him. "I want to talk to both of you." He held her arm firmly as she tried to pull it out of his grasp. "Please."

She stepped back into the office and closed the door. "What?" she said.

"I know that the two of you were expecting overnight success and I could point out how unrealistic that is, but I won't. I'm pretty sure I don't have to."

Helen frowned and looked at him crossly. "I don't want to sell insurance anymore," she said.

"You know, Helen, Gwen budgeted for a salary for you. You don't have to sell insurance. Maybe if you came on board here full time, as a salesperson, you could make a difference."

"That's not a nice thing to say and its borrowed money. Look at the business we did today. You know what? I have a family to support, an extended, extended family and I have to have an income."

"So you're just going to give up in one day."

"I thought you said you weren't going to point out how silly we're being."

"I didn't say silly." He propelled her to a chair and leaned against the wall with his arms crossed looking at both of them. "It is silly, but I wouldn't say that." Both women looked away from him. "What I wanted to point out was something I think neither of you have notices. He paused and let the silence grow.

"What?" Gwen finally said. Helen looked up at him.

"Sybil. I just had a little talk with her and she told me that there is always more marketing to be done than the artist anticipates."

"What does that mean, Phil?" Gwen asked.

"Yeah, I know she's a smart kid," Helen said. "But what does that have to do with what's going on here."

"Well," he smiled wickedly. "One, she must be some kind of an artist. Do you know of any artistic ability, Helen?"

"No."

"Two," Phillip continued. "She's had experience with trying to sell her work. Three, she knows at least something about marketing or how much marketing is necessary."

Helen and Gwen looked at him for a minute without saying anything.

"I sent out a flyer, actually a magazine. That's marketing," Gwen said. "It must have made an impression because I've gotten email responses. Some people have even requested a catalogue but there were still very few customers in here today."

"That's right, Phil," Helen said. "What more can we do?"

"I don't know. I'm an accountant. I don't know anything about marketing. I guess you could wait and see if the magazine will be enough over time. Or maybe there are other things you can do to help the magazine along. Maybe Sybil can give you some ideas, not to mention that I'm pretty sure she's got some hidden artistic talent that she can contribute to your gallery."

The bells on the door jingled. It was loud enough to hear in the office with the door shut. Helen stood up and hugged Phillip. "Thanks, Phil, I love you. I need to go out and help Sybil," she said and hurried out of the office.

"That was very nice, Phil," Gwen said. "You've picked up Helen's spirits and that's a good thing but what good is another artist if I can't even get people to come to see the artists I already have in the gallery?"

"One day, Gwen. How realistic is that?" he said. "Honestly."

"Stupid I guess." Gwen stood. Her shoulders slumped as she went out to the store.

*

"Business picked up a little bit at the end of the week," Gwen said to Helen over lunch the next week.

"Good." Helen leaned back and took a long breath. "I can't take much time at lunch today, Gwen. I've got an important client to see at 1:30. I need the sale."

"Over here!" Gwen called to Allison as she came in the door of the coffee shop.

Allison made her way over to the table. "Hey, guys. What a spectacular day," she said as she sat down at the table. She was smiling and she smelled like cool fresh air.

"I didn't realize how cool it was outside," Helen said. "In fact I don't even remember coming in here. Goes to show how caught up I am in work."

"I thought you didn't really like your job," Allison said as she picked up the menu and looked it over.

Gwen tensed. Allison never seemed to worry about what she said.

"No," Helen said. "I don't really, but I have to make a living."

"Don't we all?" Allison asked and put down the menu. "I know what I'm having. How are things going at the store?" She crossed her arms and looked at Helen and Gwen. "Oh, gosh," she said, sobering. "Is something wrong?"

"No," Helen laughed and Gwen laughed, too. "Actually, things are picking up. I think we might do alright."

"Of course you'll do alright," Allison said. "I loved the place. I've told everyone I know about it."

Gwen laughed again. "What are you having for lunch, Allison? I haven't decided yet."

"I'm having a blue cheese burger with homemade chips. This place does those really well."

"You're young. You can eat like that," Gwen said. "I can't."

"Me neither," Helen said, "and honestly, I've completely lost my appetite for eating in a healthy way."

"You've lost your appetite for anything," Gwen said. "Honestly, Helen, you look almost gaunt."

"You do," Allison said, "and you know what? I can't eat like that all the time either. I allow myself to eat something seriously fatty and delicious like that once every other month."

"But, I mean, how can you want to, when you know it's so bad for you?" Gwen asked.

"It's the human problem." Allison looked at Helen. "Do you think you'd want to eat if you could have a cheeseburger and fries?"

"Yes, as long as I could have a brownie alamode for desert."

Gwen laughed and Helen put her face in her hands.

"I tell people at work all the time. Don't pretend you don't like the bad stuff. It tastes seriously good. People who say they don't like it are lying to themselves. If you indulge now and again, the rest of the time you'll be able to enjoy what's good for you. It's what you do every day that counts and the good stuff actually tastes pretty good, just not indulgent."

"You said at work. What do you do for a living?" Gwen asked. "I can't believe I don't know. You've become such a good friend."

"I'm a dietician."

The waitress came and Allison said, "We'll have three blue cheese burgers with homemade chips."

"Wait," Helen said. "I'll have cheddar and be ready to bring me a brownie alamode for desert."

"Is blue alright with you, Gwen?" Allison asked.

"It's good, but for desert I'll have apple crisp with ice cream."

*

"That was so good." Gwen sat back patting her belly. "I've probably gained all twenty pounds I've lost."

"No. You haven't," Allison said. "Like I said before, it's what you do every day that counts. How do you feel, Helen?"

"I've probably gained back all twenty pounds I've lost, too."

"That would be good," Gwen said.

"Yes, but you probably haven't," Allison said. "Maybe you'll feel more like eating the good stuff now, though. Remember, no more of this for two months."

"Does that mean we can't have lunch with you for two months?" Helen said. "You've been good for me."

"No, but we'll go to the bluebird café. It serves the best healthy food in town." Allison put her napkin in her lap and pushed her chair back. They had already split the bill three ways. "I have to go, now. I have to walk Isabella before I go back to work."

"Oh, Allison," Gwen said. "I wanted to ask you. I want to get a toy poodle. I want a dog, but this time I want a small one. I've always had big dogs, standard poodles actually, but I'd like to have a small one this time. What breeder did you get Isa from?"

"I can get the name from her papers." Allison stood and picked up her purse. "But I've been working with rescue groups since I got her.

Maybe you'd like to look there first. There are a lot of great dogs that need homes."

"I've been thinking of getting a greyhound," Helen said.

"What?" Gwen looked at her.

"Melissa is coming back next month. In fact she's been hinting about coming back early," Helen said. "I need a dog. I love Tiffany and it will break my heart to leave her, but she has a loving owner. I've read about greyhounds. They need people. One of them needs me."

"They're good apartment dogs, too," Allison said. "Do you live in an apartment?"

"At the moment I do. I'm looking for one of my own."

"If you exercise them, they really aren't high energy dogs. Some of these rescue groups get together at the same time. I'll call you when we can see them both."

"That sounds great," Helen said. "I'm going away next week, but after that, I'm ready for my own dog."

"Call me," Allison said as she waved and left the restaurant.

"I feel like a new person," Helen said.

"Allison is great. You want a dog? You're getting your own apartment?"

"Yes and yes, Melissa is coming back at the end of October. I was planning on more time but she misses her dog," Helen cleared her throat, "and I think she misses Victor, too."

"You don't want to go back home?"

"No, no, I can't, at least not now."

Gwen took a deep breath. The silence stretched for a minute. "What kind of apartments are you looking at?"

"I'm looking in the building I'm in, Melissa's in, and I have a few others to see, similar ones."

"I don't know how a greyhound would do with an elevator." Gwen stared at the table in front of her.

"Well, we'll see."

*

"Hey, Rodney, come on up." Helen called into the intercom and pushed the button to unlock the front door. A few minutes later she opened the door to Rodney.

"Hey, Helen," he said as he leaned toward her to receive a kiss on the cheek.

"I love your beard, honey."

"Thanks, Mom hates it."

"I know she told me. It's just that she loves your handsome face and I have to say, it does kind of make you look mysterious." Helen stepped back to let Rodney enter the apartment.

"I don't want to look mysterious. I just want to hide. I don't want to look like anybody," he said. "Show me these plants you want moved."

"They're out on the balcony." Helen led the way to the door that opened onto the balcony and they both stepped out.

"Wow!" Rodney stepped back. "Are you sure it's safe to have all these plants on this balcony?"

"Apparently so. They've been there since I got here. I have to admit, though, I hadn't thought of that. I feel a little less secure standing here now." Helen laughed. "Anyway, I promised Melissa I'd move them at the beginning of October and we're already pushing toward the middle of the month. I need to get it done before I go away next week."

"Alright," Rodney picked up one of the pots and started for the door. "Do you know where she wants them?"

"Yes, but before you start bringing them in, I need for you to help me bring the plant stands up from her storage unit in the basement of the building."

"Oh," Rodney put down the plant and followed Helen out the door to the elevator.

"Why do you want to hide, Rodney?" she pushed the button for the basement.

"Did Mom put you up to pumping me for information?"

"She tried to," Helen smiled but I won't talk to her about anything you tell me. "I just thought you seem like you want to talk. You and I have always had a special bond."

"Yeah, I guess Mom and Dad really didn't want another kid when I came along. You helped a lot."

"I don't think they didn't want you, honey, but I think I envied them a little. I couldn't have any more kids and I really wanted more." She led the way out of the elevator when it stopped. They crossed the parking deck to a row of storage compartments. "But I'm enough removed to be more of a friend than a parent."

"Yeah, you are."

"So talk to me. Here," She pulled a cart over to a door and unlocked it. "We can load the shelves onto this. We'll probably have to make a couple of trips."

"I think we will." Rodney laughed as he looked into the packed storage unit. They set to work pulling the shelves out and loading up the cart. "Will this load fit in the elevator?"

"We'll take the freight elevator." Helen pointed to the far end of the basement. They maneuvered the cart into the elevator and she pushed the button.

"I don't know, Helen. I just hate my life. It's not what I want to do, not at all," Rodney said as the elevator doors closed.

"You mean engineering?"

"Yeah, and school, I hate school."

"You've done so well and you're almost finished."

"Actually, I have two more years of classes to complete. I'll die. I swear I'll die before I'm done." He shook his head and rubbed his face with both hands.

"Have you told your parents you feel this way? I can't imagine they'd want you to do something you hate that much."

"I can't tell them. Every time I see Dad, he comments on how nice it will be to have a professional in the family. He's tired of being the only one." He helped Helen edge the full cart out of the elevator.

Helen paused to think. She couldn't just tell him it wasn't true, that his father would understand. She was sure Phillip just wanted

Rodney to be happy. It had probably never dawned on him that he was pushing the boy. She looked at Rodney as he pulled the cart toward the apartment. He's not a boy, she thought. He's a man.

"...and Mom, I mean, I know she loves me, but that's part of the reason she hates my beard. I'm not as clean cut. She can't show me off. Dad was always so caught up in Andy. She was the apple of his eye. Truth is she was always very dramatic and required a lot of attention." He laughed. "....and Frankie was always the problem child. Mom had to spend a lot of time and energy on him. I was just this cute little guy that didn't need much attention and I sort of kept things on an even keel. Where do you want me to set these shelves up? I think we should set them up before we go down for the rest."

"Good plan. Here I've got instructions right here." Helen pulled a folded paper out of a drawer in the coffee table. "Melissa is so organized. Look what she's done." She laughed as she unfolded the paper and put in down on the table. "She's numbered the shelves and diagramed the apartment."

"She must be an engineer."

"No, insurance sales."

*

"What happened to Amber?" Helen asked after they had spent a quiet half hour working together to put the shelves in their designated spots. They were back on the elevator, heading back down to the basement.

Rodney took a deep breath and looked down at the empty cart.

"You don't have to tell me, Rodney."

"No," he took another deep breath. "She's very ambitious. She's studying chemical engineering. That's a really difficult major. I started out there, but had to change course."

"Does that bother you about her?"

"No." Rodney looked up and met her eyes. "I think it's great." He looked at the elevator doors as they opened. He pulled the cart out and started toward the storage unit.

"She couldn't understand your feelings?"

"Not at all, I tried to talk to her, but she couldn't stand it. When I quit school she was mad then when I lost my job, she told me she didn't want to see me again. That's the night I screwed up."

Helen unlocked the door and they loaded the remaining shelves onto the cart and went back to the elevator.

"That's the night you got arrested?" Helen asked when the doors of the elevator had shut.

"Yeah, I really don't drink much, Helen." He looked at her earnestly. "I mean I can party like anyone else, but I usually don't drink a lot and I've never been stupid enough to get into a car when I'm over the line."

"I believe you, Rodney."

"I got so bad that night I fought with my friends." He rubbed his face with both hands again. "I can't believe it. They tried to stop me, but I fought with them. I mean physically." He looked up and Helen could see the anguish in his eyes.

"We all do things we regret. Don't punish yourself. You've already been punished."

"I just remember looking back at the group of them standing on the sidewalk shaking their heads. Only seconds later I heard sirens. At first I thought they'd turned me in, but it was too fast. They didn't have time."

He pulled the cart off the elevator and went to the apartment. Working together quietly they unloaded the remaining shelves then went out to the balcony to get the plants.

"Can I pet the little dog?" Rodney said when the last plant was inside. He approached the crate where Tiffany had watched them quietly.

"Sure. Open the cage. She's pretty friendly, unless she thinks you're trying to hurt me."

Rodney laughed. "I know. Dad told me." He picked the little dog up and let her lick his face.

Helen smiled at his expression. He obviously enjoyed the dog's affection. "What do you want to do, Rodney?" she asked.

"I have no idea." He looked into her eyes. "I've spent so much time being what Mom and Dad want me to be that I don't know what I like."

"I'm sorry. I know that whatever you decide to do, you'll be good at it."

"Thanks, Helen. Like always, you've made me feel a lot better."

"I'm glad, honey. Don't worry, I won't tell your mother anything you've said to me today."

"I know. I wouldn't have said any of it if I didn't trust you."

Chapter Nine

Helen breathed deeply through the open window of the car. Victor pulled around the marina to the back of a large metal building. Through the open doorway she could see boats hanging at different levels all the way up to the top. It was probably the equivalent of three stories.

They had traveled all day from Atlanta to the coast. The conversation had been good. The silence had been soothing, and they had enjoyed the whole day.

"We park back here and carry our stuff down to the dock," he said. "I've chartered us a boat over to the island. The island boat doesn't run on Monday."

"I suppose we could have waited until tomorrow. I should pay half of the charter," Helen said as they pulled to a stop and she opened the door.

"You're supporting a huge and extended family." Victor smiled at her. "I'll pay for the charter."

"Okay, I'll let you." Helen laughed and got out of the car. "...but I'll carry my share." She started pulling bags and coolers out of the trunk.

"Okay, I'll let you."

"I love the ocean breeze," Helen said, lifting her face to the wind as they walked toward the dock with their belongings.

"I do, too. I always feel the beginning of the rush when I get to this point." Victor pushed the cart containing their belongings down a ramp to the dock. "The ride over is even more exhilarating and then comes the encompassing calm of the island. You're going to love it, Helen."

She watched the features of his face change as he described his feelings. "Wow, Victor, you're not only a painter, you're a poet."

"Shut up," he elbowed her gently on the arm. "I just love this island. That's all. Here's the boat. Start loading stuff on. Jimmy should be around here somewhere."

They loaded the boat. It was a very flat and wide boat. There were two benches to sit on in the front and a seat in front of the pilot. He stood behind a stand with a steering wheel on it.

"I'm sure there are gages and stuff behind that steering wheel, right?" Helen said as she sat in the middle of the second bench. "I have to say, Victor. The fact that there are no sides to this boat makes me a little nervous. Suppose we hit waves or something. What will keep me from falling out?"

Victor sat down beside her. "Hey, Jimmy," he called to the man that stepped on to the boat behind them.

"Hey, Vic."

"This is Helen," he said.

Helen smiled and shook his hand.

"It's kind of choppy today," Jimmy said. "Hold tight to the bottom of the bench." He started the engine of the boat and conversation became difficult above the roar.

Helen sat clutching the bottom of the bench. She could feel her knuckles going white, but couldn't relax them. They skipped across the waves and the ocean spray dampened her face, hair and clothes. They bounced over a very high wave and she wasn't damp any more. Soaked to the skin, she looked at Victor laughing and stopped. He had his face raised to the spray of the water and was gazing out to the ocean.

    She followed his gaze. "Sharks!!!" she screamed and tightened her grip. She had seen two fins above the water only yards from the boat. Oh, no, what if she fell out of the boat. She thought as they maneuvered another wave big enough to shower her with salty water.

    Victor leaned close to her ear. "Dolphin," he said. She could feel his warm breath and the comfort of his arm as he put it around her shoulder and pulled her close to him.

    "Dolphin," she repeated so quietly that she knew only she had heard it. She looked at Victor, as he beamed at her for a second then looked out to sea and pointed. She followed the direction of his gesture and caught her breath as several fins surfaced and submerged only to surface again. One of them stood completely out of the water. Then the group swam away from the boat only visible by the rise and fall of their fins.

    "Ohhh," Helen breathed. The motor slowed and they entered a waterway that led through the marsh. The edges were marked with tall grass. The front of the boat rose and fell with each wave.

    It seemed they would hit the muddy side of the marsh with each turn of the river, but the boat maneuvered back to the middle of the waterway. She could see the dock in the distance and people standing on it looking toward them.

Victor tapped her shoulder. "Alligator," he said.

She stiffened and looked at the wide scaly eyes and nose that watched the boat as it passed. He squeezed her shoulder and she realized that he hadn't let it go since they'd seen the dolphins.

"Bald eagle," he said into her ear and pointed to the sky.

Helen followed his gesture and there only yards above them soared a magnificent bird with a wide black wing span and a snow white head.

When they reached the dock, Helen felt short of breath. Somewhere along the way she'd lost her hearing, too. She was becoming aware of someone calling to her.

"Helen, could you throw that rope to Herb. Helen… Helen…" She looked at Victor. He was standing in the back of the boat and gesturing toward the front of it.

"Don't worry about it, Vic," Jimmy said as he moved past her. "She's awe struck." He laughed. "Remember your first time."

*

"Are you alright, Helen?" Victor asked as they opened the door to the house. It sat on one of the few hills on the island. It was compact, but more than adequate, all the luxuries really. They had unloaded the boat in silence and Randy, the island supervisor had taken them in a pickup truck to Victor's house. She'd ridden in the back of the truck, by her own choice, and had loved every second of the bumpy ride.

"Do you always see that much wildlife on the way over here?" she asked, tying to sound calm but hearing the shake in her voice.

"Not always, but frequently, and it's not over yet. We've got feral horses and pigs, wild turkeys, deer, of course, and uncountable birds, armadillos believe it or not, raccoons. There are also bobcats on the island, although, they're rarely sited. I can't even name everything we see here."

"What does feral mean?"

"It means domestic animals that have gone wild. You know like cattle that were herded on a plantation at some time in the past. You know, horses, chickens, pigs."

"Oh," Helen shook her head and smiled. "I think I need to shower, change, and maybe have a drink before we go any further."

"Good plan." Victor showed her to one of the three bedrooms in the house. "This one opens onto the front deck. I think you'll enjoy it. The bathroom is through there." He pointed. "I'll shower and change and meet you in the kitchen, which is over that way." He pointed again.

"Good. Thanks. I won't be long." She closed the door behind him and fell backwards on the bed.

"Helen," Victor called through the door. "I forgot to tell you. You'll need to make the bed. The sheets are in plastic bags on the pillows, which are also in plastic bags."

"Thanks," she said. "I'll do it."

*

What am I doing here, she asked herself as she emerged from the bedroom half an hour later. While she was in the shower, she had realized, suddenly, what a position she was in. She hadn't been alone with any man other than Matthew in how many years? Thirty one, she reminded herself. Would he want her sexually? Would she be happy if he did? How would she feel if he didn't?

"Over here," Victor said leaning down to look through a pass through from the kitchen. "Just follow the hall."

"I think I can find my way." She entered the small kitchen. The coolers were empty and stacked by the door to the porch. Victor looked refreshed and dressed in clean clothes. "It took me longer," she said.

"I'm much more familiar with the routine."

"You already have dinner cooking." She looked at the stove where there were a couple of pots with covers on them and something smelled really good.

"Easy stuff," Victor smiled as he poured martinis out of a chilled cooler from the freezer. "Tomorrow night, I have a fancy barbecue planned but since it's already after 8:00 I wanted to have a drink on the porch and get us fed in time to go down to the beach for a walk before we turn in."

"It's 8:00 o'clock." She looked at her watch quickly.

"Yep, you just loose time on that trip over." He laughed, "...but think of the day we've had, Helen. We drove from Atlanta. That's six hours. Then the trip over here, that's only forty five minutes, but it seems like a life time, a new life time."

"You're right but it'll be nine or nine thirty before we get to the beach. Maybe we should wait until tomorrow."

"You'll be alright with it, Helen," he said, smiling and picking up the martinis. "Open the door for me would you?" he said. She opened the door to the porch and they went outside. There were two folding chairs set up on the porch facing the marsh. There was a table set up between the chairs. "Are you right handed?"

"Yes."

"Good, because I'm left handed. That's perfect," he said as he put the drinks down and sat down in the chair on the right.

"Isn't that funny," Helen said. "I've watched you paint so many times and never noticed that you were left handed." She sat down in her chair. "Now that you mention it, though, I recognize it."

"I try not to drag my hand through everything I write, but I'm not always successful. Luckily I don't have to drag my hand through everything I paint."

"I guess not."

They sat silently and sipped their drinks. "What is the sound we're hearing, crickets or frogs?" Helen asked.

"A combination of the two."

"Is there a pond near bye?"

"No. There used to be, but it was manmade and it bothered the neighbors, so I stopped the flow to it. What we're hearing now is the marsh. It's right through those trees." Victor pointed.

"Yeah, I did notice that. It's beautiful."

Victor stood and took her hand. He pulled her to standing. "Bring your drink. Let's go ahead and eat dinner. I'm hungry. Are you?"

"Yes. For the first time in months, I'm hungry. It must be the fresh air."

*

Helen listened to the grinding of the motor of the four wheeled vehicle Victor was sitting in trying to start. She wanted to tell him that she didn't think it would ever start, but he wouldn't hear over the noise. Suddenly the motor turned over and the vehicle roared to life.

"I told you my generator would work," Victor said jumping out of the driver's seat, which was in the middle of the thing, with room for a small person on each side.

"Now we just need to let the battery charge for a minute." He pulled Helen by the arm and guided them over to sit on the steps to the house. "Finish your drink."

"You finish yours, too." Both of her hands held martinis, their second. She was feeling a little tipsy.

"Thanks," Victor said taking his drink. He sipped. She sipped, too, and the silence stretched comfortably between them.

"Just leave the glasses here," Victor said when they had finished. "I'll pick them up when we get back."

"Okay," Helen climbed carefully into the vehicle. Victor sat behind the wheel and backed up to turn around.

"Don't worry," he said. "I know how to work this thing."

They started down the sandy road. She couldn't keep track of the turns and briefly it dawned on her that if anything happened, she wouldn't know how to get back.

"Calm down, Helen," Victor spoke loudly into her ear. "Nothing will happen and I promise you won't have to run away from me."

"I'm not worried," she said, putting her face fully into the wind and feeling the glory of it.

"Ahhh," she screamed, "...a horse."

Victor slowed around a turn when a horse crossed the path in front of them. He stopped and another horse crossed with a baby horse behind it. "Remind me to tell you the story of the horses when we get back," he yelled to her.

"I will," she said.

Victor stopped the vehicle before the end of the road and turned off the motor. He got out and came around to her side to help her out.

"I'm not an invalid or anything," she said. "Why are we stopping here? It looks to me like we could get a lot closer."

"We could and it would probably be alright, but the tide isn't fully in and I don't want to lose my ride. It's not easy to get those things over here." He pointed to the vehicle.

"I guess that makes sense, but suppose it won't start again. How will we get back?"

Victor took a deep breath and looked out to the dark sea. "Helen, it's a ten minute walk, maybe fifteen. I'm hoping that before we leave here you'll have relaxed and please, don't be afraid of me. I won't hurt you."

"I'm not afraid of you." She bristled. "What makes you think that? Let's go for a walk on the beach."

*

"That was so wonderful, Victor," Helen said after they had pulled the four-wheeler into the shed and walked up the steps to the house.

"Isn't it incredible?"

"It is. I don't think we said a word to each other on that beach." She brushed her sandals off on the mat outside the door and they both walked in. "It feels good in here," she said. "It's warm out there even in October. I like coming into an air conditioned house."

"I do, too. Do you want to watch a movie or go out on the porch and have another drink?" Victor took off his shoes and sat down on the couch in the living room.

"I think I'll go to bed, if you don't mind," Helen said. "I have a feeling I'm going to sleep better tonight than I have in a long time.

Victor got up from the couch and walked over to her. He took her by the shoulders and looked into her eyes. "I hope so," he said. "You need some rest and relaxation." He kissed her on the cheek and then he kissed her on the mouth. "That's why I wanted you to come down here. There is no better place to get it." He kissed her on the mouth a little more firmly. "If I stay up and watch a movie will it bother you?"

"No," she said. "I think I'll be fine." She walked down the hall to her bedroom. I won't be fine, she thought. I wanted more than a kiss. She pulled off her clothes and put on her nightgown. "How would I have felt about more than a kiss?" she said out loud. "Shut up, stupid." I'll never sleep, she thought, as she put on her PJ's and crawled into the bed. She could hear the television going in the other room. "No way I'm going to sleep," she said.

*

"Helen!" She heard her name from the other side of the door to her bedroom. Then there was knocking. "Are you going to sleep all day?" She heard the door open and felt the weight of Victor as he sat on the bed beside her.

"I can't seem to open my eyes." She laughed and slowly pulled the weight of her eyelids up and focused on Victor's face. "What time is it?"

"It's 10:00 am. I've already gone for a run on the beach. I figured you'd be up when I got back, but you weren't so I cooked breakfast thinking the smell would wake you up."

"It didn't," she said pulling at the sheet to make sure she was covered.

Victor didn't seem to notice. "You've been in the bed for twelve hours. Did you sleep the whole time?"

"Yes. The last thing I remember is crawling into bed. Then you were knocking on the door. I don't even think I dreamed."

"Good, you needed the rest." Victor stood and went to the door. "I hope you like pancakes and turkey sausage. It's warming in the oven. Do you drink coffee?"

"Yes."

"Good, I've got it made. I'll be on the deck when you're ready to eat." He left the room and closed the door firmly behind him.

Helen jumped out of bed. She felt rested for the first time in months, maybe years. She remembered thinking she wouldn't be able to sleep. She hadn't told Victor that, because she didn't want to tell him why she didn't think she'd sleep.

She showered and dressed in shorts and a tank top. She looked at herself in the full length mirror on the back of the door. She smiled. She didn't really look bad for a fifty four year old mother of twins. Her stomach wasn't flat, but it was firm and her arms weren't flabby like some women her age. She still looked fine in a tank top.

"I'm up," she said as she carried the cup of coffee she'd poured herself out onto the deck.

"Join me," Victor said and gestured to a chair he'd set up next to the table he had a steaming cup of coffee on.

"I guess you're pretty hungry," Helen said as she sat down and sipped, "...if you've been up long enough to go for a run."

"I always get up early. I love to run in the morning." He sipped his coffee. "I had a glass of juice before I went. I don't like to eat much before a run. I'm pretty hungry now but I can wait until you've finished your coffee."

"I'm glad, because I'm really enjoying it."

"Would you like to hike to the lighthouse after we eat? I don't know exactly how many miles it is but at a casual pace it takes about an hour. We can hike inland so you can see what the interior of the island is like then we can walk back along the beach. That is if it isn't too sunny for you."

"That sounds wonderful."

*

"I'm glad you insisted that I use that insect repellant," Helen said about an hour later as they walked along the sandy road to the lighthouse. "I can see the bugs flying around me but not many of them actually bite me."

"If you're getting bitten at all, maybe you should spray yourself again. I have the can in my pack."

"No, I'm fine. I'm just really enjoying the walk. You were right. This island is beautiful and so, I don't know, serene," she said and laughed. "I don't think I've ever used that word before."

Victor laughed and took her hand in his. "You're right, though. It is serene. I love it down here. I come as often as I can."

They walked in silence for a while. He continued to hold her hand. At first, Helen felt a little uncomfortable but, after a few minutes, she relaxed and enjoyed the warmth and comfort of the contact.

"Look," Victor pulled his hand free to point to a tree branch. "…a painted bunting."

Helen looked at the tree and a beautiful multi-colored bird cocked it's head toward then took flight.

"He's beautiful," she said noticing that her hand still felt warm where he'd been holding it. "We have the indigo buntings in Atlanta but I've never seen one of these."

A few minutes later a white tailed deer leaped across the road followed by two fawns.

"This is so much fun, Victor, seeing all of this wild life."

"We've got a whole lot more to see. Sometimes the horses come down to the beach in the evening. We can see them from the deck. We'll sit out this evening and watch for them." He took her hand again and started around a bend in the road. "Here's the light house."

Helen looked up at the tall round building. "Can we go up to the top or is it locked up?"

"It's locked but the residents know the combination." He set to work opening the lock and pulled the heavy wooden door open. It squeaked eerily as it opened and she looked into the dark cave like building. The curving stairway started just inside the door.

"Ahh," she screamed and stepped back as a large snake stared at her then slithered around the back of the steps and disappeared. "I don't know, Victor. Maybe I'll just stay down here."

"Don't worry, Helen. The snakes are more afraid of you than you are of them."

"I'm not so sure about that."

They'll stay away from you," he said and stepped into the building pulling her in behind him. "Come on."

They climbed the stairway that wound around the inside of the tower a couple of times then ended with a ladder that went to a floor above them.

"The ladder is over the stairway," Helen said when she looked up at the opening to the light house then back down to the stairway below. "That's not a good design."

"I didn't think so either but you won't fall. I won't let you." Victor positioned her in front of the ladder and put his hands on it on either side of her waist. "Go on climb, Helen. You've got to see this."

"Alright," she took a deep breath and started to climb, determined not to look down. "Ohhh…" she breathed as she climbed through the opening and stood up in the top of the light house. There were windows all around the room. The windows had no panes of glass it was all open and the breeze swirled gently around the room. "You were right. I had to see this." She could see the ocean and the forest below. The view was breathtaking.

"I knew you'd think it was worth the climb." Victor joined her on the platform and put his arm across her shoulder. "Melissa won't come up. No matter how hard I try to convince her. She won't do it."

"You've brought Melissa down here?" There was a sinking feeling in her chest.

"Yes. She doesn't like it much."

"How could she not?" She hoped he didn't notice anything in her voice.

"Well, I guess I shouldn't say she doesn't like it. She seems to enjoy it a lot for a couple of days and then she gets restless. A long weekend is about all I can get her down here for."

"So you and Melissa do have a relationship?"

"Yeah, I guess so," he said and looked out the window to the ocean.

"Is that why she went away, so that you two could have some time apart to think things out?"

"Maybe," he said. "Come on, let's climb back down. The beach looks great. It's cool enough even with the sun and I brought you a hat so you won't get your face burned."

"Do I have to go first again?" Helen looked cautiously at the opening in the floor.

"No, I'll go first so I can break your fall if you slip."

"Great!" She laughed. "Thanks for the confidence."

*

"I'm going to barbecue salmon tonight," Victor said as they wiped their feet outside the door to the house.

"That sounds great. That was a great day, Victor. Thank you." Helen went into the door and sat down on the couch. "Once again, I'm very glad this house is air conditioned. It got hot toward afternoon."

"It always does this time of year. The mornings are cool. So are the evenings, but afternoon warms up nicely."

"Yeah, it was nice for it to be hot. I just loved swimming in the ocean. It really cooled me off."

"You can only swim during the day. The sharks feed off the shore at night."

"Sharks?" Helen looked at him, her eyes wide.

"Yes, sharks." He laughed. "They feed off the coast here but like I said. They don't come around in the daytime. Don't swim out there at night, though."

"Don't worry. I won't."

*

Helen ran on the sandy road toward the river dock. They had been on the island for four days and they had fallen into a morning pattern. She had hoped to run with Victor in the mornings, but he always got up before her and even though she had asked him to get her up. He never did. Maybe he wanted to be alone. That was alright, though. She'd run on the beach the first morning and found that she enjoyed the inside roads of the island more. It was like running through a tunnel of trees. There were palmettos all around her. She'd heard the rustling and snorting of pigs in the bushes once and it frightened her a little. Victor told her that the pigs could be dangerous. But he assured her that if she didn't corner them they would leave her alone.

She rounded the bend to the open area at the river dock. There were row boats and canoes turned upside down in rows. The residents of the island left their boats next to the dock. She and

Victor had lowered crab traps into the brackish water of the river that ran between the big island and the small one.

She sat down on a fallen tree and drank water from the bottle she'd brought with her. The morning was cool even though she knew it would be warm in the afternoon. She looked in the direction of the road she had just come from. There was the sound of a vehicle coming closer. It could be any of the residents. They'd met a few of them on the beach and one of Victor's neighbors had asked them over for a drink in the evening.

The four wheeler rounded the corner and Helen waved at Victor.

"I thought I might find you here," he said as he climbed down. "I was coming to harvest the traps. I'm counting on crabs for dinner. Otherwise, we'll be opening cans."

"Victor, do you have a boat down here?"

"I sure do. That's mine over there." He pointed to one of the canoes that was covered by a tarp.

"Why haven't we gone into the river with it?"

"I planned that for tomorrow." He laughed. "Crabs today and tomorrow we fish. I have one more meal planned for Friday night then we go home on Saturday."

"We fish in the river?"

"Sure but if we don't catch anything, we can go to the beach. You can catch all sorts of things there. Flounder is my favorite."

"You have everything planned out." She followed him down to the dock.

"I usually do but I keep all sorts of canned stuff down here so if it doesn't work out, I won't starve." He pulled the trap up from the water and there were six blue crabs scrambling around in it. "Look at that. Even if we don't catch fish tomorrow, we'll probably have leftovers." He looked up at Helen smiling.

"Poor things," she said.

"I know," he said, "But I don't think they have much of a nervous system and you're a meat eater. I know because I've fed you meat every night since we got here."

"Yeah, but I don't kill my own meat."

"I'll kill these. I had to get used to it but I can do it now."

"I wonder how Tiffany's doing."

Victor laughed. "You sure are an animal lover."

"I never thought I was," Helen said and watched as Victor dumped the crabs into a cooler. "Maybe I just feel bad that I'm supposed to be taking care of her and I've farmed her out to Gwen."

"Gwen will take perfectly good care of her. If I didn't think so, I would have brought her with us."

"Have you brought Tiffany here before?"

"Yes but she has to stay inside except when she goes out on leash to pee and poop. You can't let a dog run here. If they go too close to the water, they could get eaten by an alligator."

"Alligator! I'd forgotten about alligators."

"Hopefully we'll see one tomorrow when we're on the river."

"I'm not sure I'm hopeful about that."

*

Helen lifted her face to the evening breeze and took a deep breath. They were walking on the beach after eating flounder. They'd spent the day finding them in the high tide. She wrapped her arms a little tighter around herself. The breeze was cool tonight. The weather had cooled each day that they were there.

"Are you cold?" Victor asked as he moved closer to her and put his arm across her shoulder.

"A little but you're warming me up." She smiled at him and noticed again that he was eye to eye with her. It was nice and when he kissed her it was nice not to have to look up. She was a tall woman but Matthew was a tall man as well, so when they'd kissed she'd had to look up. That was nice, too. She frowned and looked out to the endless sea.

"Is something wrong?" Victor interrupted her thoughts.

"No." She smiled and said, "I was just thinking that this week has gone really fast. I can't believe tomorrow is the last day."

"Yeah, it always goes fast. I hope you've had as good a time as I have."

"I've had a wonderful time." She stopped walking and lifted her face to the cool breeze again. "I don't think I've ever felt so relaxed."

"I feel the same way. You're good for me, Helen. When I'm with you I forget about all the stresses of my life."

"Do you have stresses, Victor? You always seem so composed."

"It's an act." He smiled and stooped to pick up a sea shell.

"What stresses you? Talk to me."

"No, please, Helen, I don't want to threaten my shaky tranquility."

"Shaky tranquility? You're very poetic."

He stood back up and tossed the shell into the surf. He turned to her and leaned close to kiss her mouth. He put his arms around her waist and she circled his shoulders with hers. They stood like that enjoying the feel of their joined mouths and the pressure of their tongues. Then Victor pulled back and put his arm across her shoulders. He gently turned them around so they were walking back to where the four wheeler was parked.

"You know, during the summer the University of Georgia hosts a turtle project down here." He changed the subject and Helen shook her head to clear it. "A group of students and one of the professors come down and they stay in the cabins over near the dock. They take turns watching the sea turtles come ashore to lay their eggs."

"That's sounds like fun. Have you ever seen a sea turtle lay eggs?"

"Yeah, I've joined them a few times when I come down in the summer. It's really invigorating. You wouldn't believe how hard it is for those turtles to move on land."

Helen remembered Gwen's description of the difference between the snapping turtles clumsiness on land and their grace in the water.

"Then they dig a hole, every movement is labored. They lay their eggs and then make the difficult trip back to the sea."

"I guess turtles don't sit on their nests," Helen said.

"No." Victor laughed and squeezed her shoulder. "The students on watch that night move the clutches to a protected place. Clutches are what they call the nests and they watch them to make sure that they aren't raided by birds or raccoons or some other wild threat. Then when the eggs hatch they help the babies crawl to the sea without being attacked by predators."

"What a great project."

"Maybe, if you want to, we could come back next summer and you could observe it one night."

"I'd like that."

*

Helen woke up to the sound of something coming from Victor's room down the hall. After their walk on the beach, her thoughts of Matthew, and Victor's stimulating kiss, she'd been sure she wouldn't be able to sleep. But as usual she had fallen soundly to sleep as soon as she crawled under the sheet.

She sat up and listened more closely. She'd heard the sound before. It sounded like he was talking. She'd thought at first that he made a call at night. She'd wondered if he was talking to Melissa. They had definitely been involved with each other. Maybe they still were.

Helen swung her legs over the side of the bed and pulled on her bathrobe. She opened her door and walked quietly down the hall toward the other bed room. She stopped at the door and listened for a minute. He was talking but she couldn't understand what he was saying. He must be talking in his sleep. Maybe he was having a bad dream.

"Victor, are you alright?" she said as she opened the door and looked in. He was sitting up leaning against the wall. His hands were clutching the sheet. His eyes were closed and he was mumbling and shaking his head.

"Victor!" She hurried over to the bed and crawled over to him. She stood on her knees and took him by the shoulders. "Victor, wake up. You're having a bad dream." She shook him gently. "Wake up."

His eyes came open quickly and focused on her face. He raised his right hand and for a second she thought he was going to hit her. She winced and pulled away.

"Helen," he whispered. "I'm sorry." He put his arms out to her and she moved forward to embrace him. "I'm sorry," he said again and cleared his throat. "I didn't mean to wake you."

"Victor," Helen sat down on the bed beside him still embracing his shoulders. "I've heard you in here a couple of times. Do you have nightmares every night?"

"No. Maybe. I'm sorry. I didn't realize I made so much noise."

"Maybe it has something to do with all that stress you were talking about this afternoon."

"Probably, I can take something for it. I will tomorrow night. You need to be rested for the trip home."

"Victor," she leaned against the wall beside him and took his hand. His arm remained around her shoulders and he was pulling her tight against him. "I'm not concerned about me. I'm worried about you."

"Don't worry about me, Helen. I'm alright. I just have this recurring nightmare. It makes me call out for help only it doesn't sound like that. Melissa described it to me, too. If I take a tranquilizer before bed I sleep better. I just don't like to take them all the time. I don't need to form a habit." He smiled shakily.

"You're not going to talk to me anymore about this, are you?"

"No."

"Well, I guess I might as well go back to bed then." She started to move toward the edge of the bed but Victor stopped her.

"Helen," His voice shook. "Will you stay with me?"

"Of course, I will," she whispered as she crawled under the sheet and pulled Victor to a lying position. She put her arms around him. He rolled onto his side and put his hand on her cheek. Then he ran his fingers through her hair. The room was dark but the moonlight defined his features. She could see him smiling at her as he leaned to press his mouth to hers.

*

"I wish we'd shared a bed all week," Victor said on the ride back to Atlanta. "I slept like a baby with you beside me. No nightmares." He looked away from her but not before she noticed a blush moving up his neck to his face.

"I slept well the whole week, Victor. Thank you for bringing me down here. I don't think I've ever felt so relaxed and refreshed. I'm glad you want me to come back next summer."

"It's a great place, isn't it?"

"Umm hmm, and the company was good, too. Of course I can't complain about the food or the accommodations either. All in all, I'd say it was a wonderful trip."

Victor pulled into the parking deck below the complex. They unloaded the car into a cart and pushed it to the elevator. He pushed the button for her floor. "I'll drop you and your stuff then take mine to my apartment.

"Do you want to have dinner together tonight? It's kind of become routine." he asked when they had unloaded her bags.

"Thanks but I don't think so. I'm still full from lunch and I think I'll run over to Gwen's to pick up Tiffany. I've missed her."

"Okay. I was thinking I'd spend a little time in my studio. I've got an idea for a painting of the islands. I've got pictures of it."

"Good. I can't wait to see it." She closed the door behind him and picked up the phone to call Gwen. There was no answer so she left a message and went to the bedroom. There's no point in going over there if she isn't home, she thought. Unpacking was easy. Everything went into the laundry. She went to the laundry room and put in a load of wash then went to the kitchen to pour herself a glass of wine.

The buzzer from the front door in the lobby sounded and she went to the intercom.

"Mom," It was Daniel's voice. "Dandy and I are down stairs. We took a chance that you would be back from your trip. Can we come up?"

"Of course," she said, smiling as she unlocked the door. They'd come together. Maybe they'd missed her.

She pulled the door open as soon as the bell rang then she stepped back. Delia's face was red around her eyes. Helen looked at Daniel. His were, too.

"What's wrong?" She demanded. "Your father…"

"Dad's fine. Mom," Daniel said, coming through the door and closing it behind him. "Grampa died this morning. I called the number at the island but…"

Daniel was still talking but Helen couldn't hear him. Her ears were ringing and there was darkness creeping in around the outside of her vision.

"Mom!" She heard Delia cry and then everything stopped.

Chapter Ten

"I can't believe I wasn't here when he needed me." Helen pushed herself to a sitting position on the couch where she'd been laying when she came to. She swung her legs over the side and Daniel sat down beside her.

"Mom, it wouldn't have made any difference. He'd given up."

"He'd been depressed since Mom died, though. I didn't realize this was so much worse. I should have realized."

"Don't blame yourself. I had tried to get him to take anti-depressants. I'd called in one of the doctors I work with but Grampa wouldn't take them." Daniel handed her a glass of water. "Drink it," he said when she tried to push it away.

She took the glass from him and sipped.

"You can't make a person want to live."

"No, I know you're right." She looked across the room. Delia stood by the window looking out. "I'm sorry, honey. I know it hurts. Were either of you with him?"

"Both of us were," Delia said. "I was working and I called Danny and he got there in time."

"Good." Helen wiped her eyes and swallowed against the lump that rose in her throat when she saw the anger that remained in Delia's eyes. "I'm glad he wasn't alone."

The front door buzzer sounded again. "I wonder who that could be." Helen stood and

Daniel pulled her back down onto the couch. "You sit still. I'll get it."

"Helen, this is Gwen. I have Tiffany. Can I come up?"

"This is Daniel, Gwen," he said into the intercom. "Come on up."

"I thought you could use the company tonight," Gwen said when she entered the apartment and set the little dog on the floor. Helen wrapped her arms around Tiffany when she ran to her and buried her face in the soft coat as a new wave of sobs took her.

"I'm sorry, Helen." Gwen sat down and put her arms around her.

"I'm sorry, too, Mom," Delia said. "I know you loved him a lot."

"Thank you, honey. That means a lot to me." She didn't look at her daughter. She couldn't face the anger right now.

"Danny, we should go. Greg will be home soon and Dad will need his dinner."

"Will you be alright, Mom?" Daniel stood at the front door. "If you need me to, I can take Delia home and come back."

"Thank you, sweetheart." Helen stood and embraced her son. "I'll be alright. I need to be alone with my grief. Will you be alright?"

"Yeah," He kissed her cheek. "Greif takes time. Come on Dandy."

Delia walked stiffly by her mother and out the door. Helen closed the door behind them and leaned on it. She put her face in her hands and cried. "She's still so angry. My children hate me. I was never good enough for my father. Maybe I am just a horrible person."

"Don't feel sorry for yourself." Gwen stood and went into the kitchen.

"You're so compassionate, Gwen." Helen followed her into the kitchen.

Gwen poured herself a glass of wine. "You want some?"

"I have some around here somewhere." She looked around. "It must be in the living room."

Gwen followed her back into the living room and they both sat down. "I don't mean to be uncompassionate, Helen. I know this is hard. I remember when my Dad died. It really hurts. It's alright to hurt but don't beat yourself up. And everybody's children hate them at some point."

"I don't see your kids hating you."

"Oh yeah, they're just not as straight forward as yours are."

"Okay, I won't feel sorry for myself but I don't know about not feeling guilty. I was on vacation when he died. I wasn't even here." She put her face in her hands and gave into another wave of sobs.

Gwen moved over to the couch and put her arms around her.

"I knew he was sick. I mean he broke his hip. How could I go away?"

"You had to. If you don't take care of yourself, you're no good to anyone else." Gwen stroked her hair. "Let the guilt go, Helen. You have a big enough job dealing with the grief."

"You're right. I know. But I had so much fun and all the time he was giving up. He was dying."

"And he'd have been giving up and dying if you weren't having fun and nothing you did made any difference. Remember? Helen, let that go."

She took a deep breath and then a sip of wine. "You're right. I will." She pulled Tiffany up into her lap. "I love this little dog, Gwen." She pulled Tiffany close and buried her face again. "I think I'm a dog person. I loved Rocky, but not like this."

"Then we'll get you one of your own."

"I want this one."

"You can't have her but she has a good home and I'm sure Melissa will let you visit her when you want. So tell me about your trip. Did you sleep with Victor?"

"Yes, but I can't talk about that now. I need to face my grief."

The telephone rang and Helen picked it up.

"Heln... Matt."

"Hello, Matt. I guess you heard about Dad."

"Yes... wanted to say... you're sorry."

"Thank you, I appreciate that."

"Are you... alright... are... alone?"

"I'm not alone. Gwen is with me, but I'm alright. Thank you for calling, Matt. It means a lot to me."

"Anything... you... I ... can do?"

"No, but I'm glad you called." She hung up the phone. "That was Matt."

"What did say?"

"He said he was sorry. Actually, he said I was sorry. His speech is still so broken. Has he made any headway at all?"

"He speaks beautifully, Helen. It's only broken when he's nervous and you make him nervous."

"Why?"

"Because he loves you and he knows that you don't love him anymore."

Helen didn't say anything. Did she not love Matthew anymore?

*

"So?" Phillip said as he pulled on his jacket.

"So what?" Gwen ran the comb through her hair and put it down on the vanity. She turned and looked at Phillip.

"Did she sleep with him?"

She looked away from him and went into the walk-in closet to get her dress. "I can't believe you would ask that question on the day of her father's funeral. You really don't have any feelings for her, do you?" Gwen came back out of the closet pulling a black dress over her head.

"She did." Phillip sat down on the bed and punched the mattress with his fist. "Man, how could she do that?"

"I didn't say she did."

"You can't lie to me, Gwen."

"I didn't say she didn't either." Gwen squeezed her lips together and turned her head.

"See what I mean."

"Phil, maybe you shouldn't go to the funeral if you can't let that go long enough for her to bury her father."

He took a deep breath and stood. "You're right." He put his arms around her and rested his chin on the side of her head. "I won't let it show. Helen has been through a lot."

"She's been through hell. I don't know how she's still walking around with all she's gone through in the last few months."

*

Phillip looked across the grave site at Helen. She stood looking at the casket as it was lowered into the earth. There were tears streaming down her face but her expression was bland. Her brother, Franklin, stood beside her. His hands were crossed in front of him.

Daniel and Delia stood slightly behind their mother. Their spouses stood next to them and Matthew stood behind, a few steps back. Franklin's wife stood beside him with her hand tucked into his arm and their daughter stood behind them with her husband.

"Thank you for coming," Helen said to Phillip as he took her hand in the receiving line when the service was over.

"I'm sorry. I know this hurts." He took her hand and looked into her eyes. Immediately he wished he hadn't. He'd never seen such depth of pain. Helen was suffering. He felt a lump rise in his throat and moved on to Franklin's family.

"I'm Helen's brother. Franklin." He introduced himself.

"I remember," Phillip said. "I'm Phillip Desmond. I'm married to Helen's best friend."

"Oh yes, Gwen," Franklin smiled sadly and introduced his family.

Phillip looked around the room when he'd completed his condolences. Matthew stood at the back of the room leaning against the wall. His expression was unreadable. Phillip started toward him.

"Poor Helen, she tried so hard to make him happy," Matthew said.

"It didn't work, though, huh?"

"No." Matthew stood straight and straightened his shoulders. "He never got over his wife's death. I was surprised he lived that long after she died. He just didn't care about life anymore."

"Your speech has really cleaned up, Matt." Phillip slapped Matthew on the shoulder.

"Unless I'm talking to...Heln." Matthew dropped his chin to his chest "Or...apparently even thinking about...talking to....her."

"You still love her a lot?" Phillip looked into Matthew's eyes and for the second time in a matter of minutes he felt a lump rise in his throat. The love and pain in Matthew's eyes was unbearable. Phillip swallowed and felt the anger surface. If he had to make a choice it would always be Matthew, his best friend. He breathed deeply, happy for the anger. The anger would carry him through and he wouldn't have to feel the pain, the pain people that he knew and cared about were feeling.

*

"Phil hates me," Helen said to Gwen that afternoon in her apartment. "For just a second I saw compassion in his eyes, when he went through the condolence line. Then the next time I saw him his eyes blazed at me."

"Don't worry about him, Helen. He's having a hard time coming to terms with his feelings."

"I miss him, Gwen." Helen put her face in her hands and cried gently. "He always teased me. We had this playful bantering relationship. You'd think a friend could understand my need to take care of myself. I'm taking care of Matt, too. I've kept up the taxes and utilities on the house. I even bought him a top of the line walker. Matt's disability payments helped but now that he's working as one of the construction team, his income is even lower than the disability payments."

"It's not about money, Helen, but don't even think about him. He'll come around. Just come to terms with your grief."

"I've already done that."

"You have?"

"I've come to terms with my grief but I don't think I'll ever come to terms with my guilt."

"What do you have to feel guilty about, for heaven sake?" They opened the door to Helen's apartment and went inside. Helen opened the crate and scooped the little dog up in her arms. "I need to take her outside. Do you want to come with me or would you like to stay here."

"I'll come with you, of course. That's why I came over here. I didn't want you to be alone." Gwen heard herself sounding irritated.

"Well, I'm not alone. I have Tiffany." Helen snapped. "You can go home if you want to."

"Okay, Helen, why are we snapping at each other?"

"I don't know." Helen hooked the extendable leash to the little dog's collar and started out the door. "Maybe I'm just not fit for company right now."

They walked to the elevator and Helen pressed the button. When they had entered the elevator and the doors had closed behind them, Gwen said, "Maybe I'm just a bitch."

Helen laughed and hugged her friend. "You're not a bitch."

"Why do you feel guilty, Helen? You tried everything to make your dad happy. If anything, you should be mad at Franklin. When he visited your dad last summer, it was the first visit in a year. You told me it was."

"I tried to be mad at him but, you know, he has a life in Houston. When Mom first died, he came here every three or four months. Dad wouldn't respond to him either. Then it became every six or seven months."

"But a year, Helen?"

"Plane tickets are expensive. Why come here to be ignored? He did what he had to do. It couldn't have been easy for him to be so far away."

"I see what you mean. At least being close, you recognized the fact that there wasn't anything you could do."

They left the elevator at the plaza level and went out the front door. Gwen followed Helen down the path to the park that surrounded the building.

"So, anyway, why do you feel guilty?"

"Because, as much as I miss my dad. I mean I really can't believe I'll never see him again." Helen sniffed and wiped at her eyes as the tears spilled onto her cheeks. "...As much as all that, it's a relief. It's a relief to not have to think of him sitting over in that dismal apartment pining or grieving or just finding a way not to feel anything." Helen leaned down to scoop Tiffany's droppings into a plastic bag. "I'm going straight to Hell for saying that."

"I don't think you go to Hell for what you say, Helen."

"Yeah, but I said it because I felt it."

"I don't think you go to Hell for a feeling, either. I think you go to Hell for what you do."

*

It had been a long morning. Helen put her hands on her desk and pushed back against the chair to stretch her back and shoulder blades. There was a knock at her office door and she took a deep breath. She had appointments all morning with clients and she was feeling short tempered. I hope I don't tell this one to go jump. She thought.

"Come on in."

"Helen," Her son in law opened the door only a crack and peeked around it.

"Greg," She stood and hurried over to the door. "What's wrong?"

"Nothing, really," he smiled, came into the room and closed the door behind him. "I'm sorry to alarm you. You've had a number of shocks lately, I know." He looked around the office that she spent every day in. "May I sit down?"

"Of course," she said and went around the desk to sit back down in her chair. "What's going on? I don't think you've ever come to my office before."

"No. Maybe I should have." He looked around. Helen thought he was avoiding looking at her eyes. "I have a problem. I don't really know how to deal with it and I was hoping you could help."

Helen smiled at her son-in-law. He was a tremendously pleasant person. He had very blond hair and very blue eyes. The only thing she'd found a little funny when Delia married him was that he was at least three inches shorter that her daughter. Of course, the fact that Delia was six feet tall meant that if she wanted someone taller than her, she would have narrowed the field considerably. She looked at his face and remembered how he had won her. That smile. It was beautiful and genuine.

"I hope I can help, too, but I'm kind of struggling myself. I'm not sure I can find any answers for you if I can't answer my own questions."

"Well, maybe just someone to talk to."

"Talk away."

"Delia wants to have a baby."

"That's what she told me before she quit speaking to me."

Greg looked away from her. "I'm sorry she's being such a bitch. She's so distraught right now she can't understand her feelings."

"Thanks, Greg. You know what's funny?"

"What?" He looked back at her.

"Even though she hates me right now, I bristled when you called her a bitch. I guess mother's never stop protecting their children."

"I'm sorry." Greg took a deep breath.

"Don't be. We can all be bitches. So what's the problem? You don't want to have a baby?"

"Yes, I do. I think I'd love to be a Dad. I hope my children are all taller than me." Greg laughed, "Even my daughters."

"Well, my children are taller than me, even my daughter." She smiled at him. "So I'm still looking for the problem."

"Delia wants to have a house before we have a baby. That's why we're living in your basement. I mean Matthew's basement." Greg looked at his hands and turned red on is neck.

"Go on."

"I don't want to live in the basement anymore. I don't see why we can't start our family in an apartment."

"You really can't afford a house right now? Maybe I could help?"

"I don't want your help!" Greg took a deep breath. "I'm sorry. I didn't mean to yell. We could get a house, but we'd have to take a second mortgage. We're close to having a decent down payment. I just don't want to get us into debt problems. We can bide our time and buy a house in a couple of years. The baby won't know the difference."

"No, the baby won't know the difference. Greg, can you think of anything I can do to help?"

"No, not really, I just want you to tell me if I'm being unreasonable."

"I don't know what my word means but it sounds perfectly reasonable to me."

"I love your daughter."

"I know you do."

"Helen," Greg looked her in the eye. "If she won't see my point or at least be willing to talk to me about it, I'm prepared to leave her."

"Oh, Greg," Helen stood and came around the desk. "You wouldn't really leave her, leave us?"

"I don't want to, but I can't be controlled like that. My feelings have to be considered, at least discussed."

Greg stood and Helen looked at him eye to eye. "If you leave her will you be alright?"

"No. I love her so much that it might kill me but I need to be heard, Helen. When I talk to her, she doesn't hear me."

"She doesn't hear me either." Helen put her arms around her son-in-law and hugged him.

"I'm going to talk to her tonight. If she won't listen to reason, I'm leaving. I love her Helen, but I can't just give up myself."

"No, you can't." Helen could feel tears building behind her eyes and filling her lower lids. "I'll always love you, Greg. I pray that she'll listen."

*

She picked up the phone and dialed Victor's number. He answered "Hey."

"You knew it was me."

"I have caller ID. I wouldn't have answered if it wasn't someone I wanted to talk to."

"I'm glad to know you want to talk to me. I could use a walk in the park. Would you like to join me?" Helen said as she picked up Tiffany's extendable leash off the table and clipped it to her collar.

"Love to. I'll meet you at the basement door."

Helen carried Tiffany to the elevator and rode down to the lobby. She put the little dog down and walked to the front door. Victor was standing on the other side by a potted plant looking toward the park. The site of him warmed her heart.

"Hey," He turned toward her and smiled. "Do you want to walk in the park or should we go down the street to the mall?"

"That might be fun for a change." She fell in beside him. "The city is fun, too."

They walked in silence for a while. Helen stooped to scoop Tiffany's droppings into a bag. "The nice thing is when you walk down the sidewalk there are garbage cans." She laughed dropping the bag into a can.

Victor smiled at her. "Melissa will be back in ten days. Have you figured out what you're going to do?"

"Yes, I've leased an apartment on the third floor. You're not going to get rid of me that easily."

"I don't want to get rid of you."

"I'm glad." They walked in silence for a few more minutes.

"Helen?"

"Hmmmm?"

"You might be the best friend I've ever had."

"… but… I hear a but coming."

Victor smiled and took her hand. "I'm going to ask Melissa to marry me."

"Oh, Victor, I'm so happy for you." She turned to him and threw her arms around his shoulders. "I could tell you and Melissa had a relationship."

"You don't feel rejected?"

"You're not going to stop being my friend?" She put her hands on his shoulders and pushed back, looking him in the eyes.

"Of course, I'm not." He leaned forward and kissed her soundly on the cheek. They resumed their walk in silence for a minute. "I suppose you want to hear an explanation."

"You don't have to explain anything to me." Helen looked down. "But, yes, I want an explanation." They both laughed.

"You know, my first marriage sucked." He squeezed her hand. "I'm pretty sure I loved her when we were married. I certainly still care about her but I'm glad she moved away so I don't have to face my failure all the time."

"I'm sure you didn't fail. Maybe it just wasn't a good fit."

"No. It was definitely not a good fit." Victor stopped to scoop the little dog up and smiled as she licked his face. "Let's cross the road. There's a nice spot over here by the fountain." They walked toward the middle of the mall.

Helen followed him to the fountain and they sat down on a bench. Tiffany sat between them.

"Well, it was bad, so I always felt that I just wasn't someone that could have an intimate relationship."

"Oh, shut up. You're the most genuine person I know."

"With you," he said and looked down at the ground in front of him.

"...and Melissa." Helen prodded.

"Yeah,"

"I like her, too."

"She wanted a commitment. I told her I couldn't give her one." He rubbed his eyes. "That was stupid. I'm totally committed but marriage scares me to death, plus she wanted me to..."

Helen looked at Victor. His hands gripped the bench and his head was bowed. "She wanted you to figure out what the nightmares are about."

He looked up into her eyes. "You read me so well, Helen," he said. "But I just think some things are better left buried."

"Yeah," she said. "Some things are better left buried, but that doesn't mean you can't make a commitment. You just have to stand by your commitment to yourself."

"She'll never quit pestering me about it."

"That's because she loves you."

"What if she persists and wins and I disintegrate?"

"What if she persists and wins and you don't disintegrate?"

*

"Hey, Sybil," Helen said as she walked through the door of the shop."

"You okay, Helen. I'm doing fine with the chocolate and I think this," she pointed to her bulging belly, "is actually helping. People come in just to see if I've delivered."

"I'm so glad." Helen looked around the gallery. She felt replaced. After all she was the one that pushed Gwen into opening this place up. Apparently she just didn't matter at all anywhere. She wasn't even making her own chocolate.

"Gwen is teaching me all the ropes, though. I know how to work the front register and how to do the stocking. That's what she'll need when you can come here full time, plus, we're getting low on the boxed chocolates and I don't have any idea how to do that."

Helen turned around and smiled at her daughter-in-law. "You handled that really well. I feel better." She laughed. "However, I know what you said isn't true because I taught you how to make all the candies that I make."

Sybil laughed and came around the counter to embrace Helen. "Yeah, I can do it, but we still need you. We need your drive, organization, determination..."

"If you don't stop I think I might throw up."

"Me, too." Sybil sat down on a stool and put her hand on her belly."

Helen moved over and put her arm around her daughter-in-law's shoulder and put the other hand on her belly. "My grandson is going to be an athlete." She laughed. "Do you ever get any sleep?"

"Actually, I sleep better than I ever have. It's the being awake that's hard."

"I seem to remember that."

"Yeah, but you had twins. I can't imagine it and the way Daniel and Delia are together, I'll just bet they were squabbling in the womb."

Helen smiled and kissed Sybil on the cheek. "You know what? You are the best thing that's happened to me in a long time." She walked around the counter and looked beneath it to check her stock.

"Helen, Daniel and I are planning to move out of the house pretty soon after the baby is born. Greg is working hard on Delia to move out. Do you think you'll come back when we're all gone?"

"Oh, honey," Helen looked up. "I hope none of you thought I left because of you. It had nothing to do with you."

"Well, no," Sybil said. "I just thought that maybe the house being so full and Matthew being sick... I mean, I can see how it would be overwhelming."

"No, it had nothing to do with that. Matt and I were already in trouble."

"So, you really don't love him anymore?" Sybil asked looking into Helen's eyes earnestly.

Helen looked back at her. She had a flash memory of the twins being born and the look of wonder in Matthew's eyes. Then there was a flash of the first time she'd seen him. She'd decided then that she was going to marry him.

"I'll never stop loving him," she said. "We were married for more than thirty years. We raised twins together. We'll have mutual grandchildren. I'll always love him." Helen looked down at the shelves below her and feigned concentration.

"But you can't be together anymore?"

"No," she said looking up at Sybil. "Not right now anyway."

*

"Come on down, Helen," Gwen said into the intercom. "Allison is driving and she has a minivan. We can definitely get your greyhound and my toy poodle into that."

"I'm coming." Helen called back. "Are you sure you don't want to come up for coffee first."

"No, way, I'm so excited I couldn't swallow a sip of coffee."

"I'm on my way."

They pulled into the parking lot of the pet store and Allison parked the car.

"I can see the greyhounds," Gwen said. "Where are the poodles?"

"Look over there," Allison pointed to the far corner of the lot.

There were beautiful poodles of all different sizes and colors.

"Oh..." Gwen said softly. "I'm going to have a hard time not taking one of those standards. I always had standard poodles before we got Sandy."

"You know, if you really want one, you can have one," Helen said. "You still have a house with a yard."

"Yes, but I really do want to downsize. I just think it would be easier to have a small dog. If they don't behave, you can just pick them up." Gwen kissed Isabella on the top of her fluffy head. "And it's nice to have one that can sit in your lap."

"That's true," Helen said and nuzzled the top of Tiffany's head. "I just love Tiffany, but I'm determined to have a greyhound. That's why I brought Tif with me. I've heard that some greyhounds aren't safe with small animals. There is no way I'm bringing home one that would hurt Tif. Let's go." She opened the back door of the car and got out. Allison and Gwen followed her and they started walking through the rows of dogs up for adoption.

"I can't believe how many there are," Helen said. "I know why there are so many greyhounds, but what about the rest of these dogs. Look how many of them are pure bred."

"They come from people that thought they wanted a dog and then found out how big a commitment it is. They decide it's too much work and send it to a rescue group thinking they've done something good." Allison was leading them through the crowd to the group of greyhounds.

"Well, it's better than dumping it on the side of the road," Helen said.

"Yes it is." Gwen hurried beside Helen and Allison who both had legs considerably longer than hers.

"Yes it is," Allison said. "Of course, a lot of these dogs came from the side of the road."

They stopped at the table next to the group of greyhounds. There was a man sitting behind the table holding the leash of one of the dogs. To the left of the table another man stood with several leashes in each hand. The dogs stood together calmly. Their heads hung a little but they wagged their tails when someone patted them or spoke to them.

"I would like to look at a greyhound that will be good with small animals," Helen said, extending Tiffany in her arms toward the man. "It would have to get along with her."

"Helen, she isn't going to be living with you." Gwen whispered.

Helen ignored her. "Do you have any here that you think would be alright?"

"Yes, I think we do. We have a kind of test we do on them," the man said. "Of course, we don't allow them to devour a cat or anything but in a safe supervised situation we get an idea of how they will react to small animals. Of course, there are no guarantees. There never are with animals."

"No guarantees with children, either, are there?" Helen looked at the group of dogs.

"All of these here today pose a minimal threat to small animals. When we come to one of these things we choose the ones that are the least aggressive. It wouldn't work for our cause if one of them killed another homeless dog."

"No I don't suppose so." Gwen noticed that Helen's brows were pulled together. She looked worried.

"I think the brindle one on the end is the best bet, though," the man said. "She's very maternal. She's had a couple of litters and always cuddles and protects her toys."

"She's striped," Helen said. "I didn't know dogs could have stripes."

"That's what brindle means," Gwen said quietly.

The man behind the desk stood and took the dog he was holding over to the other man. He traded leashes and returned to Helen, Gwen, and Allison. "Lower the little dog toward her but be prepared to step back if you need to."

Helen clutched Tiffany in her arms. "I'm afraid to."

"Tif isn't afraid," Allison said. "Here let me do it." She handed Isabella to Gwen and pried Tiffany out of Helen's arms. She lowered the little dog just enough to let the greyhound stiff her.

Both dogs wagged their tails and sniffed noses.

"I'm pretty sure they'll be alright," the man said. "Do you want to walk them around together for a while?"

"I don't know." Helen still looked worried.

"You need to spend time with this dog, Helen. The chemistry between the two of you is the most important thing," Allison said. "I'll hold Tiffany and we'll walk side by side over to the poodles. When you feel more comfortable we'll let them walk together. Is that alright?" she asked the man.

"That's fine. But hold on tight to the leash. Greyhounds are runners. They're really pretty lazy dogs but if you give them the chance to run they will."

The three of them started in the direction of the area where the poodles were. Gwen was carrying Isabella. Allison was carrying Tiffany and Helen was walking beside the greyhound holding the leash. She reached down and stroked the dogs shoulder. The dog was unresponsive but tolerant.

"She doesn't seem to care if I pet her or not."

"Those dogs haven't ever had affection. Whenever they're led anywhere it's just to run a race. They have to be taught to accept your love." Allison explained.

"What if she never accepts it and I have a dog that just doesn't care? I need one that cares."

"I've worked with greyhound rescue for a long time. They all care and they all learn to accept and show affection. The only problem we have is that some of them have been so badly abused that they don't ever learn to trust. When that happens, they really aren't fit to be pets."

"I think this one trusts," Gwen said as she let the beautiful dog sniff Isabella.

"Put her down," Allison said.

Gwen put Isabella down on the ground and held her leash to keep her from running over to the greyhound.

"Let her go over. Helen, keep your leash fairly tight."

The two dogs sniffed noses, the greyhound stretching her long graceful neck down to sniff the toy poodle. Isabella turned her small body so the greyhound could sniff her bottom then they started forward as the group headed toward the poodle rescue. Allison put Tiffany down. The ritual was repeated and they all continued on their way.

"They're all so beautiful," Gwen said. "How will I make a decision?"

"Well," Allison said. "Let's narrow it down. Did you have a preference in color?"

"I was thinking white like Isa, but this little peachy colored one is awfully cute." she stooped down and extended her hand to a little poodle in one of the many crates.

"Would you like to see her, ma'am?" An attendant asked as she opened the door to the crate. She picked up the little dog and offered her to Gwen to hold. "This is one of my favorites."

"She is very cute." Gwen cuddled the dog close and it put it's little paws on her chest and pushed away.

"Hmmmm," the attendant said and reached for the dog. "She usually isn't like that."

"The chemistry isn't right for her." Allison laughed.

"I've never had a dog react to me like that before." Gwen looked hurt.

"Don't get upset. I'm sure we can find you a dog that likes you but maybe color isn't important."

They walked around looking at the crates with toy poodles in them. Gwen held several of them. Most of them reacted to Gwen well, but none of them really grabbed her. Several were adopted while they were there.

"Gwen, you don't have to get a dog today," Allison said when they'd made the whole circuit of toys and miniatures. "There are a lot of rescue services."

"I really want one, though. I'm ready."

"I'm a firm believer in chemistry. Don't just settle. These dogs will get homes because they have people helping them."

"I guess you're right." Gwen looked over at the row of large crates that housed the standard poodles.

"Gwen, those were always your favorite dogs," Helen said. "If you want one get one, at least look at them." She moved in the direction of the standard poodles and put her hand on the greyhounds shoulder. "I can tell you one thing. The chemistry is subtle with greyhounds but it is definitely here with this dog. I wish I'd asked her name. She's coming home with me."

"Really, Helen," Gwen hurried to catch up. "I'm so happy for you and it doesn't matter what her name is. She's your dog. You can name her what you want."

"Can I really?" Helen looked at Allison.

Allison laughed and scooped Tiffany up in her arms. "You don't have to get my permission. Of course you can name her yourself."

"What kind of a dog is that?" Gwen stopped short. At the end of the row of standard poodle crates was one with a huge dog that barely fit into it. It was a reddish brown color. Gwen was sure she had never seen a poodle that color. Its hair was very short, but its tail was bushy and though it was very wavy hair, it was not tightly curled like a poodle's.

"I don't know," Allison said. "But it certainly isn't a poodle. Look at this dog, Gwen. It's apricot like the toy you liked that didn't like you."

"I don't think she's listening to you." Helen touched Allison's arm and they both watched as Gwen moved toward the crate at the end of the row. "I think we've got chemistry."

Gwen approached the crate and stooped. "Hey, pup. What are you doing in this row of poodles? Surely you're not one of them."

"We're thinking at least one of his parents was." The attendant approached the back of the crate and met Gwen's eyes when she looked up.

"What do you mean?"

"We're thinking either golden doodle or labradoodle. That would mean that one of his parents was a poodle and one was either a golden retriever or a Labrador retriever. Judging by the color I'm more inclined to say golden doodle. We don't actually know anything, though, because I found him on the highway."

"You found him on the highway?" Gwen looked back at the sweet brown eyes and lolling tongue of the dog. It looked like it was smiling.

"Actually, more like in the highway. He was in the grassy median of a divided highway in Mississippi."

"Do you think someone left him there?"

"Probably, these dogs are runners so it's possible that he just escaped but judging by the condition of his coat, he clearly hadn't been taken care of for a long time."

"What do you mean? His hair is so short." Gwen leaned forward and the dog licked her cheek through the bars.

"We had to shave him down to the skin." The attendant laughed. "I couldn't even show him for adoption for two weeks afterwards. We had to let some hair grow back. I was afraid people would think he had mange or something."

"So his hair is actually long."

"Well, there is no way of knowing what his hair is like. He was encased by a crusty mat that covered his whole body." She came around the crate and opened the door. The dog immediately leapt out and started jumping up and down into the air. He was going straight up and wiggling and wagging his tail. He licked Gwen's face as she stood and then he leaped higher.

The attendant laughed and took control of him by his leash. "This is another problem. We don't know what kind of hair he's going to have and I'm not sure you'll be able to keep him in a fence."

"So he probably jumped someone's fence. Did you try to find the owner?"

"We did, but I don't think they wanted him I think they dumped him. There were no homes for miles and even with his hair that matted he wasn't thin and he wasn't weak or malnourished. I think he was just too much work."

"How do I adopt him?" Gwen said. She had taken the leash from the attendant and was pressing her hands on his shoulders to keep him from standing on his hind legs to lick her face.

"Gwen, are you crazy?" Helen asked. "Not only is that not a poodle but it's not a toy. It's not even a toy mutt. You said you wanted to downsize."

"This is the dog I want. What do I have to do to adopt him?"

"Come to our facility at your convenience and fill out the papers. Then we'll come out and inspect your home to be sure it's a good fit."

"Inspect my home, at my convenience. I want him now."

"I know." The attendant struggled to get the dog back into the crate. "I have a good feeling about you and I'd love to just give him to you but we have to do it this way. Otherwise we get too many of them back."

"Will the greyhound people have to inspect my home?" Helen asked. "Because at the moment I don't have one, I mean, I have a temporary one but I won't have a real one until next week."

"The greyhound people don't generally inspect your home but they won't let you take her home today. You'll have to go through the screening process."

"This sucks," Gwen and Helen said together.

"I guess I should have warned you about that," Allison laughed.

*

"You'll have to do something about the fence, Phil," Gwen said when they got into bed that night.

"Yeah, you mentioned that, maybe twelve times since I've been home today. I don't see why the electric wire isn't okay. It worked with Sandy and it isn't cruel. We figured that out a long time ago. Sandy only got shocked twice and she never tried to jump again. Do you think she had a bad life?"

"No. She had a good life but we didn't have to pass inspection to get her."

"No. That's true. Do we have to take the electric device off the fence or just tell them that we won't turn it on?"

"No we have to take it off. They can't think we're that kind of people."

"We are that kind of people, Gwen and our dogs live to fifteen years old and they love us and have happy lives and they don't get hit by cars."

"I know. You're right." Gwen pulled the covers over her head. "But I want this dog really bad."

Phillip pulled the covers down and looked at Gwen. "Okay, here's what we'll do. While you go to the facility and fill out the papers and arrange for the inspection, I'll remove the electric wire from the fence."

"But he'll jump it without the wire."

Phillip leaned back on his pillows. "What do you want me to do about that, Gwen? According to Helen, this dog can jump the grand canyon."

"I was thinking we could build a shelf around the top of the fence. Maybe slant it a little so it doesn't just give him something to stand on."

"I can't do that in a day and you said you wanted this dog soon."

"I want him tomorrow."

"Let's just tell them we'll keep him on a leash."

"I just think that if we have a fence out there they won't believe it."

"I can't take the fence down in a day either," Phillip said.

"No, you're right. If they won't let us have him, they won't. That will break my heart." Gwen sighed. "Anyway, I'm just glad that Matt and Sybil are running the gallery tomorrow so we can work on this."

"Yeah, me too, and with it being Matt's first day without us, it's probably a good thing that we'll be too busy to check up on him."

"I think you're probably right. I'm not too worried, though. Sybil can handle it all, if she doesn't go into labor."

"Gwen?" Phillip said after they had turned out the light and been quiet for a while. "One of the reasons you wanted to downsize your dog was because you thought you could take him to the gallery with Cole. From what Allison said, this dog will be like the proverbial bull in a china shop."

"I'll make it work."

Chapter Eleven

*Editor's Journal
by Gwen Desmond
October Edition*

I took the other fork in the trail this month. It wound up a hill and stopped at the top. There was a swing at the top and it overlooked the golf course. The hill challenged my conditioning but I managed it alright. There were no turtles to watch, but there is a bird sanctuary at the site. It's a forested area, obviously landscaped but well incorporated into the natural flora.

There were bird feeders all over. I could tell by the different seeds in them that they were specialized to attract different birds. I could also tell by the birds that fed at them. There was one that attracted a beautiful small yellow bird. I later learned they were gold finches. I should have brought my bird book but I didn't. Take yours if you go there.

I also saw robins and cardinals. There were blue birds and wood peckers. The wood peckers had a special feeder of their own. I saw one try to feed from another feeder and he wasn't able to do it because he hung off the bottom of it.

There was a hummingbird feeder. Those little birds are so beautiful. The feeder in the sanctuary had a lip on it that the bird could light on. I love seeing them fly but seeing them sit still is thrilling, too. They're beautiful and tiny.

Next month I'll have a dog to walk with. I hope he doesn't scare the wildlife. My plan is to go to one of the Chattahoochee River trails.

*

"I thought you said you weren't coming in today since I could be here," Helen said from the door of the office.

"I'm leaving in a minute. I just had to get my *Editor's Journal* done. The flyer goes to the printer on Monday morning."

"That's right. I haven't even thought about that flyer. You've done so much on this project." Helen sat down in the chair across the desk from Gwen.

"You've done a lot, too. I feel kind of bad that we've fallen into the pattern of you taking every Saturday, Helen. I mean you work a forty plus hour week."

"I want to do it. It's really the only chance I get to be a part of the Gallery, that and late afternoons after work."

"Well, I have to go." Gwen looked at her watch. "The rescue service is coming over to inspect our home, you know, to make sure it's appropriate for Henry."

"You named that dog Henry?" Helen laughed.

"Yes. I love that name. It's so dignified."

"The name is dignified but that dog isn't," Helen said. "I would have named him something like Chewbacca or Frankenstein. Frankenstein would be perfect. When he stood on his hind legs and put his hands on your shoulders to try to drown you with his tongue, he was definitely a foot taller than you."

"He's dignified," Gwen said. "I've visited him every day at the rescue and I know that he's a gentleman."

"I've visited Lila, too," Helen said. "I can't wait until I'm moved and she can come home with me."

"You move tomorrow, right?"

"Yeah," Helen smiled. "Both of your sons are going to help me and my son and my son-in-law."

"Do you have that much to move?"

"Yeah, there are some things that I have stored in the attic that I want to bring. You know Melissa's apartment has furniture. This one doesn't. Also I've bought a washer and dryer. They're still at the home store. I didn't want to pay the delivery fee."

"I'm sorry money is so short, Helen."

There was a knock at the door and Sybil poked her head in. "Can I have a minute with you two?"

"Come on in, honey," Helen said and stood up. "Here take my seat. Sybil, are you sure you should still be working? You're due in two weeks."

"Sixteen days." Sybil lowered herself carefully into the chair. "As long as I don't swell up or get anemic, I'm okay."

"You don't want your blood pressure to go up either," Gwen said.

"There's no way that could happen without us knowing about it. Dan takes it fifteen times a day." They all laughed.

"Except for the discomfort," Sybil rubbed her swollen belly. "I feel pretty good."

"So what can we do for you?" Gwen asked.

"I think I might have sold a couple of ads in the flyer. I know that it goes in on Monday and we can't get them in this month but it'll take a few weeks to design them anyway."

"You've sold ads?" Gwen leaned forward. "Do we have new artists?"

"No. No. These people don't sell things in our shop but I thought we were just a sale flyer. I didn't know we were exclusive."

"Well, no, I don't think we're exclusive," Helen said. "...but how did you manage to get people to buy advertising space."

"Just being out front and talking. Your Editor's Journal draws people and apparently you've gotten a very good circulation." Sybil grimaced and clutched her belly.

"Are you okay?" Gwen and Helen said together.

"Yeah, it's just those Braxton Hicks contractions. I'm having them a lot. My Lamaze coach says that they're practice for the real thing."

"So, Sybil, what do you mean by design the ads? I've really just been listing the merchandise. I've had a layout designer but that's just kind of technical."

"I know but these people would want a graphically designed ad."

"...and you can design one?" Helen said.

"I think I can, at least I could try. They'll give me their ideas, of course"

Helen and Gwen looked at Sybil for a minute.

"I need to go," Gwen said. She stood and put her hand on Sybil's shoulder. "I'm really impressed. I can't wait to see your ideas but I have to go home. It's taken a week for me to get this dog and I don't want to put it off a minute longer."

*

"How high is this fence?" the woman from the rescue service asked.

"Five feet," Phillip said.

"I know he can jump that." Gwen put her hand on the top of the fence. "We've already agreed not to let him run out here until we replace it with a higher one."

"I've dealt with this dog and I don't think you can put a fence in that's high enough he can't jump. For one thing, he's huge, and for another, he can climb as well as jump. He's very agile." The rescue volunteer was a tall woman and looked down at Gwen then at Phillip.

"We'll keep him on a leash forever," Gwen said. "I swear I'll take care of this dog. He and I connected. I'm telling you we did." She could feel tears gathering behind her eyelids.

"I can see that you did," the woman said. Martha pushed her walker out onto the deck above them and waved as she sat down in one of the chairs. "Did you know that he chases anything on wheels?"

"No I didn't," Gwen said, giving into the lump in her throat and wiping the tears off her cheeks.

"She will love this dog," Phillip said.

The rescue volunteer looked out at the large back yard. "If I were you, I'd electrify that fence."

*

"Morning, Mom," Daniel said to Helen as she walked into the kitchen of the house that she and Matthew had shared.

"Good morning. I rented a truck. It's out front." She sat down at the table where her son-in-law was finishing a bowl of cereal. "Are you ready to move, Greg?"

"All set."

"Good... m.m.morning, Helen," Matthew said. He came into the kitchen and filled the kettle. He put it on the stove and opened the cabinet to pull out a tea bag.

"I can't believe you don't drink coffee anymore."

Daniel and Greg both stood.

"Morning, Dad," Daniel said.

"Good morning, Matt," Greg said. "I'm going up to the attic. Do you know what stuff she wants, Dan?" They left the room together.

"I think... we... make them..." Matthew concentrated, looking for the word. He shook his head and turned sadly away.

"...nervous," Helen finished for him. "It must be very frustrating for you to know what you want to say and not be able to say it."

"No... yes," He took a cup out of the cabinet and put the tea bag into it. "Yes," he repeated.

"I'm sorry, Matt," Helen took a deep breath. "But you aren't using your walker. Things have improved there."

He poured the steaming water over the bag, turned back to Helen and smiled sadly. He sat down across from her. "Don't need the walker…" he looked like he had more to say but picked up his tea and sipped instead. His right hand shook and he steadied it with his left.

"How's work going? Do you like working on the construction team?"

Matthew smiled genuinely this time and nodded his head.

"Good, I'm glad." Helen reached across the table to pat his hand.

He grasped her hand in his and held it. "Come… home…"

She looked into his eyes and took a deep breath. "I can't, Matt." She gently pulled her hand away from his and stood. Why was there a lump in her throat? She wondered. Isn't this what she wanted to do? She turned before he could see the tears forming in her eyes. "I'm going up to supervise the kids. Goodbye, it was good to see you doing so well." She opened the door to the attic stairway and stopped to compose herself.

*

"Your Dad's speech is still so impaired. Will he ever get it back?" she asked Daniel when they got into the truck. Greg was going to follow them in a borrowed truck.

"Maybe not completely, but Dad is so smart that if he can't find a word, he can usually find another way to say it."

"He couldn't this morning."

"I doubt he'll ever be very eloquent under pressure."

"What pressure?"

"His speech deteriorates when he's talking to you." Daniel looked out the window. "Gwen's noticed that, too."

"Why?"

"Why do you think?"

*

"How's the house hunting coming, Danny." Frankie asked while they were carrying the bed mattress into the door of the apartment.

"Not so good. Sybil can't really do much walking around these days. We've pretty much decided to wait until after the baby comes."

"Let's try it on this wall," Helen said as they wedged it through the door to the bedroom. "If I don't like it there you can move it."

"Easy for you to say," Daniel grinned at her.

Her heart bounced and she smiled back. "I think we'll put the dresser over here. I hope it all fits." She looked around the room.

"I can't believe you bought a whole bedroom suite this morning," Frankie said.

"Well, I had to have furniture and besides, I didn't buy it this morning. I bought it a week ago. I just had you pick it up this morning. I'm avoiding delivery fees."

"Hey," Greg looked into the room. "Where are the washer and dryer hook ups?"

"Are you back already?" Helen said. "I'm so glad you were able to borrow that pickup truck from your friend. With two trucks we'll be finished with this move by early afternoon." She hurried out the door. "I'll show you where the laundry closet is. Danny, you and Frankie go down and get the rest of the bedroom furniture."

"You sure are good at giving orders," Daniel said.

Two hours later, Helen looked around the room and smiled. "The furniture I brought from home and the new stuff come together to look pretty good, don't you think?" She looked at the four young men.

"Looks great, Helen," Frankie said and rubbed his belly. "I'm glad we're finished. I'm starving. You guys want to get some lunch?"

"Look at the time," Helen said. "It's 1:30. Why didn't you tell me? Poor things, I'm a slave driver."

"That's for sure." Daniel teased.

"I have lunch," Helen said. "I picked up deli sandwiches from George's. Is that still your favorite, honey?" she asked Daniel.

"Sure is and I don't think I've been there since I moved back."

Helen went behind the counter that separated the kitchen from the living room. "I only got two bar stools. I should have gotten more." She opened the refrigerator and pulled out a bag.

"There isn't room for anymore stools. We can eat in the living room," Rodney said. "Don't worry we won't get crumbs on your new furniture."

"See that you don't." She smiled. "I got potato salad and slaw and chips and a whole variety of sandwiches." She pulled everything out of the bag and spread it on the counter. "I have to go out this afternoon and buy plates and flatware, but I have paper and plastic for now."

They filled their plates and spread out around the room. Helen sat at the counter with Frankie. They ate in silence for a while.

"We were hungry." Helen broke the silence.

"We were. So, Greg," Daniel said. "When are you and Dandy moving out. You said you didn't want to live in the basement anymore."

"We're not moving out. I am."

Helen put down her fork and looked at her son-in-law. "She wouldn't agree?"

"No. She wouldn't even talk about it."

"Oh, man, I'm sorry, Greg," Frankie said. "I thought you were awfully quiet this morning."

"I rented an apartment around the corner. I plan to move in next week."

"Honey, are you sure. I know Dandy can be difficult," Helen said. "But I also know you love her and she loves you. Don't you think you can work this out?"

"I'm hoping we can, but I have to make a stand. I mean, she has to consider my feelings, too."

"I don't know if Dandy's ever considered anyone's feelings but her own." Daniel laughed. "Sorry, I know this isn't funny, but she's always been self absorbed."

"Then she shouldn't have a baby," Rodney said. "Parents need to be able to focus on their children."

"What do you know?" Frankie nudged his younger brother's arm.

"Oh, I think she'll make a good mother." Greg continued. "But we have to establish our own relationship first and married people should make decisions together. I have to get through to her." He ate a bite of his potato salad and looked around the room. "I rented a two bedroom. I'm hoping she'll miss me enough to move in and we can start our family there."

"I hope so," Helen said. She felt very uneasy about this. "Greg, I'm not sure separating is the answer."

"Well, it's the only one I can think of. I've tried everything else."

*

"It worries me sick, Gwen," Helen said as they walked along the wooded path. The greyhound trotted sedately by her side.

"I'm sure it does." Gwen struggled to control Henry as he bounced in front of her. He pulled her to the right. She yanked on the leash and the dog danced around her winding the leash so that she had to turn completely around and hurry to catch up with Helen. "I would hate it if Tom and Andrea split up. I've gotten as attached to him as I am to her. In fact, in a lot of ways I like him better."

"I feel the same about Greg."

Gwen leaped forward as Henry spotted a squirrel and ran after it. She planted her feet and yanked on the leash only to be pulled forward again. Then the dog turned and leaped at her face planting his paws on her shoulders and nearly drowning her with his tongue. She staggered from his weight and felt Helen brace her from the back.

"You have got to get some control over that dog, Gwen."

"I know. I will." She moved the dog's paws off of her shoulders and pushed him firmly to the ground. "Down, Henry, now heel," she held the leash closer to his collar and they began to walk again.

"My greyhound is better than your toy poodle."

"Cute. Anyway, there isn't anything you can do about Greg and Delia. They have to work it out for themselves."

"I suppose you're right. But, you know what? I feel responsible."

"Why in the world?"

"Because when things got tough for Matt and me. I left."

"That's different."

"How is that different?"

"You don't love Matt anymore." Gwen yanked on the leash as the dog strained forward again then bounced around her. She made another turn and pulled him close to her side.

"I can't believe you just said that."

"What, that you don't love him anymore. Come on, Helen, before the stroke you made it clear to all of us."

"That's not true. Of course, I love him. I always will. You don't spend thirty plus years with someone and raise two children without loving him."

"Well, you care about him, of course, but you're not in love with him."

"I suppose that's right." Helen remembered the lump in her throat when he'd asked her to come home. I just felt sorry for him, she thought. I'm sure that's right.

"Helen, are you thinking about going back home?"

"No, I can't go back there."

"You can't go back to the house or you can't go back to Matt?"

She took a deep breath. "Either one, I can't go back to either one."

A man walking a small white dog rounded the corner of the path in front of them and Henry barked frantically. He took off at a run and Gwen had no choice but to follow. The path went downhill and just when Gwen thought she was going to be able to stop him her feet hit a patch of pine straw. She slipped and skidded down the hill toward the small white dog. She saw the look of horror on the man's face and sat down hard on the ground, grabbed the leash in both hands and yanked as hard as she could.

"God, lady," the man said scooping his dog into his arms. "If you can't control that dog, you shouldn't bring him to the public park." He made a wide pass around them and hurried away.

"You've got to get control of that dog." Helen laughed as she helped Gwen to her feet.

Phillip let himself in the back door of the gallery and stepped into the office. Helen looked up from behind the desk. "Something I can do for you?" she asked.

"I wanted to do some work on the books. Can you get up or should I come back later?"

"No, I was just looking at some of the ad designs that Sybil was doing before she had to stop working." She stood and walked around the desk. "It's all yours."

"How is Sybil?" Phillip asked taking his seat at the computer. "She must be really uncomfortable by now."

"I guess so. She's due any day but I haven't seen her since she quit working last week."

"Oh, that's right. You don't live with your family."

Helen took a deep breath. "I'm getting really tired of your anger, Phil. If you can't get over it and you're not willing to work it out with me then keep it to yourself."

"I'm sorry. I shouldn't have said that." Phillip didn't look at her. His eyes moved up and down as he looked at the computer.

"I'm serious, Phil. This gallery is my project, not yours. We can get another accountant if you can't be civil to me. Gwen will agree."

He turned and looked at her seriously.

"Are you threatening to fire me?"

"Exactly,"

Phillip laughed without smiling. "Well, I don't know how you're going to pay anyone to do this. I hate to tell you but this gallery is getting off to a very slow start."

"We've only been open for six weeks, Phil. I think it's a little early to be giving up."

He took a deep breath and turned back to the computer. "Things will probably pick up with the holiday season."

"I'm sure they will."

*

"What in the world are you doing?" Phillip said.

Gwen sat straddling Henry who lay on his back stretched out full length with his front paws up in the air. The black cat sat behind Gwen chasing Henry's wiggling tail. "I'm brushing his chest and arm pits. His hair is starting to grow out and I don't want him to get matted again. I told you they said he was matted to the skin when they found him."

"I'm surprised he'll let you do it."

"Well, it's been a wrestling match." The big dog suddenly rolled over and jumped to his feet dumping Gwen onto the floor. "Henry, no," Gwen shouted when he leaped toward the wheels of Martha's walker as she came into the room.

"Down, Lurch," Martha said and the dog dropped to the floor and looked adoringly at Phillips mother.

"How do you get him to listen to you, Mom? He won't do anything I say."

"He loves me."

"His name is Henry, Martha," Gwen said getting to her feet and straightening her pants legs.

"...and he loves everyone so why does he obey you and not the rest of us."

"I think his name should be Lurch." Martha pushed her walker toward the kitchen. Henry stood and followed her, nipping at the wheels of the walker but not touching them. "I think he knows I'll break in a million pieces if he knocks me down."

"Well, he certainly doesn't worry about me." Gwen followed them. "I'm bruised from head to toe. I don't think I've ever hit the ground as much as I have since I got him."

"You could have gotten a toy poodle," Phillip said to Gwen then turned to his mother. "Mom, sit down. What do you want? I'll get it for you."

"I can get it myself, sweetheart. You're such a wonderful boy. Have you heard from your sister lately?" She opened the refrigerator. "I wonder if I'll ever see her again. I'm not long for this world, you know."

"Don't talk like that, Mom. I'm sure Jennifer will come by soon. She's pretty busy with all that traveling she does in her job."

"Of course, I just hope she doesn't feel guilty when I'm gone and she realizes she neglected me at the end."

"You're starting to get on my nerves, Mom."

"I told you we'd get on each other's nerves."

"Okay, you two just stop it," Gwen said. She winced as she heard the snap of the electric fence outside. "He just isn't learning to stay away from that wire. Maybe we should close up the dog door, Phil."

"He's fine. He doesn't go over the fence and eventually he'll learn."

"I hate leaving him in a crate all day while I'm at the gallery, but I can't take him with me like I can Cole. He'd destroy the place."

"I'm just glad he and Cole get along. I was a little worried about that." Martha sat down heavily and sipped at a glass of lemonade.

"I was, too. Henry seems to have a problem with small dogs. Every time he sees one, he tries to attack it. I don't know if he'd hurt one or not but I don't want to find out."

"I love your dog, Mom," Rodney said skipping down the steps and around the corner. "Don't worry about leaving him in a crate. I've been taking him to the dog park. You know they've opened a new one here in Sandy Springs."

"Hi, honey," Gwen said. "I'm glad you've been doing that, but do you let him off leash at the dog park."

"Yeah, he has a blast."

"How does he do with small dogs?"

"The small dogs are separated. The only problem is that he can jump the fence into their area and that scares the owners. He doesn't hurt them, though. He just likes to stand over them and look down. It's funny, really." Rodney pulled the orange juice out of the refrigerator and drank out of the carton.

"Don't do that, Roddy. You're not a child anymore."

"Sorry, Mom," He put the carton back into the refrigerator and shut the door. "I'm off to work."

Gwen heard the front door shut behind him and said, "I'm not so sure a kid that can't drive because he got a DUI should work as a bar tender."

"At least he's working," Phillip said.

"I'm just glad he can walk to and from work and I'm glad he works during the day."

*

Martha went out on the back deck. It was late fall, but the day was warm and she liked to enjoy the morning air. Phillip went down to the garage. He'd sold the Austin Healy and bought a new car. It was an Alpha Romeo. He'd gotten a good price for the Healy and put all the profit into the gallery funds. It was the best single sale they'd made so far.

Gwen stroked Henry's soft head and leaned down to kiss him. He bathed her with his tongue then looked at her adoringly. "I'm glad you're not a toy poodle." The door bell rang and she went to answer it.

"What in the world is that?" Her mother demanded as she came into the foyer and put her arms up to guard herself from the bouncing dog. He went straight up and down almost touching the ceiling.

"I'm sorry, Mom. I forgot he isn't good with incoming people." Gwen struggled to get hold of Henry, ushered him into the dining room

and shut the door. She winced as she heard something crash then looked at her mother.
"What *is* it?"
"It's my dog." Gwen hugged her. "Why didn't you tell me you were coming? When did you get to town?"
"I got in this morning? I should have called but I just wanted to come straight here."
"Is everything alright?" Gwen showed her into the living room and they sat down.
"Not really," Gail looked tired. Gwen wasn't sure she'd ever seen her mother look tired. "I'm going to move here, honey. I wanted to be close to you."
"What's wrong, Mom?"
"I'm dying."

*

"It's called pulmonary fibrosis." Gwen told Matthew on Monday at the Gallery. Matthew liked to come in on Monday. He worked three days on the construction team and spent at least part of the other two at the gallery.
"What is that?" he said, easily.
"It's some kind of scarring in the lungs. I'm not sure I understand it. I'm going with her to the doctor tomorrow. I guess I'll have to close the gallery. There isn't anyone to cover and I have to go."
"Of course, you... d.d.d.do." He grinned. "I stutter."
"Not that much. Anyway, I guess there isn't anything they can do about it."
"Where is she staying?"

"She's in a hotel right now. She wouldn't stay with us. We have Frankie's room, but she wouldn't stay. She'd have to share a bathroom with Rodney and neither one of them were excited about that. She says that she's going to go into assisted living until she can't take care of herself anymore. Then I guess a nursing home." Gwen put her face in her hands and cried softly.

"I'm… s.s.s.sorry, Gwen." Matthew put his arms around her and pulled her into his chest. She cried into his shirt as he stroked her back.

"I think I snotted on your shirt." Her sobs slowed and stopped and she talked into his chest. "Thanks, Matt." She pushed gently away from him and looked up. "You're so tall. I don't think I've ever been hugged like that."

"I'm… glad I was here."

"I am, too."

"You know, I really like your Mom. I wish there… was… something…"

"There isn't anything anyone can do. The horrible thing is that I haven't always liked her. In fact, I'm not sure I ever have." She sat down on the stool behind the counter. "That isn't true. I've always loved her and honestly, I like a lot of things about her, but…"

"…but…"

"She overwhelms me. She's so dynamic. I can't believe she's going into assisted living. She's always been so independent. You should have seen the look in her eyes, Matt. She looked so, I don't know, tired. She looked tired."

"I guess it would be tiring to not… be able to… to… get enough air."

"…to not be able to breathe."

"Yeah,"
"I hope I can do this."
"Do what?"
"Help her die."
"Is... there a... choice?"

*

Phillip sat on the floor of the garage stripping paint off the exterior of the Alfa. He was in a foul mood. His day at the office had been grueling then he'd come home to find Rodney leaving.

"Where are you off too?" he asked trying to sound cheery.

"Out!" The ungrateful kid said as he ran up the walk and down the street. It seemed he never got more than one word out of him at a time.

Gwen had called him at the office to tell him that she was going to be late. She had a late meeting with Mr. Robbins, the shop's landlord's agent. They had been having some trouble with the repairs to the HVAC system. This didn't help his disposition. She usually closed the gallery at 5:00pm and got home shortly after he did. Sharing that evening meal with her was comforting and he didn't like missing it.

He fixed himself a sandwich then took the portable phone down to the garage so if she called he wouldn't have to run up the stairs. He shouldn't worry about her, but he just couldn't help it and with the news about her mother, she had been distant all weekend.

Unfortunately, the portable phone didn't have caller ID and he'd taken three calls from telephone solicitors in the last hour. His mood was definitely getting worse.

He jumped as the phone rang again, contemplated not answering it, but what if it was Gwen. "Hello!" he said angrily.

"Could I speak to Gwen Desmond?" The unfamiliar voice said.

"She isn't here." Phillip snapped. "This is her husband. Can I take a message for her?" He knew he sounded angry.

"I'm calling from North Side Hospital. Mrs. Riddick is here. She had a car accident earlier today and when she regained consciousness she gave us this number to call. We've tried to reach her home all day, but couldn't get anyone."

Phillip felt the blood drain from his face. "Helen Riddick?" he said feeling stupid. "Is she alright?"

"Her condition is serious, but stable. She has a head injury and can't seem to stay conscious. I just thought someone should know. She's asked for your wife a couple of times."

"I'll be right there." Phillip ran up the stairs and grabbed his keys. Wait a minute, I can't just leave. He thought as he picked up the phone and dialed Gwen's mobile. She didn't answer and the voice mail picked up.

"You didn't take your phone with you again. Gwen we've talked about this." He heard the anger in his voice and stopped. "I'm sorry Gwen. Listen. I just got a call from North Side Hospital. Helen's there. She had an accident. I'm going over there. I sure hope you get this message." He hung up, scribbled a note on the dry erase board on the refrigerator and ran back down to the garage. He started his car and tore out of the driveway.

*

Helen felt herself surfacing again. She'd been in and out of consciousness all day. "Ouch!" she said as she put her hand to her head. It was swollen right above her temple. She could feel it under her hand. Her cheek hurt, too.

"Helen, wake up."

She heard a familiar voice from somewhere above her. She opened her eyes carefully. The room was bright and it hurt her eyes, but she could see Phillip's face swimming to her right. She turned her head and tried to focus.

"Phil, why are you here?" Her voice sounded raspy and weak.

"The hospital called Gwen but she had a late meeting."

"So you came." She closed her eyes again and swallowed. The room was spinning and it made her feel sick.

"Don't go back to sleep, Helen. The doctor says you need to maintain consciousness for a while."

She felt Phillip's hand take hers and she opened her eyes. He smiled and squeezed her hand gently. "I thought you hated me." She smiled and winced at the pain in her cheek.

"I don't hate you, Helen. Now just stay with me here."

"What happened?"

"You had a car accident, probably due to the fact that you drive like a bat-out-a-hell." He huffed. "Why are you always in such a hurry, Helen?"

She smiled without opening her eyes. "There's the Phil, I know." She laughed and winced again. She waited for the pain to recede then let herself drift off to sleep.

"Don't go to sleep on me, Helen. I think I'll raise the bed a little."

Phillip's voice seemed to come from far away. Then the head of the bed dropped a few inches and Helen's eyes flew open. "What are you doing?"

"I'm keeping you awake." Phillip had the control panel in his hand and he pressed another button. The head of the bed started to rise.

"Phil," Helen said. "The foot's going down, while the head's coming up. What are you trying to do, stand me up?" She laughed and winced again.

"No, I'm trying to keep you awake," he said as he stood back to look at her.

She was sitting up at an angle and her legs were stretched comfortably in front of her. She felt more awake now and adjusted her position with her arms.

"Here, let me help you with your blanket." Phillip pulled the blanket up over her chest. "You were flashing," he said and arranged it comfortably over her.

"There isn't much to flash in this hospital gown, unless I stand up and walk away from you." She took a deep breath and closed her eyes. Phillip reached for the control panel. "Don't touch that," she said. "I'm not asleep. I'm trying to remember what happened."

"You had an accident at about 9:30 this morning. Apparently the hospital was calling your house all day, but there wasn't anyone there. You have a very busy family. At some point you came to and asked them to call Gwen."

"Where was the accident?"

"...about a block from your office."

"Hmmmm, I wonder if I was coming or going. 9:30 in the morning is an odd time." Helen reached for Phillip's hand.

He took hers and held it to his lips.

"Was anyone else hurt?"

"No, the person who hit you was driving a truck. He's fine. Apparently it was your fault, though."

"Great."

"You scared me to death, Helen. I was working on the Alfa when the call came in. I don't even know if I closed the garage door when I left the house."

"Thank you for caring that much, Phil."

They sat in silence for a few minutes, holding hands.

"I've missed you a lot, Phil. All that's happened ...I ...well ...I didn't expect it to cost me you." Helen sniffed and rubbed her eyes with her free hand.

"I've missed you, too." He gulped and dabbed at his own eyes. "I don't want to talk about the bad feelings I've had. Right now, I'm just glad you're alive."

They both looked up as Gwen rushed into the room. "What happened?"

"I'm not exactly sure," Helen said. "Apparently I had an accident this morning and I've been pretty much out of it all day."

"We need to try and keep her awake for a while." Phillip stood and put his arm around Gwen's waist.

The nurse came into the room with a new bag of fluids and started to attach them to the IV in Helen's arm. It was the first time any of them had noticed it.

"Thanks for coming, Phil," Gwen said. "I'll stay with her. You can leave if you need to." She tried to take Helen's hand from him but he wouldn't let her.

"I'm staying until she's completely out of the woods."

"Well you've changed your tune."

"I didn't realize how much I still loved her until I thought I might lose her."

"What you're saying is so nice," Helen said, "that I don't even mind that you're talking about me like I'm not here."

The door to the room opened and Delia rushed in. "Mamma." She rushed over to the bed. "Thank God you're awake. Daddy called me. He got home and found out what happened. He's on his way."

"Oh, man. I'm so embarrassed. Is Danny coming, too?"

"If he can, you're not going to believe this but he and Sybil are here in the labor and delivery suite."

"The baby!" Helen tried to sit up, winced and fell back to the bed. "How close is it? I want to go over there."

"You're staying right here for a while." Delia smiled down at her and Helen's heart thumped.

She took a deep breath. "Thanks for coming, honey."

The door opened again and Matthew rushed over to the bed. "HHHHelen ..." He stuttered. "You ...I ..." He shook his head and furrowed his brow. "Damn it."

"You don't have a problem swearing." Helen laughed. "I'm alright, Matt. In fact, I'm feeling pretty good. I guess I know how to get people to forgive me. I just have to wreck my car."

"Don't even think about doing this again, Helen. You took a year off my life," Phillip said. "In fact, I think we should take your driver's license away."

"Not only that," Delia said, "but I haven't forgiven you. I'm just calling a truce."

A nurse came into the room and said, "I hate to be a party pooper but there are too many people in here and there's someone else outside that wants to come in."

"Who is it?" Delia asked.

"His name is Greg Spears."

Helen watched as Delia grimaced. "What's he doing here?" Apparently his plan wasn't working too well. He had moved into his own apartment two weeks ago and Delia was still mad at him.

"Well, let him come in. I'll leave," Delia said taking Matthew by the arm. "Come on Daddy, let's go over to labor and delivery and see how things are going."

Matthew hesitated looking at Helen with a worried expression.

"She'll be fine, Dad." Delia tugged on him. "Now that she's awake, they'll probably release her or they might admit her. We can find out later."

"I guess she's still not speaking to Greg," Helen said when the door had closed behind them.

"No, she isn't," Greg said pushing the door to the room open. "I can't believe she doesn't care enough to even miss me." He walked to the side of the bed. "I'm sorry. You don't need to hear about that stuff right now. How's your head, Helen."

"Throbbing, but I don't care. I can't wait to be a grandmother. Greg, maybe you should move back to the house."

"No way, if that's all she cares then it's not much of a marriage, is it?" He took a deep breath. "I don't want to talk about this. I want to know how you're doing."

Helen looked at Phillip. "I'm doing fine. You know what Greg," she said and looked back at him. "Maybe you should wreck your car."

Chapter Twelve

"Mom," Daniel rushed into the room pushing a wheel chair. "Come on, I'm taking you to see your grandson. He's beautiful, Mom." He locked the wheel chair and headed in the direction of the bed. She was staying overnight for observation. Gwen had gone home and gotten her a night gown and robe and slippers.

"I'm so excited, Danny." Helen struggled to swing her legs over the side of the bed. "I can walk."

"Nope," he scooped her up in his arms and put her into the wheel chair. "God, Mom. You're skinny as a rail. Don't you eat anymore?"

"Just get me to the nursery. I want to see my grandbaby."

Daniel hurried down the hall squealing around corners and rushing into an elevator just as the doors were closing.

"That was some ride." Helen laughed. "You drive like I do."

"You taught me." Daniel grinned. His smile was completely unchecked. He looked so happy.

"It's a great day, isn't it, son."

"The best ...the best. His name is Gabriel. Did Sybil tell you?"

"Yes, that's a wonderful name."

They rushed off the elevator nearly knocking over a nurse and doctor who were waiting to get on. Danny hurried to the nursery window. "That's him, Mom. They're just finishing his clean up." The nurse put the baby in the crib on his side and wheeled the crib over to the window.

"Oh, Danny, honey, he is beautiful. I think he looks like your dad already and maybe a little bit like Sybil."

"Yeah, I thought he looked like Dad, too." Daniel's face was glowing.

Helen looked up as Matthew approached from the back and put his hand on her shoulder. "Our first grandbaby," he said clearly.

"He looks like his dad did when he was born, remember," Helen said looking up at Matthew's glowing face.

"Yeah, a little like me ...some like you ...some like ...Mr. MMMcGoo." Matthew finished with a laugh.

"Sybil is probably in the room by now." Daniel turned and took a long happy breath. "I'm going to scrub and go there. They'll bring the baby in soon. She's nursing. You can all join us, but you'll have to scrub first. They're pretty strict about that these days." Daniel turned to Matthew. "Can you help Mom with all this, Dad?"

"I'm fine," Helen said.

"Don't get out of that wheel chair, Mom, regulations." Daniel hurried off.

"I can handle this myself, Matthew." Helen reached down to the wheels of the chair and tried to maneuver herself down the hall. The chair turned back and forth, then into a full circle.

Matthew took the handles on the back and steered her toward the wash room. "Stubborn ...mule." He laughed quietly.

They both silenced as they passed Delia and Greg. The two of them stood at the nursery window looking in, their heads close together and their expressions wistful.

"Do you think they'll make it?" Helen asked when they'd passed by.

"Hope so. They're good for ...each ...other ...both very stubborn ...though."

"I wonder if they'll ever be able to compromise." Helen reached into the sink to scrub her hands.

"Were we?" Matthew scrubbed in the sink beside her. They worked together to wash and dry their hands. Then Matthew pushed her toward the hospital room where the baby had just been taken. Greg and Delia took their places at the sink and they went into the room.

"Sybil, you look so good. I can't believe you just delivered that big baby."

"I can't either." The tired looking, but happy girl laughed. "I'm not going to think about it too much."

Daniel sat on the bed beside her and kissed her forehead. "She was great. We're going to have a dozen."

"Let's not talk about it for a while, Dan. Let me recover from this one first." She smiled down at the baby she held in her arms.

"Do you want to hold him, Mom?" Daniel stood, took the squirming infant from Sybil and handed him to Helen.

"Oh gosh, it's been a long time since I've held a baby," she said looking adoringly at the small bundle. "You know what, Matt? It still feels right."

Matthew squeezed her shoulder.

*

"Don't look at that magazine, Gwen," Gail said the next day in the doctor's waiting room. "You'll catch a disease. People lick their fingers to turn the pages you know."

"Gross." Gwen dropped the magazine back onto the table.

"Here, I brought magazines." Gwen watched as her mother reached into her bag and pulled out two magazines. "Take your choice."

Her mother was breathing heavily when they first got to the waiting room, but she was starting to catch her breath now.

"When did this start, Mom?"

"I've noticed that it's hard for me to catch my breath when I do something strenuous for several years, but only recently it's been hard for me just to walk around." She opened the magazine on her lap. "It's my own fault. I smoked for forty years."

"I looked it up on the internet. They don't think it's caused by smoking."

"I'm sure it didn't help." Gail looked up briefly at her.

"Probably not." Gwen opened her magazine and turned the pages without really looking at it.

"Mrs. Saunders." A nurse opened a door and called her name. They both stood and walked toward her.

Chapter Twelve

"This is my daughter. She's coming with me," Gail said not looking at the nurse for any kind of objection.

"Of course, this way," she took them to an exam room and took vital signs. Gwen noticed again that just the walk from the waiting room to the exam room had caused her mother to lose her breath. The nurse put a devise on Gail's finger and read the number. "Eighty seven," she said and frowned.

"Is that bad?" Gwen asked.

"It should stay above ninety," Gail said.

"The doctor will be in soon." The nurse left the room.

"Are you sure you want me here with you, Mom? I mean medical stuff is very personal."

"I'm asking you to help me die. You'll need to know what's going on and I'm not sure I can tell you accurately."

"Alright," Gwen said. She could almost feel herself shrinking in size. How in the world could she help her mother die? She'd never been able to help her mother do anything. She'd never been able to even do anything right for her mother. I hope I don't have that affect on my children. She thought.

There was a knock at the door and the doctor came in. She was a young woman with curly black hair and a bright smile. Not what Gwen would have expected of a pulmonologist. Of course, Gwen had no idea what a pulmonologist really was. A lung expert, she supposed.

"Hello, I'm Dr. Pramm." She held her hand out to Gail then to Gwen. "I've looked over the records and X-rays that were sent to us. It looks pretty clear. Of course, I'll do the tests over again, but if these are accurate, I think the diagnosis is correct."

"I don't have a question about the diagnosis. I just need a physician here in Sandy Springs. I've chosen to move here and live the rest of my life close to my daughter."

"I understand. Are there any questions I can answer for you?"

"Not for me, but I'd like for you to explain to my daughter what exactly is going on. I'm not sure I can."

"Alright," Dr. Pramm turned to Gwen. "What we have here is scar tissue on the lungs. We don't know exactly what causes this. There are some indications that it's hereditary. Don't worry about it, though. It is rare. We have no indication that smoking causes it, however I'm pretty sure it doesn't help."

"That's what I figure," Gail said.

"Dr. Pramm," Gwen said. "I saw my mother six weeks ago and she looked fine. How could this happen so fast?"

"It didn't happen fast. I'm sure you had some indication of it before, didn't you Mrs. Saunders?" The doctor looked at Gail.

"Yes, but I just didn't think it was important. Then it got a lot worse suddenly."

"That's the way this disease works. You feel it then you go along without any change for a while. Then it suddenly gets worse. You go on like that for a while. It sort of gets worse in increments."

"And there is nothing you can do?" Gwen asked.

"There is a lot we can do to make your mother more comfortable. In fact, right now I'm going to order a portable oxygen devise for her so that when she is active she can get better oxygenation. As the disease progresses we'll get her more oxygen to make her more comfortable."

"But you can't do anything to fix it."

"No, we can't. I'm sorry. I wish I could say we could. When you get to the end, though, there are drugs that we can give to make you more comfortable, Gail."

"You mean you can drug me up so I don't know I'm dying."

"I hate to put it that way."

"…but that's the way it is."

"I'm afraid so."

*

"She takes care of herself pretty well." Gwen laughed as she, Helen and Allison watched Isabella, the small poodle, successfully snarl the huge floppy dog down onto the ground and over on his back.

"Isabella is a very dominant female." Allison laughed.

"She sure is. It's funny, but Phil's mom can control Henry, too. This little old lady on a walker just tells him to sit and he sits. He won't do anything for me."

"Are you taking him to obedience school?" Helen asked.

"Phillip? I don't think there is obedience school for husbands."

"I meant Henry, of course." Helen laughed.

"Rodney is. I don't know when I'd have time. I have to move Mom in to the assisted living. I'm so glad she chose the one by my house. I can walk there. It'll be much more convenient to have her so close. Then, of course, with Sybil out, I'm pretty much alone at the shop. Matt can relieve me on Mondays. He can do it alone pretty well now and Phillip can get by for an hour some afternoons and close for me, but other than that, I'm pretty much on my own."

"I thought we were going to hire someone."

"We did, we hired Sybil."

"Weren't we going to hire someone else, too?"

"No, you were going to join us."

Helen stroked the greyhound's neck and looked at the forest around them. "That won't be happening for a while, I guess. I still have a household to support."

"Didn't you say Daniel and Sybil would be moving out soon?" Allison asked. The three dogs were trotting along pretty nicely in front of them now, the little poodle leading the way and snarling at Henry from time to time to keep him in his place.

"As long as we walk with Issa," Gwen said. "Henry's under control."

"Danny and Syb will start looking now. No telling how long that will take. Of course, I don't want to rush them. And who knows, Delia may live there forever. Greg isn't coming back and she isn't going to live with him. What a mess. And of course, Matt's still there and he can't support the place. He can only manage a couple of days of the construction team."

"You know, Helen, Matt's talked about giving up the construction team and coming on full time at the Gallery. I wouldn't have to hire anyone if he did," Gwen said. "Has he mentioned it to you?"

"No!" Helen looked horrified. "That's just great. This was my project. He fought it every step of the way and now he wants to work there while I support him."

"Okay, I'm sorry I brought it up, Helen. We'll talk about it later. This isn't fun for Allison."

Helen took a deep breath. "No, it isn't. I'm sorry, Allison."

"I'm just sorry you guys are having such a tough time. I didn't realize how really difficult mid-life is. It makes the dramas of youth seem easy." Allison sat down on a swing next to the river. "What do you think of this trail, Gwen? Will it be in the next Editor's Journal?"

"I've been so busy feeling sorry for myself, I forgot to notice it. I'll have to notice on the way back."

"Let's just sit here for a while. I brought water." Allison pulled three bottled waters out of her pack and passed them around. "...And fiber bars and rawhides for the dogs."

They sat quietly for a minute then Allison pointed across the river to a rocky spot. "Look, a Great Blue Herron."

"What a beautiful bird," Helen said. "How do you know what kind it is?"

"I have a bird book. I looked it up. Of course, there are the mallards and that over there is a Canada goose. They're coming south this time of the year."

"Yeah," Helen munched her fiber bar. "We have a family of them in the pond at the office complex where I work. They walk around with their babies in the road. It scares me to death."

"They're pretty safe out here," Gwen said. "What kind of a bird is that?" She pointed to the sky.

"It's a red tailed hawk."

They all sat quietly for a minute. "I'm starting to relax. Thanks Allison."

A squirrel scurried across the path. Henry jumped to his feet and leaped in the direction of the squirrel. Gwen grabbed the leash with both hands as she was pulled to her feet then over to land flat on her face and slide a few feet forward before bringing the dog to a stop. He danced back to her and bathed her face with his tongue.

"I don't know, Gwen," Allison said. "I think you'd better make time for obedience school."

Helen agreed.

*

"Gwen, this dog is just not going to work out." Gail balanced herself against the front door jamb as Henry bounced from floor to ceiling, licking her face as he went by.

"Lurch, down!" Martha's voice rang out from the living room. The dog dropped to the ground and crawled on his belly to the walker.

"You'll have to get rid of him, honey," Gail said, gripping her oxygen canister and pulling it to the living room. She sat down in a chair, breathing hard. It took a minute for her to catch her breath.

Gwen held her breath until Gail's slowed. "I'm not getting rid of him, Mom."

"Am I just not supposed to visit? Is that it? You'd choose a dog over your own mother?"

"Oh stop being such a selfish toad, Gail," Martha said. "Give the girl a break. The dog doesn't bother me. Just tell him what to do and he'll do it."

"Stay out of this, Martha. This is between my daughter and me."

"No it isn't. I'm a part of this household and so is that dog. What matters to them, matters to me." Martha sat back down and moved her walker to the side of her chair.

Gwen's hands were shaking. She didn't know what to say. "I'll ...ummm ...lock him up when you come over, Mom. Just warn me first."

"You mean I can't just walk in and out of my own daughter's house?"

Martha huffed. "Not unless you can deal with the dog. Come here, Lurch." She signaled. He stood, put his head in her lap and stared up at her. "After all, Gail, this is your own fault. It was those nasty cigarettes that you were so belligerent about."

"Martha, please." Gwen pleaded. "Let's try to be civil to each other."

"No, she's right. I know that's what brought me to this." Gwen looked at her mother's bowed head and tired face. She felt a stab of fear. This is really happening and she believes she's responsible.

"Mom, you know the doctor said they hadn't correlated it to smoking."

"Come on Gwen, think about it."

The silence grew strained as Gwen sat down on the couch next to her mother and took her weathered hand. She looked at the veins and lines in it. Why hadn't she noticed her aging before? Was this disease aging her faster?

"Well, whatever caused it," Martha broke the silence. "We'll all be dealing with it, so I think the best way for you to proceed is to try to fit into the family instead of trying to control it."

"Oh, you're one to be talking about control, Martha. You've made such a mamma's boy out of Phil he's even got you living with him. How did you manage to get them to move out of their bedroom for you?"

"That was not my idea."

Gwen took a deep breath. "I'll get us some tea. Then I have to relieve Matt at the gallery. He has a doctor's appointment this afternoon. How did you get here, Mom?"

"I walked. It's less than a quarter of a mile through the woods."

"Oh, Mom, I don't know if you should walk through the woods. What if something happened? Nobody would see."

"I haven't gotten to the point that I can't walk in the woods. Don't be over protective. I'll know when to stop."

"Alright," she hurried from the room to make some tea and gather up some cookies. Life is going to be a bumpy ride for a while. She thought. I hope I'm up to it.

*

Matthew looked at his watch. There was still enough time to get to the doctor's appointment, but he wondered where Gwen was. Daniel was going to pick him up and take him. He'd been driving for about a month now and felt fully confident, but Daniel said he wanted to talk to his doctor. I'm a grown man. I can talk to my own doctor. He thought then shrugged. He shouldn't complain about people caring about him. He was truly blessed.

"I'm here, Matt." Gwen hurried into the store. "Mom had walked to my house. Can you believe that? In her condition, so I had to take her home. It took longer to get her out of the car and into her apartment than I expected. I hope you're not late for your appointment."

"No," he said easily. "Danny is coming to pick me up. He wants to go with me, talk to the doctor."

"You didn't bring your car today?"

"No, he dropped me off."

"Hey guys," Phil said as he came into the room from the back door. "I thought I'd come by and keep you company, Gwen. I have some work to do on the books anyway."

"It's awfully early, Phil. You don't usually leave work by 3:00 o'clock."

"I was in good shape at the firm and I have the time." Phillip looked at Matthew. "How're you feeling? This doctor's appointment isn't something bad, is it?"

"No," Matt frowned. "I wish people would stop …treating me like …an invalid." He noticed his speech getting broken and took a deep breath.

"Sorry," Phillip said.

A gust of cool air blew in as the bells jingled on the front door and Helen hurried into the room. She looked angry. Her hands were fisted at her side and she went straight to Matthew. "I can't believe you're thinking about quitting your job and working here full time. How can you do that when I've worked so hard to support you?"

"Helen, I …you …damn it." He scowled at Gwen. His speech was completely gone. He shouldn't even try. He bit his lip and looked back at Helen. He wanted to say he hadn't been planning to do it right away. He'd only thought about when the store got fully under way.

"You're kidding!" Phillip said. "How can you think of anything like that before Helen's been able to work here? After all it was her shop. Matt, I don't know what's come over you. Don't you think of anyone but yourself? This damn stroke has made you selfish."

Gwen and Helen were looking at Phillip with wide eyes. Matthew tried to say he was not selfish, but only an unintelligible sound came out. Damn it, I hate this aphasia.

"Thanks, Phil," Helen said.

"Well, you've really changed your tune, Phil. You weren't even speaking to Helen a week ago," Gwen said.

"Look at her, Gwen." Phillip raged. "She's exhausted. She thin as a rail. She needs to quit that damn job and come here full time, but she can't, can she? She's got to support the whole damn world?"

"That's right and this idiot is planning to quit his job, the job that pays a fraction of the bills." Helen put her hands over her face and took a deep breath.

"I ...I..." Matthew scowled at Gwen. Why had she told Helen that? He hadn't meant he wanted to quit now. He'd been thinking of a time when the four of them could work in the gallery together. He tried to say something, but he wasn't even sure he knew what it was.

"Shut up, both of you," Gwen yelled. "Look what you've done. He was talking just fine before the two of you came in here."

"Gwen ...shut..." He couldn't say anymore. Why can't she shut up? Hasn't she done enough damage?

"God, I just can't believe this," Helen said. "I'm leaving. What's the point of me being here? It's his damn shop." She stormed out the front door.

"I have to say, Matt," Phillip said. "I've been on your side from the beginning of this thing, but this is just selfish. Poor Helen, I'm worried that she's about to snap." He turned and stormed to the back door. He pulled his jacket off the peg and said, "I'm going home. I don't feel like working on the books for this damn place. It's a disaster anyway."

Matthew turned to Gwen angrily. He wasn't in the wrong here, but he couldn't say anything to defend himself. "Damn ...why..."

"I didn't say you were going to quit. We were talking about hiring someone. I was saying I wouldn't have to if you came on full time." She looked up at his angry eyes and winced. "Okay, Matt, just shut up."

Shut up? As if he could say anything anyway.

"Hey, what's going on here?" Daniel stood in the front door. "I saw Mom screech out of the parking lot. I waved, but I don't even think she saw me." He looked at the angry faces of Matthew and Gwen.

"Nothing," Matthew said, marveling at how his speech had come back when he didn't really need it anymore. "Let's go."

*

"What happened?" Daniel asked when they were in the car.

"Shit!"

"Well, that happens sometimes. Tell me about it."

"Oh, I don't think so." Matthew looked out the window. "You know I speak pretty well when it doesn't matter ...but when I need to talk..., I'm useless."

"I'd like to say that'll get better, Dad, but I don't know if it will or not."

"It ...sssssucks."

"Yeah,"

"I can't believe that all four of us were arguing with each other... What's happened to us? We were such ...good friends."
"It's a rough time. Your speech may not come back completely but I think things will get better." Daniel smiled. "Let me distract you with stories about Gabriel. That'll cheer you up."
Matthew smiled sadly at his son. "Okay, tell me stories."

*

Gwen pulled into the spot where she parked her car on the back driveway. She couldn't park in the garage because Phillip's latest sports car was in there. Never mind that it was an Alpha Romeo, her favorite. She was delegated to the driveway and it was pouring down rain. She didn't go in the garage door. She hurried up the back steps to the deck and unlocked the back door to the kitchen.
Frankie and Rodney were standing by the sink scowling at each other.
"Don't call me a dimwit!" Rodney said. "You're not in a position to criticize me. You never even tried to go to college."
"Well, at least I didn't waste thousands of dollars of Mom and Dad's money and then quit."
"That's enough!" The steel in Gwen's voice startled her. "I've heard enough arguing for one day! First your grandmothers, then the fearsome four, now you two, if you can't get along then just get out of my house."

Both of them looked at her warily. She could hear Phillip hammering on something metal in the garage.

"Go ahead! Get out!"

"Want to take that big stupid dog for a walk?" Rodney asked Frankie.

"Sure, let's go."

"You can't go for a walk." She put her hands on her hips. "It's pouring down rain."

"I think it's letting up." Frankie pulled the leash off the hook on the wall and struggled to clasp it to the bouncing dog's collar. "Oh Mom, who are the fearsome four?"

*

Gwen let herself into the gallery the next morning through the back door and flipped on the light. The place looked like a museum. Like nobody ever touched anything.

"This place is lonely," she said. "Nobody ever does touch anything. I think it's time to admit that my great idea and huge investment is a big fat flop."

"Who are you talking to, Gwen?" Phillip came out of the office.

"Ahhhh..." She jumped. "Phil, I thought you had gone to the firm."

"I told them I wouldn't be in today. I've got tons of vacation time built up and I needed to do some work in here." He sat down on the stool behind the candy counter. "I also need to apologize to Matt. I can't believe I lit into him like that yesterday."

"We all acted stupid." Gwen unlocked the front door and turned the open sign around.

"I can't believe what we've come to. We've always been such good friends."

"It's my fault. I should have listened to you. This gallery was a big mistake."

Phillip moved around the counter and put his arms around her. "It's way too early to be saying things like that. Give it a chance, Gwen." He pulled her close despite her resistance until she relaxed. "I feel terrible about going to bed without talking to you last night. I hate it when that happens."

"Judging by the snoring, you didn't have any trouble sleeping."

"No," he laughed. "Sorry, I never do."

"I hardly slept a wink."

"Well, I'll stay with you and we'll run the place together. I'm not going over to the job site where Matt is until this afternoon. He probably needs time to settle down. I do think that working with his hands helps him."

"Yeah, and working in his garden." Gwen pushed away from Phillip and turned on the computer at the checkout counter. "We treated him like a cripple yesterday."

"He couldn't talk."

"He's not a cripple."

*

Matthew wiped the sweat off his brow. He'd like to take his hard hat off but that would be stupid on this job site. There were too many things that could fall on his head and his head had become dear to him.

He couldn't quit going over the scene that had taken place the day before between him, his wife, and his two best friends. What a mess and it was all his doing. He put the top tray into his tool box and closed the lid. It was 4:00 o'clock. He was the only one still on the job and he was tired. He'd worked in his potting shed on wintering his bonsais until well into the night. It helped.

"Matt," he heard Phillip's voice and turned around. "Are you the only one here? The place looks abandoned."

"I told them I'd lock up." He watched the concern enter Phillip's eyes and said, "I'm not a child, Phil."

"No, of course you can lock the place up." Phillip sat down on the bench that Matthew had set his tool box on. "I came to apologize, Matt. I was way out of line yesterday."

"We were all out of line."

"I think you were the victim."

"No, I have thought about going into the gallery full time." He took a deep breath. "I'm talking just fine now."

"That's got to be hard for you."

Matthew looked at Phillip and smiled sadly. "It's very hard. I could have defended myself, if I'd had the words. Let's go." He motioned toward the door and Phillip followed him out.

It was cool outside and Matthew took off his hard hat. The cool fall breeze felt good in his sweaty hair. He didn't know why they'd kept the job site so hot today. They could have cooled it just by opening a door.

"I'm trying to work up the ...cour ...c...c ...strength to go and talk to Helen. I had no intention of taking over her ...p.p.project."

"I know. Gwen told me. You were thinking of a time when you and Helen could work in the gallery together." Phillip followed Matthew to his truck and stood next to it while Matthew put the tool box into the lockbox in the flatbed and secured the latches. "Matt, do you think Helen and you will ever get back together?"

"I hoped."

"You don't hope anymore?" Phillip waited but Matthew didn't respond. "She went to that island with that man. I don't suppose you can forgive her for that."

"I don't give ...a ...d.damn about that."

"You don't?"

"Well ...I hate it ...but don't give a damn." He blanched at the fact that his speech suffered even when he was talking about Helen.

"So you still love her."

The look on Matthew's face was so incredulous that Phillip laughed. "So why don't you do something about it?"

"What?"

"Take her back."

"Can't ...take ...her..." Matthew opened the door to his truck and climbed in.

"Well then, win her."

*

"Hey, Helen," Victor's voice sounded on the other end of the telephone line. "I wanted you to be the first to know that Melissa and I have set a date."

"That's wonderful, Victor. What's the date?"

"March fourth."

"That's not far off. Are you sure you can arrange a wedding in that amount of time?" Helen thought it was a long way off, but if that was okay with Victor, what did it matter to her?

"It seems like forever to me, but it's important to Melissa to have her family there. What's important to her is important to me."

"You're a good man, Victor."

There was a pause before he said anything. "I wanted you to be the first to know." He laughed. "I want you to be my best man."

Helen felt the delicious laughter before it came then enjoyed every chuckle. "I think that's great. You know I'm not a man, right?"

"Of course I do but you're the best friend I've ever had. You'll stand with me, won't you?"

"You bet. I can't wait."

"We're taking Tif for a walk. Come along."

"Thanks but no. I just got in from work. I walked Lila right away and I'm beat. I'll join you another time."

"I love you, Helen."

"I love you, too."

*

Chapter Twelve/ 347

She stood at the window and looked out over the park. This apartment had a better view than Melissa's. Victor and Melissa came into view below. Tiffany ran ahead on her extendable leash. They held hands and, though Helen couldn't see their faces, she knew they were smiling.

The buzzer from the front door of the apartment building sounded and Helen turned and went to the intercom. She was so tired she hadn't even thought about what to eat. She didn't have much appetite these days.

The buzzer sounded again and she pressed the button to answer it.

"It's ...m.me, Matthew."

"I'll buzz you in." She pressed the button to release the lock on the door then she hurried out of the apartment to wait at the elevator.

"What's wrong, Matt? Are you alright? How did you get here?" She backed up as he came out of the elevator smiling. Then she noticed that he had an arrangement of flowers in one hand and had the other hand behind his back.

"I ...drive," he said extending the hand with the flowers in it.

"These are beautiful, Matt." She took the flowers and went to her apartment. "You didn't buy these, did you? You grew them," she said taking a vase out of a kitchen cabinet.

"I did," Matthew said from behind her. She turned around and he extended the other hand to her. In it was a small box of her candies and a small vile of Gwen's bath salts.

"What's the occasion?" she said as she took the items from him and put them on the counter.

"I'm sorry ...about ...yesterday. I ...didn't..."

"I know, Matt. I was too fast to react. I should have talked to you about it before I got so fired up. I'm sorry, too."

"Dinner ...steak place ...over there." He pointed to his right.

"Well, that would be nice, but how can you drive? Can you read the street signs and all?" She stammered.

He grinned at her and she had a fleeting memory of the handsome young man she had married. Unable to help herself, she smiled back.

"I ...read ...I ...understand," he said tapping his temple. "Don't write ...don't talk."

"You do a pretty good job with only a few words," she said. "Well, I guess dinner would be nice. Let me get a jacket. The nights are cold these days." She went to the coat closet and pulled out a sweater. She wondered what they would do at dinner if they couldn't talk.

"Beautiful dog," Matthew said. Helen turned around to see him stooped in front of Lila stroking her shoulder.

"That's Lila. I'm just thrilled with her. I didn't know how close you could get to a pet. Not that I didn't care about Rocky," she said.

"I love dogs."

"I didn't know that. I thought you were a cat person."

"Love dogs ...love cats."

*

Chapter Twelve/ 349

"I like ...your ...appointment," Matthew said as they were seated in a booth inside the small steak house down the street.

"My appointment?" She questioned. Matthew looked concerned his brows were pulled together and he seemed to be deep in thought.

"Oh!" she said. "My apartment...thanks. I think it's nice."

"Lonely?" he asked

"Sometimes I am." The waitress approached the table and Helen noticed the concern in Matt's eyes as he looked at the menu. "I suppose you'll have the surf and turf," she said casually. "Is that still your favorite?"

Matthew smiled, nodded his head and said, "No."

"We'll both have the surf and turf," she said to the waitress then closed her menu and gave it to her. "Do you want to go to the salad bar?" she asked. "I've heard it's very good here, or I could just get you something. I know what you like."

"I'll go," he said and stood up.

She walked to the salad bar ahead of him, but in the line, she watched out of the corner of her eye. He had really gained control of his right side again. He didn't walk with a limp and his hand shook only a little as he dished up his food.

"You've done really well, Matt," she said when they got back to the table.

"Therapy,"

She smiled. "And good friends, all those walks with Phil help I'm sure. Are you still going to the Gym?"

He nodded. "Three ...times a ...week," he said holding up three fingers.

Helen thought for a minute as she munched her salad. It had been months since the stroke. "Three times a week," she said. "When do you go? I never see you there and I'm pretty much going every day."

"Morning ..." he said.

"Oh. You go while I'm at work."

Their dinner came and Helen picked up her lobster tail to break it in half but struggled. The shell hadn't been cut quite enough.

"Help?" Matt offered.

"Well, if you can." He took the tail from her and easily broke it apart releasing the tender meat from inside.

"You're strong, too." She smiled. "I'm so glad, Matt."

He picked up his lobster tail and broke it in half releasing lobster slime in a stream over his face. He sat up straight looking startled then laughed.

Helen laughed, too and took her napkin from her lap to clean his dripping face.

When they got back to her apartment, Helen stopped at the door. "Matt, this was nice but I think we should say goodnight now."

"Coffee..." he said holding out his hand for the key.

"I have to walk Lila."

"I'll walk with you. Keep you safe."

She smiled and handed the key to him. He unlocked the door and they stepped inside.

Helen called the dog and they attached the leash to her collar and went down to the park outside the building. When they got back to the apartment, Matthew took the key he had kept in his pocket and unlocked the door.

They went inside and he locked the door from the inside then handed the key back to Helen. "Not coffee," he said, "peppermint tea." He pulled two tea bags out of his jacket pocket.

"Good, much healthier," she said and took the leash off the collar of the dog. She dropped the key in a bowl on a table in the foyer and took the tea bags. "I'll make it." She turned to go to the kitchen but Matthew stopped her with a hand on her arm.

"Not peppermint tea ...you," he said and dropped his hands to her waste to pull her close. He kissed her and she melted against him for a minute, remembering the feel of his lips on hers, the perfect pressure of his tongue. She inhaled the scent of him. This was what she'd fallen in love with. She could remember it now.

"Matt," she tried to pull away feeling short of breath. "We can't ..."

"We ...can..." he said holding firm against her resistance. Then he dropped his lips to her neck and nuzzled her chin. "I want..." he whispered. "I want ...you."

"Matt, you just had a stroke. I'm afraid." She whispered. "What if this brings on another one?"

"Will ..." He shook his head from side to side then kissed her again.

"It will?" She tried to resist, but he picked her up in his arms.

He shook his head and said, "Yes." Then grinned at her again, that beautiful boyish grin. "Sex ...is good for your ...heart."

"Matt, how can you pick me up, you're thin as a rail."

"I go to the gym ...and you're thin as a rail." He settled her on the couch and knelt beside her. His speech was improving as his heart beat increased. He kissed her again and gently started to pull her blouse off.

"Oh, Matt," she whispered and wrapped her arms around his neck. They took their time undressing each other, kissing and caressing each other as they went. Matthew stretched his body above hers and parted her legs with one knee.

"Are you sure this won't hurt you?"

He nodded and she guided him gently to her. He eased inside and began the gentle motion that they both knew so well.

*

"Matthew," Helen ran her hand through his thick grey hair. "Are you alright?"

"No...." He whispered into her neck as he nodded his head. He propped himself up on his elbows and kissed her again then sat up and pulled her into a sitting position beside him. "I meant yes."

"Matt," she said. "This doesn't change anything. We can't solve our relationship problems with sex."

He looked directly into her eyes and stroked her cheek with his hand.

"You need to know," Helen said pulling her head away from his hand and looking down at the floor, "that I have thought terrible things about you."

"I've...thought...terrible things about ...yourself," he said, laughed, and shook his head.
"...didn't say it ...right."

Helen smiled. "You said a lot. I understand what you meant, but what you said was good. I've thought terrible things about myself, too. However, Gwen says I can't just let you say it wrong so let's try it again." She turned herself so that her body was facing him and looked into his eyes.

"I have thought terrible things about myself," she said. "I'm talking about you, of course, but repeat it exactly."

"I've...thought t.terrible things ...about ...y.y.y ...my...self." He grinned at her and she melted.

Matthew tightened his left arm around her shoulders, scooped his right arm under her knees and pulled her into his lap. He lowered his mouth to hers and kissed her.

"Seriously, Matt," Helen pulled a long breath. "I'm not just going to come back to you now and go back to the way we were before. Things have got to change."

"Change...is good...like sex." He smiled and kissed her again.

"I'm not going to watch you destroy yourself again. I won't! I mean it!"

He pulled away from her a little so that he could see her face.

"And I don't want to work at this job anymore," she said. "I want to work in the gallery. It's not fair that you're there more than I am." She looked up at his face and saw love and comfort. "Oh God," she said and looked down at the floor.

Matthew put his hand under her chin and turned her to look at him. He took her hand and placed it on his chest, holding it there firmly with his large warm one. "You're...sorry," he said.

She felt the tears spilling over as she rested her forehead on his chest. "*I'm*...sorry." she corrected and let him fold her into his arms.

*

"Well, we don't have to put up Holiday decorations. The two of you are lighting up this holiday season just fine," Gwen said the next morning when Helen and Matthew came into the gallery through the front door. "Does this mean what I'm hoping it means?"

"Probably," Helen said as Matthew wrapped his arms around her waist from behind and kissed her neck.

"You're going home."

"No, Matt's moving into my apartment with me."

"Oh." Gwen scowled.

"We're going to sell the house," Matthew said clearly.

"Selling the house?" Phillip came out of the office. "What about your garden, Matt. You can't live without a garden."

"I have bonsais."

"He's going to develop his bonsais while we live in the apartment. I only signed a six month lease." Helen smiled at Phillip. "Don't worry, Phil. I won't try to take his passion away from him." She looked adoringly at Matthew. "It's his passion that I love. We're looking at one of those town houses on the street next to yours."

"That would be so nice. I'd love for you to live close to us," Gwen said.

"Well, if the courtyard isn't big enough, we won't buy it. Matt has to have a garden."

"What about the kids living in your house?" Phillip asked.

"If we can ever get them out of it, we'll sell it." Matthew marveled at his easy speech.

"We'll get the kids out of it," Helen said. "And, Gwen, you don't have to hire anyone for the store. I've quit my job. Matt went with me this morning to give my notice." She looked back at Matthew smiling. "He's going to continue to work on the construction team until we can both depend on the shop."

"Oh, shit," Gwen said and ran into the office.

Phillip watched her go and turned back to Helen and Matthew. "The books don't look so good," he said. "She's feeling defeated."

"We're not going to be defeated before I even get a chance to work here," Helen said starting toward the office.

"Sweetheart, you have an appointment with the lawyer on your dad's estate," Matthew said, again marveling at the ease of his speech, "twenty minutes from now…your brother."

"Oh man!" Helen stopped on the way to the closed office door. She looked back at Phillip. "Don't let her give up. I won't give up, so it really doesn't matter but I want her support. Don't let her give up." She hurried back to Phillip and put her hands on his shoulders. She kissed his cheek and hurried out the front door with Matthew right behind her.

*

"So we have about one million dollars to split between us," Helen said to the accountant that they had hired to deal with their father's estate.

"We also have some properties that Dad owned," her brother said. "They're commercial properties. There is one that Dad left specifically to you. The other's we're to split between us."

"One he specifically left to me?"

"Yes," Franklin laughed. "He's been your landlord since July. You are now the proud owner of the strip mall that the gallery is in."

*

"Gwen, you're not going to believe what I have to tell you." Helen hurried into the shop two hours after she had left. She stopped short.

Gwen sat behind the register and on the stool behind the candy counter Delia sat looking tired and something else. Something was wrong, Helen realized. "What is it? What's wrong?" She looked from one to the other. "Did something happen to Matt?" She felt a current of anxiety.

"No, Mom. Dad's okay," Delia said and stood. "But I need to talk to you, alone."

"Of course, we'll go into the office. Will you be alright out here alone, Gwen?"

"I'll be fine."

Helen shut the door to the office after they had both gone through. Delia sat down on the chair inside the door and Helen went around the desk to sit in the office chair.

"I suppose you'll be moving home now." Delia frowned and looked down at her hands.

"You don't sound happy about the thought."

"I just have a hard time forgetting how much you hurt him."

Helen took a deep breath. "Well, we aren't moving back to the house," she said. "Your Dad is moving in with me."

Delia looked up, shocked. "You can't ask him to give up his garden. God, Mom, you have no heart."

Helen swallowed. "Delia, if you've come here to abuse me then you should just leave. I don't deserve your hostility and I won't accept it."

Delia sighed and looked back down at her hands. "He loves his garden."

"We've talked about that and Dad's excited about moving his bonsais over to the apartment. After my lease is up, we plan to find a townhouse. We won't buy one that doesn't have a decent size courtyard."

"So you're really going to sell the house." Delia's voice shook. "It's the house Danny and I grew up in."

"I know honey. It'll be hard for you. It'll be hard for all of us, but it's time for this family to move on."

"You mean break up."

"No. I mean go on to the next stage."

Delia's face crumpled and she sobbed into her hands. Helen was reminded of the little girl she had comforted so many times and she suddenly realized what was going on. She stood and rounded the desk to sit on the arm of Delia's chair. "You're going to have a baby, aren't you honey?" She put her arms around her daughter and rested her cheek on the top of her head.

"Yes," Delia sniffled.

"You're scared to death."

"Yes, especially since Greg and I aren't speaking. And now I'm just so humiliated. I have to move out of the house if you and Dad are going to sell it. What will I do, get my own apartment? That would be stupid. How will I raise a baby by myself?"

"I don't think Greg will let you raise that baby by yourself." Helen felt Delia stiffen in her arms and held fast not allowing her to pull away. "Don't you think you should talk to Greg about this?"

"It would be saying I'm wrong."

"It would be compromising."

"How is it compromising if I go to live with him in his apartment? He will have won." Delia straightened her shoulders and dried her eyes. "I want to raise my children in a house."

"I'm sure you will, but I'm sure you'll get there faster if you and Greg work on it together." Helen kissed the top of her head. "Delia, this isn't a competition between you and Greg. It's the beginning of your family."

"So you think I should just crawl back to him." Delia tried to shake her mother's arms off but failed. "We'll never save enough money to buy a house now. Having a baby costs money. I didn't plan to get pregnant this fast."

"Are you still on birth control?"

"No, but I thought it would take longer. My friend Jessica is still trying after a year and a half."

"You know what? I was surprised, too." Helen pulled her even closer and kissed her again.

"Honey, you don't have to crawl. Tell him about the baby and watch the excitement on his face. He loves you and he wants to start a family, too." Helen stood and pulled Delia to her feet. She hugged her and kissed her cheek.

"Don't you think a child should have a yard to play in?" Delia sniffed again.

"It's nice, but it isn't necessary. There are parks and playgrounds and, besides, like I said, you both make good money. If you work on it together, you'll have a house soon enough." Helen stepped back. "And, at the risk of making you mad at me again, I have to say that your dad and I are selling the house. So that yard isn't available."

Helen met her daughter's eyes and saw the anger come and go.

Delia took a breath and said, "So, what do you think I should do?"

"Well, that's up to you, of course, but what I'd like to see you do is; first tell Greg about the baby and watch the thrill in his eyes. It'll warm your heart, I promise." Helen smiled up at her tall beautiful daughter. "Then move into his two bedroom apartment with him and decorate the nursery." She laughed. "And let me help."

Delia sniffed and Helen handed her a tissue from a box on the desk. "How are you feeling?" she asked. "Are you sick?"

"I throw up in the morning." Delia sat back down. "Actually, I feel pretty queasy all the time."

"I was like that, too. Don't worry it goes away after a few months."

Chapter Thirteen

Editor's Note
By Gwen Desmond
December 1

  Today I took my dog to the mountains of north Georgia. Sandy Springs isn't the only nice place in north Georgia. I love our city but having such good access to the rest of the state is one of the reasons.
  We have Interstate 285 which can get us to any highway leaving the city of Atlanta and of course we have Interstate 400. That's the one I took. I found a state park that had a road leading to the top of the mountain. I went by myself so I didn't take abandoned forest trails. I didn't want to get attacked by a bear or worse a human.
  My dog, who was supposed to be a toy poodle, but isn't, accompanied me, so I'm pretty sure that I would have been safe from any predator. He stands about 38 inches at the shoulder, weighs about 85 pounds and looks like a walking shag carpet.
  We found a swing at the top of the mountain and just trying to hold Henry (said dog) still propelled me higher and higher. The mountain breeze was energizing and the call of wild birds and chatter of crickets relieved any stress I may have felt.
  Give it a try. I'll include on the last page of this edition a map of my adventure. Take advantage of our wonderful location.
  For the first of the New Year issue, I plan to go to the new Sandy Springs dog park. My dog has

been there with my sons, but I plan to experience it for myself.
Talk to you then.

*

"So Dandy is pregnant," Phillip said to Gwen that night over dinner.

"Yep, of course I knew it before Helen told me. She came into the shop with her eyes swollen and looking pale. I knew as soon as I looked at her she was pregnant."

"I guess women can tell that kind of thing." Phillip sat back and looked at Gwen. "That's two grand babies for them and one for us."

"It's not a competition, Phil. I love Trevor but I don't want any babies that their parents aren't ready for."

"You're right.

They were sitting at the kitchen table eating pizza. The door bell rang and Henry ran to the foyer barking loudly. Gwen could hear the whish and thud of him jumping up and down.

"At least he just jumps up and down and doesn't put all of that energy into charging the door," Phillip said. "I don't think the door would hold him."

"Come with me, Phil. Someone has to control Henry while the other opens the door."

"I'm right behind you." Phillip picked up the plates and put them in the sink where neither of the animals could knock them to the floor. He grabbed the dog by the collar, pulled him into the dining room and shut the door.

"It's Amber." Gwen whispered as she unlocked the front door to open it. "Hello, Amber," she said. "Rodney isn't here. He got off work about an hour ago but he doesn't always come straight home." She stepped back and Amber came into the house.

"He got off his bar tending job." Amber sneered.

"Yes, come in and sit down." Gwen took her to the living room and offered her a chair. "Can I get you something?"

"No, I came here hoping I could talk some sense into him. If he applies now I think he could be back in school next semester. His grades were good up until the end."

"He doesn't want to be an engineer, Amber. He knows he won't be happy doing that," Gwen said, sitting down. "We were disappointed, too, but we want him to be happy."

"He told me he loved me. If that's true how can he be happy without me and I will not marry a bartender!"

Phillip took Gwen's hand and squeezed it. She hadn't been aware that he was sitting on the couch beside her until then. She smiled at him. If he hadn't taken her hand, she'd have slapped the stupid girl and told her to get the hell out of her house.

Gwen took a deep breath and squeezed Phillips hand back.

"He told us that you loved him, too," Phillip said. "If you really do, you'll want him to do what makes him happy."

"That's just stupid," Amber said and Gwen and Phillip squeezed each other's hands firmly again.

"Of course it takes hard work to achieve what we want." The girl continued. "But once we've done it, we'll have money and prestige. Then we'll be happy."

Gwen took another deep breath and felt her head spin a little bit. She was hyperventilating. She breathed slowly out through her mouth and said, "Amber, you'll spend a good half of your life making your living. It needs to be something you like doing."

They heard the front door open and close. "Mom, Dad, I want you to meet someone," Rodney said as he rounded the corner into the living room. He was holding the hand of a small woman. Her hair was brown and her eyes were almost the same color of brown, light brown. She looked shy and a little bit frightened. Rodney stopped short and the girl stopped slightly behind him.

"Amber!" he said. Gwen couldn't tell by his tone if he was happy to see her or not. "I wondered who's car that was at the curb. I didn't recognize it."

"It's new," she said, and turned to the girl who stood behind Rodney looking uncomfortable. "Don't believe anything he says. Apparently the word love doesn't mean anything to him." Amber stormed to the front door, opened it and went through.

Rodney looked at his parents and propelled the shy looking young women to stand in front of him. "Take care of Lilly for a minute, would you." He looked at her and said, "I'll only be a minute." He ran out the front door.

Gwen couldn't help but notice the difference between the two girls who had just stood in her living room. Amber was tall and slender, perfectly proportioned. Her hair was dark, long and straight. Lilly was very small. She seemed stocky at first but on second look, which Gwen was mad at herself for, she had a full figure with a slender waist and legs. She was not heavy, just curvy. Her hair was brown and a little bit frizzy, even in cool weather. Gwen thought. I hate to think of what it's like in the humid Atlanta summer.

"Come in, Lilly," Phillip said, breaking into Gwen's thoughts. "I guess we haven't been properly introduced but I'm Phillip, Rodney's dad and this is Gwen, Rodney's mom."

"I'm sorry," Gwen said. "Was I staring? That was really a dramatic scene." She smiled at the girl. "Can I get you something, Coke, lemonade, hard liquor?" She laughed.

Lilly smiled as she sat down on the chair Amber had just left. "I'll take the hard liquor."

Phillip noticed that there were dimples in her cheeks and her eyes danced when she spoke.

"I'm kidding, of course," she said. "Rodney and I work at the restaurant together. We've become really good friends." She looked toward the window to the front yard where they could see Rodney and Amber obviously arguing. "I'd leave but we walked. My car is at the restaurant and I'd have to walk by those two to go back."

"Don't leave, Lilly," Gwen said. "Do you like dogs?" Henry was pawing at the dining room door. Nothing had crashed. She and Phillip had removed anything breakable.

"I love dogs, cats, too." She scooped Cole up in her arms from where he'd been rubbing on her leg.

"Well come outside with me to let Henry, AKA, Lurch out for a run." Gwen stood. "How about lemonade, I made it myself. It's not from a carton."

"That sounds good."

All three of them were out in the yard with Henry when Rodney joined them again. "I'm sorry, Lilly," he said right away. "Mom, Dad, I hope Amber wasn't rude to you."

"She wasn't rude, son," Phillip said. He took the slimy tennis ball from the excited dog and handed it to Rodney. "You throw it this time."

Rodney smiled and threw the ball. "I wanted you to meet Lilly because she's become my best friend." He smiled down at her and she smiled back. "I wanted my best friend to be here when I told you that I'm not going back to Tech." He looked at Gwen and Phillip and fell silent for a minute then said, "I want to open my own restaurant."

Gwen looked back at him then looked at Phillip. Neither one of them could say anything. Finally Gwen took a deep breath and made sure to breathe slowly out through her mouth. "Have you looked into it? Do you know what it involves?"

"Yes," Rodney took Lilly's hand and Gwen saw the girl reach for his. "The owner of the place where we work has made me his apprentice behind the bar. He's going to help back it. He wants to branch out. This wouldn't just be a bar and snack kind of place. We want a real family restaurant."

"Rodney," Lilly said. "You don't have to justify yourself."

"No, you don't," Phillip said.

Gwen smiled and put her hand on the back of her son's neck to pull him down for a kiss on the cheek.

"I've looked into loans." Rodney hurried on. "I can get one for this, but I'm not ready for that yet."

Phillip said, "We were planning to pay another...two years at Tech. We'll invest that money in your business, unless you don't want us to."

Gwen noticed the squeeze between hands again as Rodney said, "I'll take your money unless I screw up again. Then I'll never ask for another dime."

"If it's really what you want to do. You'll do fine," Gwen said.

"Rodney," Lilly said. "I need to go back. My sitter needs to leave by 7:00. I know my way. You don't have to come with me if you don't want."

"No, I'll walk you back to your car."

"You have a child?" Gwen said feeling her heart begin to pound. She didn't know why.

"Yes, William is 18 months old." Lilly smiled proudly.

"He's really cute, Mom," Rodney said and Gwen detected pride in his voice, too. "We'll bring him by to meet you some day."

"That would be nice."

*

"A child," Gwen said when they'd left. "I guess she must be a single mother if she's hanging out with Rodney."

"Not necessarily," Phillip winced as the electricity snapped at the leaping dog. "Men and women can be friends without being lovers. I've had a real lesson on that recently." He put his arm across Gwen's shoulders and they walked to the stairway.

"Do you really think they're only friends?"

Phillip looked thoughtful. "No, they held hands like lovers but what do I know? Would it bother you if she was a single mother?"

Gwen thought about it. "I'm not sure. I mean if they're nothing but friends then it wouldn't but…"

"…But what?"

"I feel guilty about what I was just thinking. I shouldn't stereotype. I'm ashamed."

"I feel really guilty, too, but not about that, even though I know what you were thinking." Phillip smiled.

"Tell me why you feel guilty."

"I was so excited about him being an engineer," Phillip said, "…and honestly, I was excited about Amber. She's so beautiful and she's smart and driven, too."

"So, why did you marry me?" Gwen opened the back door and Phillip followed her through. "I'm none of those things."

"Yeah, but I fell in love with you so what could I do."

"Screw you," she said and turned to the sink to wash the dishes.

"That's what I was hoping you'd do." Phillip moved up behind her, put his arms around her waist and pulled her back against his chest.

"Now, or when you fell in love with me."

"Both."

Gwen sighed. "I don't know, Phil. I'm just so preoccupied. Do you think we should really encourage Rodney to do this? Suppose he does have a drinking problem. That would be the worst job he could have."

Phillip huffed. "So I guess you're not going to screw me?" He grunted as she jabbed an elbow into his ribs. He pulled her close again and kissed the back of her head. "I don't think we have a choice, Gwen. He's a grown man. There isn't anything we can do."

"He's only twenty two."

"That makes him of age to make his own decisions. Did you notice that he didn't ask us for permission? He didn't even ask us to for money."

"No, but you volunteered."

"I guess I should have talked to you first. Do you wish I hadn't?"

"No." She turned to face him and put her arms around his neck. "I'm just very uncomfortable about it."

"So am I." Phillip kissed her on the mouth. "Let's see if we can distract each other."

*

"Honestly, Allison, I just wish I hadn't gotten myself into this stupid Gallery business. I'm failing at it and I'm not happy either," Gwen said as they walked around a pond waiting for Helen to arrive.

"I love the gallery. I think it would be fun to work there every day." Allison picked up Isabella to jump across a small stream that ran into the lake. "Why do you say you're failing? I thought you said that you were making enough to pay the overhead on the place."

"Yeah, but next year I have to start paying off the loan. And when the loan money runs out, we won't be able to pay ourselves salaries. Helen will have to go back to work and she'll be miserable. Ahhh..." Gwen said as Henry pulled her into the stream splashing excitedly and digging at the water. "Henry, stop that." Gwen stepped on the dry ground and pulled the soaking dog out with her. She looked down at herself. She was splashed up to her waist and both feet were soaked through. "I need to go back to the car. I have an extra pair of shoes in the trunk. It looks like I'm a failure in the dog department, too."

"Feeling a little sorry for yourself, aren't you?" Allison laughed and followed her back across the stream.

"Yes, I am. I'm lonely. Since Sybil is out on maternity leave it's just me in that store and not only that but I have to work all the time. I was looking forward to Helen working with me in the shop. I was looking forward to having a day off now and then, too." Gwen opened the trunk of her car and pulled out the spare shoes that she kept in the trunk. "Helen's here," she said as a car screeched into the gravel parking lot spraying small rocks up behind it. "We'll have to stop talking about this. She's excited about starting in the shop next week. I don't want to bring her down. Not yet."

"Gwen, I'm sorry you feel so defeated," Allison said sympathetically.

"Hey you two," Helen said getting out of her SUV and going around to the back to get the

Chapter Thirteen

greyhound out. "What happened to you? Do you need to go home and change? It's only 45 degrees out here.

"No, I'll be fine. I just need to change my shoes." Gwen looked at Helen. She was glowing. Her reconciliation with Matthew had done wonders for her. "You look happy."

"I am happy. So what happened?"

Gwen pointed to Allison struggling with Henry's leash and holding Isabella in her arms so that Gwen could put her shoes on. "I'll give you one guess."

"Henry, you're such a bad boy." Helen stroked his head and the big dog licked her hand. "Yuck." She wiped her hand on her jeans. "That's one thing I can't get used to. Luckily, Lila doesn't lick me."

"So has Matt moved in yet?" Allison asked as they started down the path. They were walking on another of the trails along the Chattahoochee River.

"He hasn't moved all of his stuff, but he's staying with me. Little by little he's getting everything moved over. We've contacted a real estate agent to sell the house. We're meeting with her on Monday, tomorrow. It's good that you didn't want Monday off. I have a million things to do before I start at the gallery on Tuesday."

"You're absolutely beaming, Helen," Allison said. "She'll cheer you up, Gwen."

"Why do I need to cheer you up, Gwen? You're not feeling defeated again."

"No, of course not," she looked down at the path ahead of her. Henry yanked on the leash threatening to trip her as he veered in front of her.

"Stop it!" she shouted and yanked on the leash. The dog fell back in beside her looking hurt. "Oh, I'm sorry, Henry, but you have to behave." She stroked his silky back.

"His hair is beautiful. I didn't realize it would grow out that much," Helen said.

"I don't think it's finished growing." Gwen smiled. "I love brushing it. Rodney helps me with exercising him but he won't brush him."

"I don't suppose that's the kind of thing a kid likes to do," Allison said.

"He's really not much of a kid anymore."

"How's he doing these days? I haven't seen him since he helped me move." Helen stepped across the stream and Lila crossed in one leap without a single splash.

Gwen stood holding Henry as he strained toward the water. "Let's try this again," Gwen said commanding Henry to sit. The dog sat and Gwen backed toward the stream. She hopped across with the leash stretched over the stream between them. Henry fidgeted and whined. "Come!" Gwen commanded and Henry bounded into the stream and started to dig at the water again. Gwen yanked on his leash and said, "Come!" He bounded over to her and shook, spraying her with drops of water.

She turned back to Helen and Allison and frowned as they tried to control their laughter. Finally they stopped trying and all three of them laughed heartily.

"He actually did obey your command, Gwen," Helen said.

"That's right," Allison said between giggles. "You're making progress."

"Rodney's making progress. He takes him to obedience classes and to the dog park and on walks. He spends more time with him than I do." Gwen fell back in step with them as they went down the path.

"You'll have more time to spend with him soon," Helen said. "Now tell me about Rodney."

"He's going to open a restaurant and he's dating a single mother."

"Wow, things have changed. When did all this happen?"

"Well, he told us about opening a restaurant last week. I don't actually know about the single mother. When he came to tell us about his plans, he brought a girl with him. Her name is Lilly. After they'd been there for a few minutes, she said that she needed to go so that she could relieve her sitter. She has an 18 month old son. I guessed that she was single."

"What happened to Amber?"

"Stupid bitch didn't love him enough to want him to be happy."

"Wow, get back, mother bear." Allison laughed. "One minute you don't seem happy with him. The next minute you're ready to kill to defend him."

"That's about right." Gwen looked down at Henry and stroked his wet coat. "And the emotional roller coaster ride is about to kill me." She wiped her hand on her jeans. "The other day he came down the steps to go to work. He'd shaved off his beard and he looked so handsome." She paused thoughtfully. "But you know what? I didn't recognize him."

"He hasn't had a beard that long," Helen said.

"I don't mean I didn't know who he was. Of course I recognized him but he didn't look like my Rodney. He didn't look like my baby."

They all walked in silence for a while. The sounds of the forest surrounded them. Gwen noticed the difference in the bird songs and jumped as a small rabbit skittered across the path in front of her. She took a deep breath and relaxed a little. I'm glad I've learned to appreciate the world around me. She thought.

"I know what you mean about Rodney," Helen said after a few minutes. "Sometimes I have the same feeling about the twins. They're just not my babies anymore. They're grown people and you know what? I love them but sometimes I don't like them very much. Then they'll do something, like when Danny took me to see Gabriel the first time. He was so excited and I saw my child again."

"Yeah, I didn't expect that. I thought I'd always have that fierce mother love," Gwen said. "But now that I'm getting to know my mother I'm realizing that she really didn't like me much at all. I don't even think she liked me when I was a child. I doubt she ever had fierce mother love."

"I know what you mean there, too." Helen stepped on a fallen tree to get to the other side. "Do you remember the way my dad criticized me. I couldn't do anything right. Sometimes I think Franklin was right to just ignore him. I'm starting to see his love for me now, though."

"I can't ignore Mom. I'd like to sometimes but she needs me." Gwen sat on the tree trunk and crossed to the other side. Henry bounded over after her. "I wouldn't feel good about myself if I ignored her."

"You know, Gwen. I didn't start controlling my own life before my dad died. I don't think I really started living until then," Helen said. "And I'm going straight to Hell for saying that." They both laughed.

"I'll be in Hell with you. I wonder how I'm going to do the things that are required of me for Mom now. Honestly, I wonder how long it will take. Now that's just evil. I hope I don't have to die before my children start to live." Gwen scrubbed at her eyes as tears threatened to spill over onto her cheeks.

"I'm sorry, Allison," Helen said. "This can't be fun for you."

"Actually, it's very enlightening. When I get home I'm going to call my mother."

*

The next morning Gwen let herself in through the front door of the gallery. She always came in through the front door, even though she parked in back of the shop. She wasn't sure why, maybe she just wanted to be sure somebody came through that door. Even though business was picking up for the holidays, she couldn't help but remember that there had been some days when nobody came in.

She put Cole down and went into the office to start up the computer. She probably wouldn't be using it but it was good to be logged in. Phillip could come by on his lunch break or after work or anytime, really. *I hope he does.* She thought as she went back out to the shop to log in the computer at the checkout desk.

"It's another day all by myself," she said to Cole as she picked him up and put him on the counter. He was really a great cat. At only five months old he was so calm that she could bring him to the shop and he played with whatever customer liked him or he slept on the counter next to her in a decorated bed she had bought for him. "I wish I could bring your brother," she said to the cat. "I guess I could if I'd adopted a toy poodle."

The bells on the front door jingled as someone came into the gallery. "I've heard a lot about this place," the man said. "I need to get something for my wife. She and I are having a little trouble and she loves holidays. I thought since next week is Thanksgiving, maybe I could get her a fancy decoration."

"We have plenty of those." Gwen smiled.

*

"So, how's business?" Helen breezed through the door letting a gust of cold wind in as she came. "I thought I'd come in and help you close."

"Thanks. Business has actually been pretty good today," Gwen said. "Maybe the holiday season will pay off. I've sold six of Grace's cross stitch items, two pillows, a wall hanging and, two place mats."

"Cross stitch place mats, wouldn't those have to be dry cleaned?" Helen said. She looked around the shop and smiled.

"Yes, we don't sell a lot of them but she doesn't make many either. We also sold a bunch of your chocolates. Everyone is looking for a simple desert. The kudzu baskets are going fast. People tell me they'll put colored leaves in them or corn or gourds. I've never done that kind of decorating. Maybe I'll do that this year. Victor sold several prints. It's been a good day."

"It sounds great, Gwen," Helen walked around the candy counter and sat down on her stool.

"We haven't sold any soap. I think it'll sell better for Christmas and Honokaa when people are giving gifts."

"I think you're right." Helen stroked Cole when he jumped from Gwen's desk to hers. "I'll bet we'd be in trouble if the authorities checked. I probably should put up a shield so the animals can't get near the chocolate."

"I've already talked to Matt about that."

Helen smiled to herself and stroked the cat.

"You're back in love with him, aren't you?" Gwen said.

"I'm pretty sure I never stopped being in love with him?" Helen looked at her best friend and smiled. "But I can't remember feeling this way for maybe fifteen years." She looked down at the candy machine. "...Maybe twenty, maybe more." She switched the machine on. "You didn't turn the machine on?"

"I don't know how to use it. Why should I turn it on?"

"Sybil knows how to use it."

"Sybil isn't here." Gwen pulled Cole off of Helen's counter and put him in her lap. "Helen, you're not going to hurt him again, are you?"

"That's what Delia said. Has anyone thought about how much he hurt me?"

The silence went on for a few minutes and Helen looked up to meet Gwen's eyes.

"No, I guess I didn't. Tell me about it."

"I don't need to." Their eyes met and Gwen smiled at her.

*

"I think business has been great today," Helen said. "I'm so excited about the fact that we had to wait to close the door until people left. If anyone else had come in, I'd have waited until they left.'"

"You haven't worked here full time yet," Gwen said and closed the cash drawer. They had counted the money and balanced it. Gwen had yawned about ten times. It was only 5:30. Helen was pumped up and ready to go.

"No, but tomorrow is my first full day." She smiled and looked around. "Gwen, I need to tell you something."

Gwen looked at her. She couldn't tell what the emotions behind the look were, fear, ambivalence, or maybe excitement. "I still cook for Phil at night," she said. "Closing at 5:00 o'clock has been one of our compromises."

"I think Phil will be okay with this." Helen put her hands on Gwen's shoulders and looked intently into her eyes. "I own this property."

"You own this property." Gwen repeated.

"That's right. Mr. Robins is…was…my dad's agent. Dad left it to me. He has other properties but Franklin and I are supposed to split them." She looked into Gwen's eyes and saw confusion. She let go of her shoulders and stepped back.

"What did you say?" Gwen sat down on the stool behind the checkout counter.

"When I saw my dad's lawyer he told us we would split the money in his estate between us but that there were also some commercial properties that Dad had. He left this one specifically to me. The others Franklin and I will divide up. I don't really care about them. All I want is this one."

Gwen sat quietly staring at the wall across the room.

"Isn't it great?"

"I guess."

"You guess. Gwen, we can start by terminating the lease. All we'll have to cover in here is overhead." Helen turned toward the office. "The first thing I'll do is get rid of Mr. Robins and find out what is involved in managing this property. I guess I need to get hold of the books. Of course, none of this can start for a couple of months because we have to go through all the red tape." Helen was talking from inside the office now.

Gwen got slowly to her feet and followed Helen to the office. She sat down heavily in the chair across from the desk where Helen was booting up the computer.

"And with the money I inherit, I can pay off the loan. We can start from scratch with no debts or obligations." Helen typed something on the keyboard and watched the screen."

"If I don't pay rent and you pay off the loan, you'll have bought me out. It won't be my shop anymore." Gwen's voice shook and she turned to look away from Helen.

Helen stopped typing and looked at Gwen. It was the first time she'd noticed how tired her friend looked. Her face was drawn. Her eyes lacked their usual sparkle. Even her frosty blond hair was dull and limp.

"Opening this place all by yourself has been hard on you, hasn't it Gwen?"

"It was a stupid mistake."

Helen felt herself flare with anger at Gwen's remark but took a deep breath to suppress her reaction. "It makes me angry to hear you say that, Gwen. I know it shouldn't but you're giving up before I even have a chance to start."

Gwen looked at Helen. Her eyes were watery but her voice was steady. "I think it's great for you to buy me out. It's probably the best thing that can happen. Then the shop has a chance."

"I'm not buying you out. You're my partner." Helen leaned forward across the desk and looked at Gwen. "What's going on, Gwen? You were so excited about this project. We've been open for almost two months. I know it had a slow start but that was expected and the holiday season is going great. Why do you feel so defeated?"

"I don't know." Gwen looked down at her folded hands in her lap.

"Since I'm here full time now, why don't you take a few days off? You haven't had time off since this started. I won't have a problem and Matt can help me if I do." Helen was unable to suppress a smile when she thought of Matthew.

"That would be just great, Helen," Gwen said, a hint of sarcasm in her tone. She yawned and pushed herself stiffly to her feet. Putting her hands on the small of her back she stretched her shoulders. There was a popping sound from her spine.

I could spend some restful time watching my mother and mother-in-law argue with each other about whatever they can find. Or let's see, I could listen to my son's argue about which one of them is the greatest failure. Then of course, there's Andrea. The way she and Tom argued about whether to spend thanksgiving with us or his family, I expect her to show up at my door any day saying, I've left Tom." Gwen sat back down in the chair and buried her face in her hands.

"Oh, honey," Helen stood, rounded the desk and knelt beside the chair to put her arms around Gwen's shoulders.

"I suppose I could take a restful walk with my toy poodle." Gwen continued. "I don't even have to walk. He'll pull me face down along the trail." She could control the tears no longer and let go, sobbing into Helen's arms.

"I can't believe what a selfish bitch I am," Helen said. "I was so caught up in my own misery that I didn't even see yours."

"You're not a bitch."

Helen laughed. "...but I am selfish."

"You've had a lot going on."

"I love you, Gwen." The phone rang and Helen leaned across the desk to pick it up. "Local

Talent," she said. "Hey, Phil, she'll leave in just a minute. We have just a few more things to discuss. Then I'll let her come home."

Helen looked at Gwen and rolled her eyes. "Eating dinner at 7:00 o'clock won't give you heartburn if you stay up long enough afterwards. Even better take a little walk after you eat." She waved Gwen's hand away as she tried to take the telephone. "She'll be home soon. Why don't you surprise her and have dinner ready when she gets there. See ya, Phil."

"Helen, you should have let him talk to me."

"Probably, but you know how I like to irritate him." Helen smiled devilishly.

"You definitely are feeling better."

"I am, Gwen. Matt and I are back together to stay and I can't tell you how good things are. It's like he's a different person but the same person, the old person, no, the young person." Helen looked thoughtful. "That didn't make much sense. Then this thing with my dad's estate, do you realize what it means that he left this mall to me?"

"He was telling you he was proud of what you were doing."

"Yeah, only he couldn't say it so he did this instead. You know, remember I found this place. Well guess what? It was Dad's suggestion. I didn't even think about it at the time." Helen smiled. "I still wish he could have been open with me, but I'm okay. Now what can we do to make you okay?" She turned her attention to Gwen.

"I still have to pay rent."

"We'll both pay rent. I mean the shop will continue to pay rent, at least until the red tape is taken care of and the place is officially in my name. Then we'll renegotiate."

"Okay, but I won't sell my part of the lease. If I don't pay for this space, it isn't mine."

"Alright, I'm convinced the shop is going to do well so we can afford rent. What about the loan?"

"You can pay off half of it if you want. The rest comes out of my salary."

"That isn't fair. If I didn't pay off half of it we would pay it as overhead with gallery funds. It wouldn't come out of anyone's salary. Why should that change?"

"Because if it doesn't it's not a 50/50 partnership. I want 50%."

Helen frowned. "You want 50%. I really am not trying to take your cut in this, but okay, how about I pay off my half and loan you the money to pay off your half. You can pay it into an IRA in my name so it doesn't get taxed until we retire. That way there is no interest. We really don't need to be paying interest if we don't have to."

"That's true. I'll talk to Phil about it and see what he thinks. He'll know how to do that legally and all." Gwen stood and smiled. She looked better to Helen and she stood too. They gathered their coats and headed for the door, turning off lights as they went.

"You sure do spoil Phillip. He was all upset that he'd get heartburn if he ate too late." Helen laughed as they walked together toward the back parking lot.

"I like cooking for him."

"I'm enjoying cooking for Matt, too. Although, he's very picky about what he eats. Did you know that he makes his own veggie burgers? They're good, too. I've never really liked veggie burgers before, but his are good."

"Yeah, we liked them too."

*

Thanksgiving morning was cool and clear. Gwen shivered as she walked out onto the back deck with a cup of steaming coffee. She pulled her bathrobe a little tighter around her and sat down in a sunny spot at the table.

"Aren't you cold?" Phillip stuck his head out the door.

"A little but the sun is warming me. Put on your slippers and bathrobe and join me. It's lovely out here."

A few minutes later he appeared at the door carrying a steaming cup of coffee and wearing jeans and a sweater. "I just figured I'd go ahead and get dressed." He shivered. "Are you sure you want to sit outside. We could put a fire in the woodstove and sit in the kitchen."

"No, I always have to be outside for a little while first thing in the morning. I don't know why."

"Well, that's okay. I'm warming up now. Gwen, how did you end up having everyone here for Thanksgiving this year? You've been working so hard. Why didn't you just take the day off and relax?"

"Oh, I can't do that, Phil. I at least have to invite the kids and their families and when Rodney asked if Lilly and William could come. Well, could I say no?"

"I guess not. Where was Rodney all week anyway? Was he staying with Lilly? If so, maybe this thing is more serious than we thought."

"I asked him, but he wouldn't tell me. He came home early this morning. He's upstairs taking a shower. Like you said, he's a grown man. I asked him to at least let me know he's alright and he has called me every day."

"I know. I talked to him about it, too. What about the Riddicks? Shouldn't Helen be providing dinner for them?"

"She was going to but it was stressing her and she's been so happy since she and Matt got back together and she came to work at the shop full time. I just didn't want her to stress. Their family has been through a hard time. I think getting together on neutral ground is the best idea."

"You're probably right but what about Victor and Melissa? What about Allison? Didn't you say she was coming, too?"

"No, I asked her but she's going home for the holiday. Her family is in North Carolina somewhere." Gwen sipped her coffee and looked at the back yard where Henry was digging a hole.

"It's a good thing our back yard is all forest." Phillip followed the direction of her eyes.

"Yeah," she smiled and turned back to Phillip. "Victor doesn't have family here and neither does Melissa. They were going to go out. Helen asked me before she invited them." Gwen watched the furrow between Phillip's brows grow deeper. "You'll like Victor, Phillip. He's a really nice guy."

"She slept with him, Gwen. Do you really think it's appropriate to have him to a social event that includes Matt?"

"I know that's hard to come to terms with but we have to. Victor is Helen's best friend, besides us, of course. She's going to be the best man at his wedding. We all just have to learn to live with what happened between them." Gwen stood and carried her empty cup into the kitchen. Phillip followed. "Besides, I didn't tell you that she had slept with him. You jumped to that conclusion."

"You don't keep things from me very well, Gwen."

"Obviously, well, I need to get started if I'm going to pull this huge meal together before guests start to arrive."

*

At 2:00pm the doorbell rang and Gwen hurried to answer it. She wiped her hands on her apron and looked out the window to the front stoop. Helen and Matthew stood there, hands full.

"What are you two doing here?" Gwen said as she pulled the door open. "I said 3:30 for guests to arrive."

"We came to help out," Helen said pushing her way past Gwen into the house.

"Brought…decorations." Matthew handed her a basket full of an assortment of fall ornaments in orange, red and yellow. "Look!" Matthew turned back out to the front stoop and reappeared with a terrarium of tiny trees with brightly colored leaves.

"Oh Matt!" Gwen said reaching for the glass house. "It's a miniature forest, all fall colors."

"I'll carry…..heavy." Matthew entered the house and looked in the direction of the dining room. "Good centerpiece…don't you think."

"Perfect," Gwen opened the door to the dining room. "Don't worry. Henry's out back."

"Martha!" Helen's voice sounded from the direction of the kitchen. "I told Gwen I would bring my Dutch apple pie. Why are you making pumpkin?"

"There are more than twenty people expected today." Gwen hurried into the kitchen to head off any fireworks. "Everything will be eaten."

"I still don't understand why anyone would want to eat pumpkin," Gail said wheeling her oxygen tank behind her into the crowded kitchen. "It tastes like mush to me. My maple shortbread cookies are going to be the hit for desert."

Gwen took a deep breath. "Now let's all remember that we are here today to give thanks for all we have. That includes each other. Let's all try to get along so that I don't have to throw anyone out."

Phillip laughed as he came through the door from the garage. "I have a feeling she'll do it, too, if you all don't behave. Come on down to the garage, Matt. Let me show you the Alpha. I actually already have a buyer for it. It won't be ready before Christmas but I created a projected picture of it on the computer and advertised it in the Gallery. I agreed to custom paint. Some woman in Buckhead wants to buy it for her husband for Christmas."

"Sounds great!" The two of them disappeared down the steps to the garage and a moment later their voices were heard in a low hum as Phillip described the features of the car.

"Gwen," Helen said. "I brought sweet potato soufflé like we agreed and my green bean casserole. What else can I do?"

"Sweet potatoes and pumpkin, yuck," Gail said. "Okay, I'm sorry." She winced at Gwen's glare. "Can I make some roasted white potatoes, too? You know that was always my tradition."

"I was hoping you would, Mom." Gwen put her hand on her mother's shoulder. "I like them too, but you're better at it than I am."

"I'm a little tired today, honey. Can I just tell you how?"

"That'll work." Gwen rolled her eyes at Helen as she turned to the stove. "Helen, the turkey should be ready at about 3:00. It'll need to sit to let the juices settle. Then I'll make the gravy. I told everyone to come hungry. Dinner will be around 4:30 so the children don't get grouchy."

"Good planning." Helen turned to Phillip's mother. "I love pumpkin pie. I didn't mean to snap. I was just surprised."

"I understand." Martha stood. "I think I'll put on my coat and go out back to see what Lurch is doing. Would you care to join me?"

*

"Hey, Mom, smells great in this house." Rodney bounded down the steps and turned the corner into the kitchen just as the front doorbell rang. "I'll get that."

"Hey, Mom!" Andrea hurried into the kitchen from the direction of the front door. "No need to let me in, Roddy," she said as she bumped into him turning the corner. "I have a key." Tom came into the room behind her looking sullen and holding Trevor. The baby had been crying. His lips were turned down and folded in the middle and his skin was blotchy.

"Aww," Gwen said. "What's wrong?"

"I think he gets car sick," Andrea said, taking the infant from his father. "Lately, whenever we go more than a couple of miles, he throws up and screams the whole way."

"Yeah, and since I was holding him, I'm not at all sure I can do justice to your thanksgiving meal, Gwen." Tom looked down at his soiled shirt and pants.

"Don't be rude, Tom," Andrea said. "Go and get the bags and go upstairs to shower. You'll feel better after one of Mom's hot buttered rum drinks." She turned back to Gwen dismissing Tom. He scowled at her and went back out the front door.

"Honey, he was covered with vomit. He wasn't being rude. He was being disgusted and I don't blame him." Gwen took a mug out of the cabinet and turned to the stove where she was warming hot buttered rum.

"He was acting like a spoiled brat. It seems to be his usual mood these days."

"I don't think I'd like being covered with vomit either," Rodney said.

Tom came through carrying two overnight bags and a diaper bag. "Andy, bring Trev up. He can shower with me."

"I'll be up in a second."

"There are things you can give babies for car sickness, you know," Helen said. "Dandy used to have that problem, too."

"I know but we got a late start. I didn't want to stop. I'll be right back." She hurried up the stairs.

"Same old selfish Andy," Rodney said. "The world revolves around her." The doorbell rang and his face lit up as he hurried to answer it. "That'll be Lilly."

"I can't believe my kids are grown and they still bicker like children."

"Siblings are siblings. Mine aren't much better," Helen said.

"Look who I found on the front stoop with Lilly and William." Rodney came back into the room holding a round faced bald headed toddler with Lilly beside him and Greg and Delia right behind.

"Hello, honey," Matthew said coming through the door from the garage. He hurried over to Delia and put his arms around her. "Feeling okay?"

"This late in the day, I'm usually alright. I don't think I can stay in here, though, with all these food smells." She looked past Matthew to Gwen. "I'm sorry Gwen. Smelling food makes me feel queasy. I think I'll step outside for a minute."

"That's alright, Dandy," Gwen said and smiled. "I remember the feeling. You go outside with Martha. She's been out there for a while. We got her one of those outside fireplaces and she loves it. I don't suppose you can drink rum. Could I bring you some tea or something?"

"I'll make you some...p.p.peppermint tea," Matthew said.

Delia went out the back door. "Don't worry," Greg said. "Smelling food makes her queasy but she doesn't have a problem eating it." He was beaming.

"Looks like things are going well with the two of you," Rodney said. "Greg, I know you met Lilly at the restaurant the other day, but I want you to meet William." Rodney looked down at the baby on his hip and grinned. "Will'm, this is your uncle Greg.

"Lallo," the baby squeeled and giggled.

"Hello," Greg said and stretched his arms toward the child. William grinned and buried his face in Rodney's shirt.

"He didn't used to act shy." Lilly smiled. "I guess it's a stage."

"Come see?" Greg persisted and William shyly stretched his stubby arms toward him. "I think we can find toys in the den. We can can't we, Granny?" He looked at Gwen.

"Yes, they're in a box in the corner." She turned back to the stove as Greg, Lilly, and Rodney left the room with the baby. "Granny?" she said glancing at Helen.

Matthew and Helen burst into laughter at the same time as Phillip came through the basement door. "What's going on?"

"Go into the den and meet William, Gramps," Gwen said.

*

When all the preparations were completed and Gwen had a chance, she and Helen went out onto the back deck with steaming mugs of hot buttered rum on a tray.

Helen put down her tray and reached for Gabriel who slept in Sybil's arms. "I'll hold him for a while so that you can warm yourself with some holiday cheer."

"It's pretty warm out here anyway," Sybil said. "That outdoor fireplace is delightful. It's too bad Gail can't get too close with her oxygen tank."

"She's not much of an outdoors person anyway," Gwen said as she handed out the steaming mugs. "She's better off in the house."

"When do you think you'll come back to the gallery, Sybil?" Gwen asked.

"Gabe's only three weeks old, Gwen," Daniel said. "I want Sybil to stay home for at least six weeks."

"I'll go nuts, Dan." Sybil sipped her rum. "I can take the baby with me remember. That's still alright isn't it?" She looked pleadingly at Gwen.

"Of course, I hope he isn't allergic to cats. I guess I could leave Cole at home."

"I don't want him exposed for at least the first year," Daniel said. "That way we can avoid any allergy problems."

"That's stupid, Dan," Sybil said surprising everyone. "I'm not going to shelter him from life just because he's a baby. He's strong and resilient. He'll be fine."

Delia and Greg exchanged an uncomfortable look. Phillip squeezed Gwen's shoulder. The whole group was quiet.

Martha cleared her throat and stroked Henry. "He doesn't seem to have a problem with dogs."

"He's teasing me." Sybil smiled. "He likes to see me become a mother bear."

"That's true." Daniel smiled. "She'll take care of Gabriel."

"I can't wait to watch Delia become a mother bear," Greg said. He arranged a sweater over Delia's shoulders. "I can't wait for our baby."

Delia smiled. "Did I tell you we've come up with a compromise on our living arrangements?"

"Remember now," Helen said. "Our house is not available."

"I remember, Mom." Delia sounded slightly annoyed. "We're going to look for a townhouse. We agree that it would be a good first step and we can probably afford a down payment on a townhouse now. We can build equity."

"I...don't know," Matthew said. "Mom and I have been looking. Th...they're pretty expensive."

"We'll look in the suburbs, not around here. This area is out of our reach," Greg said. "We were thinking of starting in the Kennesaw Mountain area."

"That's so f...f...far away."

"Don't worry, Dad. It's not that far. I'll make sure you get to know your grandchild." Delia smiled adoringly at her father.

"What's wrong with that nice little apartment you're in now?" Helen asked. "It's right around the corner."

"I don't want to live there, Mom. We've talked about this." Delia snapped.

Greg put his hand on her shoulder. "It's okay, sweetie."

Helen bit her tongue. It was clear that Delia hadn't forgiven her completely yet. At least she'd come to her when she needed her. They were making progress.

"Besides, Mom, Dad," Daniel said. "We suggested Kennesaw because Sybil and I have found a house there. We're waiting for approval on the loan. It's exciting."

"Won't that be a big commute for you?" Phillip said. "You and Delia both work in hospitals over here. Where do you work, Greg?"

"I'm about half way in between. The only difference will be that I go with traffic instead of against. That'll be an adjustment but I don't mind. It means a lot to Delia."

Helen was pleased that Greg clearly still loved Delia. "Well, I'm glad you'll be close to each other. If everything works out that is."

"I'm excited about it," Delia and Sybil said together. They laughed and Sybil blushed.

"Hey, everyone!" Frankie opened the door to the back porch and came out carrying Trevor on his hip. Grace came out behind him holding William. "We've got the monsters."

"Uncle Motser!" Trevor said and pinched Frankie's lip.

"Poof!" Frankie smiled at the child.

"I'm so glad you're here, honey. Now all we're waiting for is Victor and Melissa." Helen stood and hugged Frankie. "Hello, Grace. You look natural holding that baby. Will we have an announcement soon?"

"No announcements about children at least until I finish medical school." She laughed and handed William to Rodney. "Hello, Gwen." She hugged Gwen, then Phillip.

"Let's go inside," Gwen said. "We'll join the rest of the group in the living room and wait for Victor and Melissa."

"They're here," Rodney said. He was standing at the door holding it for the group to file through. "They've been here for about twenty minutes. Let's go into the dining room."

"Can you believe that I managed to put tables together to feed us all?" Gwen smiled. She had opened the living room and dining room up so that she could put tables end to end. Everyone could see each other. The table was set for twenty people. There were two high chairs. "I didn't set a place for Gabriel but I can if you want me to."

"Not necessary." Daniel smiled. "I'm just hoping he sleeps through dinner so his Mom and I can eat. If not, we'll take turns. We're getting used to that."

They all sat down. Gwen had felt a little dizzy when she looked at the long table. There were three generations of her family there. There were friends, friends of friends, children, grandchildren, parents, parents-in-law, and children-in-law. "What did I do to deserve such a wonderful support group?" She could feel a lump forming in her throat. "Let's say grace." She bowed her head and led them in thanks.

"We'll serve buffet style," she said and pointed to the loaded buffet table at the end of the room. "We'll start at the end of the table with the children and work our way around."

"Before we start," Frankie said. "I have an announcement to make." He stood and pulled Grace to her feet. "Grace has agreed to become my wife. We'll be married on June sixth."

Gwen's ears started to ring.

"That's fantastic!" Rodney stood and shook his brother's hand.

"Go ahead and make your announcement, Rod. You're not steeling our thunder." Frankie smiled back.

"You're sure."

"Positive!"

Gwen heard the exchange with difficulty. The ringing in her ears had gotten so loud. There was a dark rim around her vision that seemed to be getting smaller.

"Lilly and I were married last Saturday. I'm adopting William. We go to court on Monday."

Gwen heard a rumble of voices as the room slowly dimmed. The last voice she heard was Phillip calling her name.

Chapter Fourteen

Gwen pulled the knit scarf up to her ears and pulled the cap down low to meet it. The wind was cold. December could be cold in this part of Georgia, but she didn't remember it being this cold before. She looked up at the sky hoping to see snowflakes but the sky was blue, sparkling blue with only a few white wispy clouds anywhere in sight.

"Hoping for snow?"

She jumped as Helen appeared in the small space Gwen had left to see through her scarf and hat. "Yes, that was exactly what I was looking for. It's seriously cold out here."

"Yeah, it is." Helen looked around. "Where's Lurch? I don't think he and Lila have ever played together off leash. Lila will be disappointed if he isn't here."

"Of course, he's here. Why would I come to a dog park without my dog?" Gwen said looking anxiously around. "The truth is I haven't seen him since I got here."

"That's because he's in the small dog run." Helen laughed and pointed.

"Oh no, I hope he hasn't hurt anyone." Gwen hurried over to open the gate to the small run allotted for little dogs. "His name is Henry." She scowled at Helen as she signaled Henry through the gate.

"I hate to tell you, Gwen, but Lurch fits him better."

"What are you doing here anyway, Helen? Do you come here a lot?"

"No, it's my first time, but you said this was the place you were going to visit for this month's *Editor's Note* and since you've been avoiding me so well for the last few weeks. I figured this would be the place I'd find you on your day off. I called Martha to find out if you'd gone out with Henry and she told me you had."

"I'm not avoiding you. Why in the world would you say that? We work in the same store. How could I avoid you?"

"I don't know but you definitely are. Are you embarrassed because you passed out at Thanksgiving dinner?"

"No, I think it was understandable under the circumstances."

"That's what I was going to say. This family thing just keeps getting more complicated. I thought it would get easier." Helen looked in the direction of the two running dogs. "They're having a great time. I like this dog park. It's amazing there aren't any fights." Even with the big floppy Henry bouncing all over her. The greyhound managed to look graceful.

"Rodney says fights break out every now and then but the owners are expected to take care of it. I haven't seen one since I got here."

Helen directed them to a bench and pulled a thermos out of the bag she was carrying. "Talk to me Gwen. I know you. You're hurting."

"You brought coffee. I love you," Gwen said reaching for the cup with her gloved hands.

"Sorry," Helen laughed. "…Chamomile tea."

"It's hot. That's all that matters."

"Like I said, talk to me." Helen sat back and sipped her tea. The two dogs were inspecting something in the corner of the run.

"I'm not sure I can. All I know is that I want out?"

"Out of the shop, you don't want to be part owner anymore?"

"Well, no, I want to shut it down."

"Selfish bitch!"

"That's exactly why I didn't want to talk to you about it." Gwen took a deep breath and sipped her tea. "I knew you'd call me out on it and you're right. I am a selfish bitch."

"I know you are; from one selfish bitch to another."

Gwen laughed and wiped a tear that had leaked over the edge of her lower lid. "My soap isn't selling."

"I sold some this morning, right before Matt came to relieve me so that I could chase you down here."

"Yeah right, maybe a whole cake of soap."

"No, three, one of bath soap, one of face soap and a shampoo bar, all shaped like sea shells." Helen leaned forward and put both hands around her cup to warm them. "Even if it isn't ever our best seller, Gwen, the gallery is doing well. The holiday season has been pretty good and it isn't even over."

"Next week is Christmas." Gwen sipped at her cooling tea. "The Honokaa season was the best and it's over. We still haven't made back half of our investment."

"Should we have? I don't think so. I think what's bothering you about the shop is that your soap isn't selling. That and you like instant gratification."

"So what's wrong with that? If your candies weren't selling you'd feel the same way."

Helen laughed. "Yeah, but chocolate is always instant gratification. I don't have to do anything to make them sell but put them in front of people. How much marketing have you done for your soap?"

"I publish a magazine every month."

"I won't point out what an accomplishment that is and I won't mention that people are subscribing to it as well as buying ads. Where does it mention your soap?"

Gwen put her cup on the bench next to her and covered her face with her hands. Her shoulders shook as if she was crying.

Helen set her cup on the bench and put her arms around Gwen's shoulders. "Talk to me, Gwen."

Gwen looked up. She was laughing not crying. "Nothing's happening the way it should, Helen. My mother is dying and it should be breaking my heart. Of course it is, but not like it should be. I don't really know her that well. She was always so caught up in herself that we just never really knew each other. It breaks my heart to see anyone suffer the way she is, but she obviously loves me since she chose to come here to die. I'm just not sure I have those same feelings for her."

Helen pulled her closer and leaned her head against Gwen's. "She thinks you love her. You're taking good care of her."

"I'm going straight to Hell for saying what I just said." Gwen and Helen laughed together. "I love Phil's mom to death, but she criticizes everything I do and she can't get along with my mother. I know they never liked each other but you'd think she could make allowances for a dying woman. Sometimes I wonder how long this will last and if I'll still be sane when it's over. I'm going straight to Hell for thinking that."

"I don't think you're going to Hell, Gwen."

"Well, I am, because I'm so distressed about my children. Helen, I love them dearly, but I had completely different plans for them."

"I know what you mean." Helen let go of Gwen and stroked Henry as he nuzzled Gwen with his head and pushed between them. "Henry loves you, Gwen. He noticed your distress. So did Lila." Helen laughed as she stroked the greyhound.

"Why do you know what I mean about your kids? They're both so successful. They're highly trained health professionals."

"Yeah, but I always saw them as loving me dearly, crediting me with their success, and thinking I'm the most wonderful mother in the world."

Gwen laughed and Helen nudged her with her shoulder. "Your kids are successful. They just aren't what you had in mind."

"No, the only one that's on a good track right now is Frankie and I think that's because he met up with Grace and she has nothing to do with me. Her parents created her." Gwen rubbed her face again. "Of course, I'm going straight to Hell for saying that. My kids are living their own lives and that's what they're supposed to do, right?"

"Yes, it's what they're supposed to do but the ungrateful brats should at least consult us about how to do it." Helen laughed and took a deep breath. "Who knows what the grandchildren will do."

"Let's not think about that now. We don't have to think about that for a long time." Gwen stood and snapped the leash to Henry's collar. "Let's take the dogs home and go out for some real coffee."

"Great idea."

*

"I've left Tom." Andrea stormed into the kitchen and handed Trevor to Gwen. She sat down at the table, crossed her arms and dropped her head.

Gwen rocked the sleeping baby back in her arms and put her hand on her sobbing daughter's shoulder. I'm going straight to Hell. She thought as she rolled her eyes at the ceiling. "Andy, honey, what happened, what's wrong?"

"The truth is," Andrea sat up and rubbed her eyes and nose with a paper napkin from the holder. "He left me."

"He left you, why? Honey, tell me what's going on."

"I'm pregnant." Andrea sniffed and blew her nose. "Shit!" She jumped up. "I'm going to throw up, Mom." She ran for the powder room and slammed the door behind her.

"You're sleeping soundly," Gwen said to Trevor. She was glad he wasn't witnessing this.

He opened his eyes and said, "Mommy not poo!" He started to cry weakly.

"No, honey, Mommy not poo but she'll be alright. I guess you're going to have a little brother or sister." She sat down and settled him in her lap. She rocked back and forth until his sobs subsided.

"Would you like some juice?"

"Juice," Trevor nodded his head and let her put him down on the ground. They walked over to the refrigerator together, the toddler staggering slightly.

"You've had some medicine haven't you?"

"...Medicine to not poo the car."

"I guess you not throw up."

"Not frow up...no frow up."

"You're not a baby anymore, Trevor. You're a little boy." Gwen felt her heart flip at the realization. "This all goes by so fast. I need to slow down a little and pay closer attention."

"Attention to what?" Phillip asked as he came through the door from the garage.

"Look, Phil, Trevor has gone from being a baby to being a little boy."

"Trev buddy, when did you get here? Where are your parents?" Phillip picked the toddler up and nestled him on his hip. "Your Granny's right. You're a big boy now." He looked at Gwen. "Where's Andy?"

"She's in the powder room puking. She's pregnant."

"That's great." Phillip beamed. "Not that she's puking, of course, but that she's pregnant."

"I would have thought so but apparently Tom has left her because of it. Either that or she has left him because of it. I haven't gotten the full story yet."

"Rampa," Trevor pulled Phillip's lip. "Aw wanna go...raaage!"

"You want to go to the garage. You're a man after my own heart." Phillip put him down on the ground and took his hand to help him down the steps. "I'll take Trev down to the garage." He looked over his shoulder at Gwen. "You get the story from Andy."

She nodded. He acted like he was watching a mystery on TV. Gwen turned to the stove and started the kettle. Maybe some peppermint tea would settle Andrea's stomach.

"Is that peppermint I smell?" Martha said as she pushed her walker into the room.

"It sure is." Gwen closed her eyes, took a deep breath and turned around to smile at her mother-in-law. "Andrea's here and she isn't feeling very well. I thought it might help."

"Is she pregnant?" Martha asked quietly as she settled herself at the kitchen table.

"Yes, she is but that's about all I know. She had to run to the bathroom right after she got here."

"I was never sick with my babies." Martha looked thoughtful. "I remember how sick you were, though. I never believed in morning sickness until I saw how sick you were."

"You didn't think I was just being a baby?" Gwen sat down across from her with the teapot full of hot water and sunk three bags of tea into it.

"I did at first." Martha reached across the table and put her hand on Gwen's arm. "But nobody could have faked that green color you took on."

Gwen laughed. "I could feel that color. I don't suppose you can actually feel a color on your face."

"I think you could have felt that one. I've never seen anything quite like it." Andrea came into the room and dropped into a chair at the head of the table between her mother and grandmother. "Until now," Martha stroked Andrea's cheek. "Poor baby, you look like you feel terrible."

"I do." Andrea started to cry weakly. "I don't remember feeling this bad with Trevor."

"Sip some peppermint tea, honey," Gwen said. "Matt says this will help with whatever ails you."

Andrea sipped.

"Get her a ginger snap, Gwen," Martha said.

"Actually, Mom, do you have any olives. I want an olive."

Martha and Gwen laughed. Andrea looked up and reluctantly laughed with them. "Sharp flavors really do seem to help."

After she had gotten a jar of pickles out of the refrigerator and they had watched silently as Andrea ate three of them, Gwen asked. "Tell me what's going on, Andy."

Andrea looked at Martha.

"I'm not leaving, honey. You're my baby, too."

Andrea took a deep breath. "Tom accused me of tricking him. He says I tricked him into this pregnancy. He packed a bag and left three days ago. I haven't heard from him. I kept thinking he'd call or come back or something, but he didn't."

"Did you trick him?" Gwen asked.

Andrea sniffed. "Yes, I did." She crossed her arms on the table and put her head down. "I justified it a million different ways. The pills made me sick. Every kind of birth control was too hard for me. "The truth is. I tricked him.

Gwen and Martha were silent. Andrea sat up and looked at them. "I know. That was stupid. I wish I could go back and change it but I can't." She looked from one to the other.

"No you can't," Martha said.

"I tricked Gwen's father, too," Gail said. She came into the room pulling her portable oxygen tank behind her. "And he loved her more than anything in the world."

"Hello, Mom," Gwen said getting up to get another cup. "Did you walk through the woods again?" She rolled her eyes and noticed this new habit was giving her a headache. "I wish I didn't know you'd tricked Dad into having me."

"Well, I did but like I said. He loved you."

"Did you walk here through the woods again, Mom?" Gwen repeated her question.

"Yes and you'll have to drive me home. I'm just glad that stupid dog isn't loose. Where is he anyway?"

"Lurch is not a stupid dog," Martha said. "He's actually brilliant. Where is he, Gwen?"

"Rodney and William have taken him to the park." Gwen looked back at Andrea. "Honey, do you know where Tom is?"

"I suppose he's at his parents, unless he is actually having an affair."

Gwen, Martha and Gail looked at her.

"He's at his parents."

The sound of Trevor crying from the garage stopped the conversation and the wails moved closer as Phillip carried the toddler up the stairs.

"Mommy." Trevor appeared around the corner with his arms outstretched to his mother. She stood, took the baby from his grandfather and ran up the stairs to the bedrooms above.

*

"Well it seems she tricked Tom into getting pregnant. He's furious. He packed a bag and left three days ago and hasn't called or anything."

"I guess I'd be pretty mad, too," Phillip said as he got undressed for bed. "Does she know where he is?"

"She figures he's at his parent's house."

"I guess one of us should call him, find out how he's feeling. Maybe this really is the end of their marriage."

"I hate that. I was so comfortable with Andrea's choice. She always seemed like the sensible one, you know Gwen. She hasn't been very reasonable since she started this family, though."

Gwen crawled into bed beside him and picked up her cup of night time tea.

Phillip sipped his. "You know, I'm starting to enjoy this tea almost as much as that large glass of wine I used to drink at bed time."

"Almost," Gwen laughed. "Lifestyle changes are hard."

They sipped quietly.

"The marriage may be over," Gwen said. "But the relationship isn't. No matter how he feels, that's still his child she's carrying. He won't abandon the child. He won't abandon Trevor."

"Should I call him or should you."

"How do you feel about it?"

"I think I'll call him." Phillip pulled the covers up to his chin. "I hate the thought of loosing Tom. I love him like a son."

"I do, too. I love my daughter and she'll always come first, but he deserves our support, too. Why don't we both call him?"

*

"You're here early," Gwen said as she went into the office and sat down in the chair across from Helen.

"I guess the excitement will wear off after a while, but I just love my gallery. I like to get here a little early and just meditate in the quiet for a while. I even pray a little. It's a great way to start the day." Helen leaned forward. "I wish you were feeling the same way."

"I have to admit." Gwen stood and turned to go out to the shop. "It's better since you got here." She switched on lights and turned on the candy machine. Helen came in behind her. "If I'd realized how long these machines take to warm up, I'd have made a habit to turn them on first thing every morning. Of course, when Sybil was here she did it."

"She'll be back in January. Don't worry, Gwen, I talked to her yesterday and she can't wait to come back. I guess we'll need to make room for a basinet."

"Yes we will. Next year we may need to make room for two."

"Why would we need to do that? Even if Sybil had another baby by then, Gabriel won't still need a basinet."

"That's true, but I was thinking about Andrea's baby. She's pregnant again."

"Congratulations, that's wonderful but why would she be here?"

"Apparently, she and Tom have broken up over this baby. It seems she tricked him. She didn't tell him she was off birth control. He left her and she's at our house." Gwen sat down in front of the checkout and started up the computer.

"As soon as one of them moves out, another one moves in. I'm sorry Gwen. The drama just never stops does it?"

"No, but I don't think I want to talk about it for a while. I had bad dreams about it all night. I feel like I must have walked a couple of miles last night. With my sleep walking problem, I probably did."

"Well, I have something more exciting to talk about."

"Tell me something exciting." Gwen picked up a dust cloth from under the counter and started to dust the shelves. "You know it is hard work to keep this place clean, but you can't let dust collect on and under the merchandise. I hate dusty stores."

"I'll help. Do you have another cloth?"

"They're under the counter."

"Anyway, I was thinking that we should extend our hours two days a week. I get such a crowd at closing time. I think we need to be available for the after work crowd." Helen carefully picked up one of Matthew's bonsais and dusted beneath it.

"I've thought about that, but I just don't think I can stand another hour in the store. By the time 5:00 pm rolls around, I have a hard time not pushing people out the door."

"Gwen, do you really hate this place so much?"

"No, I love this place." Gwen turned around and looked at Helen. "I just don't have that much attention span and I am disappointed about my soap." She sat back down behind the checkout counter. "I've been thinking about taking them out of the shop."

"No way, I've got Sybil working up an ad for the next flyer. Gwen you've never even advertised. People don't know what your soaps can do. I can't wash my hair with anything but your shampoo bar and those bath salts that Matt brought the night he took me back are fantastic. I think I'll buy some more." Helen smiled at the memory of Matt's seduction. She went to the display of soap and picked out a handful of products. "Ring me up." She put them on the counter. "Then restock."

"You don't have to pay, Helen, and I'm not taking them out of the gallery. I'm just expressing my frustration."

"I insist, ring me up or I'll do it myself. While you're doing that let me tell you why I think we can stay open late and not inconvenience you."

"Tell me." Gwen punched the codes into the computer.

"Don't forget, Gwen. You're not alone anymore. I'm thinking that you and I can work shifts on those days. That way you can leave at 5:00. Actually you could leave earlier that day. You could have a half day off. Honestly, honey, I wouldn't want to work open to close if we stayed open to 8:00pm, either."

"I thought you said two days and besides, I like working with you. I get so lonely in here by myself. I have to work alone one day anyway, so you can have a day off."

"You've really become starved for company working alone here for the past few weeks, haven't you?"

"I guess I have. That's pretty silly since I'm certainly not starved for company at home."

"Gwen, remember Sybil will be back soon. We'll schedule her with you. I was thinking we'd try it out with one day first and if it works we'll go to two."

"Won't you be lonely here in the evening all by yourself?"

"I won't be alone. Matt will join me. We'll plan it so that it's not on one of the days he works on the crew. This is a good idea, Gwen. Please agree."

"Why do I have to agree?"

"Because you're my partner,"

"If I didn't agree would you still do it?"

"Not until you agree, but I won't stop working on you."

Gwen laughed. "I give up. I actually do think it's a good idea. I've thought of it myself, but with just me to do the job, there was no way."

"Well, there's a way now. I have some other ideas. I thought we'd try to have an evening with the artists. I was thinking once a month we'd feature one of the artists so people could meet the people who make these things. It'll give them a little more thrill. People could even get things signed."

"Have you brought this up with the artists? We have a number of them that may not want to be a part of that."

"Well, Matt and Victor have agreed. In fact, I've gotten them to agree to do it together the first time. I was hoping we could be set up for it in January. I thought we'd serve wine spritzers and lemonade and dipped fruit."

"You've got all sorts of ideas. I'm starting to feel more energized." Gwen turned as the bells on the front door jingled and the first customer of the day came in. "Good morning,"

She was a tall heavy set woman with wispy blond hair. She smiled at Gwen and Helen and looked around the shop.

"Have you been in before?" Helen asked.

"No. But I've been getting your flyer and I've been planning to come in for a while."

"We're glad you came." Helen stepped a little closer to the customer. "Let me give you a short tour so you know your way around. Then I'll leave you alone. You can read about the artists if you want. We have a write-up on them at each display."

Gwen smiled as she watched Helen lead the woman around the shop. Helen is really good with people. She thought. It's nice having her here. I'll try the tour idea with the next customer.

Helen asked Gwen a couple of questions as she made her way around the room keeping her involved.

When they had rung up the sale of one of Victor's prints and some of Gwen's soap which Helen had strongly urged the woman to buy, Gwen watched Helen sit down behind her candy counter and start to work.

"Helen, don't you feel uncomfortable when Matt and Victor are together. I mean I know it's none of my business, but you've had sex with both of them." Gwen could feel herself blushing.

Helen looked up her eyes wide. "I haven't had sex with both of them. For heaven sake, Gwen, I've only had sex with Matt."

"You told me you slept with Victor."

Helen looked up to the ceiling trying to remember. "That's right I did. I was playing with the words." She looked at Gwen. "I'm sorry. I should have straightened that out a long time ago."

"So you didn't sleep with him?"

"Oh yes, I did. He has terrible nightmares. I'm sure Melissa is going to make him get help for them, whether he wants to or not."

"So you did sleep with him."

"I slept with him, literally." Helen's eyes softened. "It was so nice, Gwen. I can't tell you how pleasant it is to cuddle up to a man without anything sexual between you. We just held each other. We kissed a few times and we slept. I don't know if I've ever woken up so rested." She started back to work on dipping fruit.

"So there's really nothing sexual between you."

"No," Helen's eyes were still soft as she spoke and she had a smile on her face. "I think we both went down there thinking, maybe even hoping, that there would be. We kissed a few times, maybe trying to start something."

"But nothing started."

"It just wasn't there, probably because we're both in love with someone else." She looked up at Gwen. "But there's something else there. I don't think I've ever felt the same about someone. We're just so comfortable."

"What about me?"

"Except for you, of course," Helen laughed. "But it's still different. I don't think I can explain it."

*

"Tom," Phillip said over the phone. "Thanks for talking to me."

"Of course, Phil, I don't have a problem with you." Tom sounded angry. "I just talked to Gwen. I guess she called me from work."

"Yeah, she said she was going to. I don't really know where to start. Tell me what you're thinking."

"I'm not thinking very clearly right now, Phil. That's why I left. I'm just so angry."

"Andrea admits that she was wrong."

"Good for her but we've still got a baby on the way. She knew I didn't want more kids."

"You're right. She got her way. It's easy for her to say I'm sorry now."

"That's right." Tom took a deep breath. "And I hate to say this to you Phil, but that seems to be the way she operates, as long as she gets her way to Hell with the consequences. She's a spoiled brat."

Phillip was silent. Yes, he had to admit that made him mad.

"See what I mean. I'm too angry to deal with this with you or Andrea."

"Yes, I can see that you're angry but at some point some decisions have to be made."

"I'm not coming back for a while. I'm not making any decisions for a while."

"Tom you're not thinking about abortion or anything like that?"

"That's not up to me but no, I wouldn't suggest it. I won't say I haven't thought about it, but I won't suggest it."

"So you'll love the baby?"

"Of course, and I'll love Trevor. I don't have any choice. It's just the way it is. I don't have any choice about Andy either. I love her. It's just the way it is."

"You have to maintain a relationship with the kids."

"Yes but I don't have to maintain a marriage."

*

Editor's Note
By Gwen Desmond
January 1

I visited the new dog park in our new city last month. I liked it very much. So did my dog Henry.

Being an eighty five pound Toy Poodle, he felt that the best place for him was the small dog run, so he cleared the five foot fence without difficulty and joined the other toy dogs. They, of course, all being little tyrants and not liking his presence proceeded to unite and order him onto his back with his legs in the air.

By the time I arrived, the owners of the toys, who were not happy about Henry's presence either, were trying to rescue him from the pack.

I managed to get him out of the small run when my friend arrived with her greyhound. Henry was happy to romp with her in the open field for the larger dogs.

The dog park was a lovely experience. Helen and I sat on a bench, enjoyed warm tea on a cold day, and talked while we watched our happy dogs enjoy a free run.

I can see a problem, though. Some dogs don't get along. Luckily ours are okay with everyone, but it was cold and there weren't very many more patrons. I can see why my friend who is a Veterinarian calls dog parks a veterinary nightmare.

If your dog is appropriate take him there. You'll love it. If your dog doesn't like other dogs, don't be mad at him. He is what he is and you love him. But don't go to the dog park.

Next month I plan to walk in the new park. It has a two mile paved walking path. I'm going to take my grandsons who are about the same age, both just a little less than two years old. I think we'll leave Henry at home for this one. I know January is cold, but my kids have fancy strollers and I'm hoping for a warm snap.

*

"I'm going...l.l.love." Matthew kissed Helen on the cheek and she opened her eyes and blinked.

"Ummm...I was sound asleep." She sat up. "What time is it?"

"It's...six..."

"You're working on the construction team all day?"

"No...half day...that's why I'm...early."

"Are you coming to the shop? I relieve Gwen at 2:00. I think she has William and Trevor this afternoon."

"Thought I'd catch...up with her...after I get off... We need too...talk."

"You and Gwen really got close in all that's happened this year didn't you." Helen put her arms around Matthew's neck and rested her face on his chest. He was so strong and so solid. She loved the feel of him.

He kissed the top of her head then eased himself away from her and kissed her salty mouth. "Love...the...taste of...sleep."

"Gross, Matt." She turned her head. "I have morning breath."

"Love...it. Love...you." He stood. "Gwen and I...always close. More aware now...She needs some support...I need to give it to her."

"I've been trying to be supportive." Helen got up and went into the bathroom.

"Her spirits...are...better because of you right now but she needs to understand that she's making it on her own." Matthew smiled. "I talk better when I'm warmed up."

Helen was brushing her teeth and looked at Matthew's face in the mirror. He looked so pleased, so free and unbothered. She smiled with foamy lips. "I love you, Matt. Will you come to the shop this evening? It's the first late night and I need your support."

"I'll be there, don't worry."

*

Matthew opened the door and loosened his scarf. The weather had warmed considerably since he'd arrived at the job early that morning. There was a breeze that was almost balmy. The sky was cloudy. The moisture was warming the atmosphere. He glanced at his watch, 2:15. Gwen was relieved at the gallery at 2:00. He would go straight to her house. She was supposed to be babysitting. They could talk and play with the boys together.

"Lurch..." The huge dog met him at the door bouncing up and down, his head barely missing the ceiling with every leap. "Down...Lurch." Matthew subdued the dog with his hand.

"Sorry, Matt." Frankie pulled Henry back by his collar."

"Not a problem. I didn't realize you would be here." Matthew closed the door behind him. "Hello...Martha," he said as he entered the living room. "Gail..." He waved at Gwen's Mother. Both women were frowning. "Your...mom here?"

"No," Frankie said. "When she got home from work, I was here and Rodney had come by to drop William. Of course, Rodney and I got into a fight. Then Gran arrived and she and Nana started into each other. Andrea's upstairs asleep, not feeling too well." Frankie laughed. "Mom scooped the kids up and ran out of here."

"She didn't...take...Lurch?"

"I don't think she could have handled all three of them."

"I'll take the dog." Matthew took the leash off the hook on the wall and snapped it to Henry's collar. "I...have a feeling...where she is. You okay here?" he looked around at all the angry faces.

"I'm ready to go home!" Gail got up and pulled her oxygen tank toward them.

"I'll take you, Gran," Frankie said. "I need to leave anyway." He turned back to Matthew. "We'll be fine."

*

Matthew stopped the car and got out. He unzipped his jacket. The balminess was persisting. He thought for a minute of leaving his jacket in the car but decided against it. It was the third week in January and this time of year warm weather could last a week or an hour. You just never know.

"Come on...Lurch...guess I should call you Henry?" He smiled as the excited dog bounded out of the car. The two of them started down the path. Matthew picked up his pace to a brisk jog, being careful to direct the big dog to stay beside him.

"You must have a death wish." Gwen's voice came from behind him as he rounded a thick hedge on the side of the trail.

He stopped running and turned around. Gwen sat on a swing with one child in her arms and the other sleeping in the double stroller in front of her.

"They're asleep," she said. "William woke up for a minute but when I started to swing he went back to sleep."

Matthew approached the swing and commanded Henry to lie down. The big dog smiled and wagged his entire back end. "Down..." Matthew commanded louder and gestured to the ground. This time he tugged on the training collar. The dog reluctantly lowered himself to the moist pine straw beneath the swing. Matthew sat down and stroked the sleeping baby's cheek with his finger.

"What are you doing here with my dog?" Gwen asked.

"Looking for you,"

"I figured." Gwen looked away but not before Matthew saw her eyes cloud with tears.

"What's going on in that sweet head of yours, Gwen? Why...you...trying not to cry?" Matthew put his arm across her shoulders and pulled her against him.

"You have the nicest shoulder to cry on; Matt, but this will probably break the damn. You may go back home with a wet shirt."

"Not a pro...problem."

"But, you know what? The lump in my throat is gone and I don't feel much like crying anymore. Thanks, Matt. I guess I just needed some company." She looked down at the sleeping baby in the stroller. "These strollers they have these days are fantastic. They can attach together or be separate. These actually have a waterproof cover you can pull down so if the weather doesn't hold and it starts to rain, they won't get wet."

"Tell me about Christmas. You've seemed sad ever since the day after."

"And you've seemed like you were in heaven ever since that day."

"The kids went to the in-laws. Helen and I spent the day completely alone." He smiled broadly. "I am in heaven."

"I'm so glad about that, Matt. You two scared us to death for a while there."

"I was...scared...too." He leaned forward and unbuckled the squirming Trevor. "Stay Henry!" The dog settled back to the straw and Matthew started to bounce Trevor on his knee. "So tell me what happened at your Christmas."

"Frankie and Rodney were at their in-laws. We saw them on Christmas Eve. So that was one less argument we would have to deal with."

"The Mothers...squabbled?"

"Yes, but that's not the problem. I'm getting used to it. In fact, I'm starting to think it's just a way for them to get along. You know what I mean. They actually seem drawn to each other, but they don't know how to do anything but disagree." She put William down as he struggled to walk around the forest.

"It was Andrea that upset me. Matt, she's so miserable. I know what she did was wrong. She shouldn't have been dishonest with Tom, but what he's doing to her now is cruel. He called on Christmas day to talk to Trevor. He wouldn't even say Hello to her."

"Phil says he's talked to him a couple of times. I suppose you have, too." Matthew stood to follow the two year olds around the opening. He handed the leash to Gwen and she stroked the dog's head.

"Yes, he just can't seem to deal with that anger. I don't think they're going to get through this."

"And you're…attached…to Tom, too."

"I'm starting to get over that." Gwen got up and went to where the kids were stooped over a pine cone. Henry put his floppy head down to examine the object and both kids squealed and fell on their rumps. Gwen and Matthew laughed and picked the kids up to set them on their feet.

"The thing is," Gwen frowned and looked at Matthew. "She's not well. I'm really worried. She's sure it's just morning sickness but she wasn't like this with Trevor. Phillip wants to believe everything will be fine but I'm worried, Matt."

"What does the physician say?"

"I don't think she's been to one."

"I'll talk to Daniel and Delia." Matthew picked up Trevor and fastened him back into the stroller. "I think it's going to rain. We'd better go on back."

They walked down the path. "Daniel and Delia are Andrea's friends. Maybe they can help," Matt said.

"Maybe," Gwen looked at the back of the stroller.

"Granny," one small voice piped

"Granny?"

She smiled. "Trevor used to call me Ramma but William has changed it to Granny."

"Do you mind?"

"No. In fact, I like it."

"Gwen, you and Phil come and have dinner with Helen and me tomorrow night. I'll make veggie burgers and sweet potato oven fries. It's been ages since we've eaten together. I mean...just the four...of us."
"Alright, that sounds nice."
They walked quietly to the car. "Do you want me to take Lurch home?"
"His name is Henry."
"Sorry,"
"I can manage. I'll see you tomorrow night."

*

Phillip pulled into the garage. He still felt a pang of guilt that he occupied the space next to his pet project. He'd tried to make Gwen use it but it was just easier if he parked there. He got out of the car and took a walk around the Alpha. It was a beautiful car and it was almost finished and already sold.

He smiled proudly and started up the stairs to the kitchen. They were having dinner with the Riddicks tonight. That would be so nice. The four of them together after all they'd been through. He had to admit he was excited about it.

Rounding the corner from the steps he stopped short. Andrea sat at the table with her head in her arms and his mother sat next to her stroking her shoulder.

"Oh, I'm so glad you're here, Phillip," Martha said. "You've got to take Andrea to the hospital. She's very sick."

"What's going on, Andy," Phillip sat down beside his daughter and lifted her chin. Now he knew what "white as a ghost" means. "What is it, honey?" He tried to sound calm but his heart was beating in his throat.

"I'm losing the baby, Daddy. I'm bleeding. I tried elevating my feet but it won't stop."

"Take her to the hospital, Phillip. I'll stay with Trevor. We'll be fine."

"I can't reach her. She must be busy at the shop." Gail came from the living room dragging her oxygen tank. "Oh, Phil, I'm so glad you're here. Take her to the hospital. I'll keep trying to reach Gwen."

"I'll pull the car around front so that you don't have to go down the steps." Phillip stood and headed for the garage. "Can you walk, honey?"

"I don't know."

"I'll come back for you." Phillip pulled the car around as close as he could get to the front door and ran in. Andrea sat on the foyer bench, Gail and Martha on either side of her. "Are you two sure you're alright with Trevor?"

Gail pulled herself up straight. "We've both raised children of our own, you know."

"That's right, Phillip," Martha said. "Don't forget, I'm your mother. Now go on. Do you need our help getting her out to the car?"

Andrea began to whimper softly and Gail put her arm around her and helped her to stand. She passed her off to her father then listened. "Trevor's up. I think I can get him Martha. I can still do stairs. You warm his bottle." Both Great-grandmothers headed in the direction of the stairs and the kitchen.

Phillip would have smiled if his own child hadn't been clinging to his shoulder and crying weakly. "You'll be alright, baby." He whispered and helped her to the car. "The hospital isn't far away."

"I'm losing my baby, oh Daddy, I'm losing my baby."

He felt the tears pushing at the back of his eyelids as he drove to the hospital. He hoped he wasn't losing his grandchild. Suddenly the child seemed so real to him, so much a part of him. Until now, he hadn't really thought of it as a child, a real person. This baby had been a pregnancy, a problem for his daughter, for him.

"Oh, I hope not, honey." It was such a useless thing to say but he couldn't think of anything else. He scrubbed at his cheeks as the tears fought their way to freedom.

*

"Phil..." Gwen called across the emergency room waiting area. He heard her and looked up. He'd been sitting with his head bowed staring at his hands in his lap. He stood and hurried over to her. She threw her arms around him and he buried his head in her hair. He was crying. "The baby..?"

"She lost the baby." He melted into a new wave of sobs. She held him tightly and buried her head in his shoulder. They cried together until a nurse put her hand on Gwen's shoulder.

"You can go in now if you want. We've got her all cleaned up and she's sedated. She was so upset we had to do something."

"I called Tom," Phillip said. "He's on his way."

"Good," Gwen stopped outside the door to the hospital room they'd been shown to. "I feel terrible. I hadn't thought of this baby as a person yet. Now I'll never get a chance to."

"That's the way I feel, too," Phillip said. "You look fine, Gwen." He stopped her hand as she tried to smooth her hair. "We're not supposed to look good right now."

She pushed the door open and went in. "Andy…"

"Mamma…" Her daughter's voice sounded so small, like when she was a child. Gwen hurried to the bed and took her hand. "I'm being punished. I killed my baby."

"No, honey, it doesn't work that way. The baby died. I don't know why but you didn't kill your baby." Gwen lowered the bed rail and sat down next to Andrea.

"It's not your fault, Andy." Phillip took her other hand and stroked her cheek.

"I messed the whole thing up." Andrea's words were slurring now. The medication was taking affect. "I ruined my marriage and I killed my baby."

"Andy, oh honey, I'm so sorry." Gwen squeezed Andrea's hand but she pulled it away and put it to Gwen's lips.

"Hope…that's the baby's name." She whispered.

"What if it was a boy?" Phillip asked.

Gwen slapped his wrist with her free hand.

"The baby's name is Hope," Andrea said again and closed her eyes.

*

The front door bell rang at Gwen and Phillip's house two hours later. Gwen hurried to open it. They had come home to relieve the great-grandmother's. Gwen took a shower and was about to leave to go back to the hospital.

"Tom..." she stretched her arms out to him when she saw his tear stained face.

"I killed my baby." He cried and Gwen felt the weight of him as he sagged into her arms.

"That's how Andrea's feeling, too, but it isn't true, Tom. Andrea let us talk to the doctor and he explained what happened. There was a medical reason for it." Phillip pried Tom from Gwen's shoulder and directed him to a chair in the living room.

"Andrea's been here a month." Tom continued. He scrubbed at his eyes and sniffled. Gwen offered him a box of tissue. "How could I have stayed away so long?" He breathed deeply. "I was just so angry."

"Daddy..." Trevor ran into the room from the hall.

"Trev..." Tom swept the child into his arms and held him close to his chest. He sobbed softly into the child's hair.

"Daddy...not...cry." Trevor squirmed. "Daddy...too...tight."

"I'm sorry, son," Tom loosened his hold and looked down at Trevor's face. "I've missed you so much, Trev." He looked up at Gwen and Phillip. "I guess I've destroyed my marriage and my relationship with you."

"We're family, Tom. We can get through this. I don't know about the marriage but I can tell you that Andrea feels the same way. She's blaming herself for everything," Phillip said. "Can I get you something to drink, some tea or coffee?"

"No, I haven't been to the hospital yet. I need to go there. Will Andrea be alright?" His voice sounded weak as he asked the question.

"Physically she'll be alright," Gwen said. "You should know. She named the baby Hope."

"It was a girl?"

"I think it was too early to tell but it doesn't matter. The baby's name is Hope. Do you want me to come with you?" Gwen stood to gather her purse and coat.

"No, I need to go by myself."

"I go see Mommy, too." Trevor held on to his father.

"Not tonight, Trevor." Gwen pried him away from Tom.

"You stay here and take care of Gramma and Grampa." Tom kissed the top of his son's head.

"Granny!" Trevor screamed and started to cry.

"We'll be alright, Tom," Phillip said as he walked him to the door.

*

"I'm sorry we had to cancel dinner last night," Gwen said when she arrived at the Gallery the next morning. It was before opening and Helen was starting the computers and getting ready to dust the shelves.

"I'm so sorry about the baby." She stopped what she was doing and put her arms around Gwen.

"Thanks," Gwen rested her head on Helen's shoulder and let her hold her tightly. "I can't believe how deeply I'm grieving. I never even thought of Hope as a person. Now she'll never be a person."

"She named it Hope. It was a girl?"

"Don't know but Andrea named the baby Hope. So I'm saying a girl." She stepped back and headed for the office.

"Why are you here, Gwen? Shouldn't you be at the hospital?" Helen followed.

"Tom called this morning. They're going to release her. They don't keep people in the hospital very long these days. He said that he'd bring her home. Phil's at home with Trevor. I'll go home at lunch and give them both a break. I don't think they slept much last night. Tom sounded tired and Phil looked tired." Gwen put her purse in a desk drawer and started back out to the gallery.

"What happened, Gwen?"

"Apparently when the fetus fused to the uterine wall it went too deep and broke through to the outside. It's a dangerous pregnancy. It's not only bad for the baby but for the mother, too. If she'd gone to the doctor he'd have encouraged her to terminate the pregnancy. It was never a good prognosis."

"I've heard of that."

"I think that's why Andy wouldn't go to the doctor. She knew something was wrong. I did, too." Gwen sat behind the checkout counter.

"Will she be able to have more children?"

"The doctor assured us she can. I don't know if she will. I'm not even sure if the marriage will survive this." Gwen took a deep breath.

"Go on home, Gwen." Helen put her hand on Gwen's shoulder. "You look like you could use some rest, too."

"I think working this morning will provide what I need." Gwen looked around. "Phillip wants to meet with us and talk about the books, you know; how we did over the holidays, cost analysis, something like that."

"You're not feeling discouraged because if you are…"

"I'm not. I love this place." Gwen smiled at Helen. "We'll do whatever we have to. We'll make it work."

Helen took a deep breath and sat down behind the candy counter. "It's good to hear you talk that way."

Chapter Fifteen

Matthew spotted his children across the crowded café. Sybil sat at the end of the table with the infant seat in a chair next to her. Daniel sat on the side with an empty chair next to him and Delia and Greg across the table on the other side.

Delia caught his eye and waved. Daniel turned around and stood to greet him as he crossed the room. "Hey, Dad,"

Matthew smiled and hugged his son. "Hey, son…I'm so happy…to join you all…today."

Delia rounded the table and hugged him holding tight for a minute and then returning to her seat. Greg shook his hand across the table.

"Don't get…up…Sybil." Matthew went to where she was sitting and bent to kiss her cheek, then kissed the top of the sleeping baby's head. "He's growing…f…f…quickly." Stupid words, he thought. He sat down next to Daniel. "What's the occasion?"

"We just wanted to get together with you," Delia said.

"…without…your mother?" Matthew looked around the table. All eyes were averted except Sybil's.

"They're very protective of you." She laughed. "They want to make sure she isn't hurting you again. I didn't recommend it, but Dan and Delia are stubborn."

"Understated nicely, Sybil." Greg smiled at Matthew.

Matthew threw back his head and laughed. He put his arm around Daniel's shoulders and reached across the table for Delia's hand.

"Thanks...kids..." The waitress came to their table and everyone ordered lunch. "I don't know what I would...have...done..."

"It's okay, Daddy. We know what you mean," Delia said.

"Don't protect me, baby." Matthew smiled. "All of you were great, Greg and Sybil, too. I...it...would mean..." he looked down at his place as the waitress put down their order. He took a deep breath. "I hope you'll mend...with...your mother."

"Sybil and I have nothing to mend," Greg said. "At least I hope I can speak for you, Sybil."

"Absolutely, I consider myself lucky to have such a mother-in-law." Everyone looked from Daniel to Delia.

"Don't worry Dad, we love Mom," Daniel said. "In fact I feel bad sometimes about cutting her out of my life so completely. But, Dad, you have to admit, she's a little overwhelming." He put his hand on Gabriel's belly as the child started to fuss. "Let your mother eat her lunch, Gabe." He smiled at the infant.

"I'll hold him." Matthew took the baby from Daniel as he pulled him out of the infant seat. He pushed back from the table and put the baby on his knee to bounce. "When you two were babies we couldn't...take...turns. There was a baby for...each of...us."

Daniel and Delia both took a deep breath. Matthew noticed how even as adults they moved with each other. He'd observed the bond of the twins right from birth but it always gave him a warm feeling.

"Maybe...you'll have twins, Dandy." He smiled across the table at his daughter.

"No, it's just one baby, Daddy. I had an ultrasound. It's a girl."

"Wonderful!"

"I love Mom, too, Daddy," she said quietly. "I have to admit she's always there when I need her. But I agree with Daniel. She's overwhelming. I mean she's so dynamic."

"I guess I like dynamic." He looked around the table at his children, children-in-law, and grandchild. "Good...thing...surrounded by dynamic."

*

"So Nanna and Gran took care of Trevor?" Frankie asked Phillip. They sat in the kitchen sipping lemonade while Trevor smeared macaroni and cheese on the high chair tray.

"They did a great job. I think they have actually formed a new bond. They were exhausted when we got home, but neither one could stop talking about all they'd done. It took the two of them. Gail is a little more mobile than Mom, but she's not as kitchen savvy." Phillip wiped Trevor's face and hands.

"So are they actually getting along now?"

"I'd be more inclined to say they're arguing peacefully. Mom slept for twelve hours after we relieved her. Your mother took Gran home and checked on her about eight hours later. She was fine, but not up to breakfast."

"Can I go up and see Andy?" Frankie looked timidly toward the steps to the second floor.

"I think that's fine. Rodney's up there. Tom went out to get her some flowers. He's worried because she's so depressed. He's depressed, too, but I think it makes him feel good to try to do something about it."

"Do you think their marriage will survive this?" Frankie stood and started toward the steps.

"I hope so. I love them both. Maybe they'll start talking to each other instead of trying to manipulate each other and read each other's minds." Phillip smiled at his tall son. Frankie was his black sheep. He winced to even think that. He'd grown into such a good man.

"I'll tell you what. Grace and I will never stop talking. She won't allow it." He grinned and disappeared up the stairs.

Phillip put Trevor down on the floor. "You can go into the living room and open the toy box, Trev," he said. "But stay out of trouble until I get there. When I come in, we'll look on the internet for a new sports car to rebuild."

"Ports Car...grraage."

Phillip took the removable tray off the highchair and rinsed it in the sink. He could hear his three grown children talking upstairs. Andrea was crying but the boys deep voices rumbled in comfort. His grandson chattered to himself in the living room.

"Are you alright, honey?" His mother asked from behind him.

He jumped. He usually heard the wheels of the walker before she got close. Henry bounded in the back door as she opened it.

"I'm pretty good right now, Mom." He stroked the big dog and leaned down to pet the cat that weaved through the dog's legs. "I was surprised by the intensity of the grief for my unborn grandchild, but hearing my children upstairs comforting each other is heartwarming."

Martha cocked her head toward the stairs. "I can hear a low murmur. I'm glad to know they're there for each other." She approached Phillip from behind as he finished drying the table. "Why don't you let your own mother comfort you? She reached up and touched his shoulder.

He turned and put his arms around her. He was surprised again by the tears that sprang so easily to his eyes. They held each other for a minute enjoying the familiar warmth.

"Rampa...don't...cry." Trevor tugged at his pants leg.

"Okay, you two, cut it out or you'll have me blubbering in a minute," Gail said from behind them. "What kind of grandparents are you. I found Trevor in the living room all by himself. Down, Lurch!" she commanded the bouncing dog.

*

"Andrea wanted to have a funeral," Gwen said as she and Helen sat in the office. They had just closed the shop and were waiting for Phillip. They were going to go over the books and the holiday sales. "But there isn't really anything to bury and a memorial service doesn't seem right. We never got to know Hope. How can we remember someone we never got to know?"

"Danny and Dandy have a service planned," Helen said. "They wanted to talk to Andrea about it first but I think they're planning it for Saturday. Everyone will come to our apartment for an early dinner."

"Really?" Gwen looked puzzled. "Now that you mention it, Tom said something about that. He plans to take the family back to Charlotte on Sunday. I hope they're ready."

"I hope so, too, but there isn't anything we can do if they aren't."

"Yeah, I'm coming around to that fact. All we can do is be here to help pick up the pieces if it doesn't work."

"Yeah, but don't pick them up too fast." Helen laughed.

"So, I guess your kids are speaking to you now if you know about the plans for the service."

"They talk to me when they need to. I guess things are getting better but they still don't really like me very much. They went to lunch with Matt today. I was definitely not invited. I think they want to make sure I'm not mistreating him in some way."

"How would you mistreat him?"

Helen sighed. "I guess they do have reason to worry. I did leave him at his lowest point."

"I just think that's what needed to happen. Things have changed so much for the better."

"Part of me thinks that and part of me thinks I'm going straight to Hell."

"See you in Hell." Gwen laughed.

Helen stretched and looked at her watch. "Where is Phil? I'm tired and Lila probably has to pee. I don't know if Matt got home to let her out after lunch."

"Helen…" They both looked at the door of the office as Matthew spoke. His eyes were very bright and he seemed to fill the room as he stepped through the door.

"Matt," Gwen said. "Are you mad about something?"

"Mad about Helen." He rounded the desk and took Helen's hands to pull her to her feet.

"What's wrong, Matt?" Helen asked. "The kids didn't tell you something to make you angry with me, did they?" Her mind was racing. Had they talked mistakenly about Victor?

"Matthew," Gwen said. "Calm down and tell us what's going on."

"I said 'mad about you' not 'mad at you." He pulled her into his arms and kissed her.

"Matt…" Gwen said then noticed the way one of his hands held Helen's waist and the other hand loosened her hair. She backed toward the door. "We'll talk about the books another time," she said as she shut the door to the office. She wanted to move away from the door but couldn't resist listening to the soft lover's voices from behind it.

The back door opened and a gust of cold air swept in. Gwen was grateful. The cold air mobilized her.

"I'm sorry I'm late, Gwen," Phillip said. "The kids were all at the house and I lost track of time. Let's go into the office. Is Helen still here?"

"She's here." Gwen smiled. "But we're not going into the office. We'll talk about the books another time." She stopped him with a hand on his arm.

"I know you don't want to talk about this, but as long as we are all here..." Phillip stopped as she guided him away from the office door. His face registered understanding and he smiled as he heard the quiet voices. "Matt is with her."

"Um...hmm... He just rushed in and swept her away. So I think we'll leave them alone."

"We'll talk about the books another time." Phillip pulled her into his arms and kissed her loosening her hair.

*

"I'm going now, Mom," Andrea said.

They were at Matthew and Helen's apartment. They had enjoyed a short service. All the kids had read passages on love and comfort for the lost child. Matthew had made a beautiful speech that brought tears to everyone's eyes.

The company of friends and loved ones had warmed everyone's hearts. Even Tom and Andrea were smiling, if a little sadly.

"We'll take Nana home with us." She hugged Gwen then Phillip and Helen. "Thank you, Matt," she said as he held her tightly in his arms. "The meal was delicious. You'll have to give me your recipe for veggie burgers."

"I will...honey." He kissed her temple. "I'm sorry for your loss."

"Thanks."

Tom held a sleeping Trevor over his shoulder as he shook hands with Phillip and Matthew.

"Thanks for all your support," he said to Phillip. "You've had every reason to be mad at me but you've been nothing but supportive."

"We're family." Gwen kissed the tall handsome young man that loved her daughter.

"We'll see you at home."

Frankie approached the group. "We're going home, too, Mom. We'll drop Gran on the way." He kissed his mother and Helen then shook hands with Matthew and Phillip. "Rodney came with us so as soon as he gets William off the playscape we'll go."

"Come by again soon, honey," Gwen said as he and Grace left. "Thanks for coming, Grace."

Gwen turned as the door closed behind the last guests. "It was nice of Victor to drop by," she said. There had been no awkwardness between him and Matthew. In fact, Gwen had been impressed with their easy relationship.

"He's a good guy." Helen laughed. "He isn't going to make me wear a tuxedo to his wedding. You know I'm his best man."

"That's what I hear." Phillip joined the laughter. "I guess we should go, too, Gwen."

"Not yet," Matthew said. "I made a pitcher of Martinis. Join us."

Phillip frowned. "I haven't had a martini since…"

"Since the last time the four of us got together," Matthew said and the room fell silent. Matthew looked at his wife and his two best friends. So much had happened since the night he'd had the stroke. He looked at Helen.

She looked back at him with a smile. He stroked her cheek. He'd lost her and won her back. If not for that terrible night he may have lost her and not won her back.

Helen looked at Matthew. His handsome face beamed at her and there was a new glow to it. He was healthy and fit and beautiful. Thank God he hadn't died that night. She winced to remember a fleeting wish that he had. She put her hand on his and squeezed.

"We're not going to cry or anything, are we?" Phillip laughed nervously. "I'm getting just a little too close to my feminine side."

"Crying is healthy, Phil," Gwen said fighting the lump in her throat. "I'd love a martini, just one, though, everything in moderation."

"Everything in moderation," Matthew said. "Well not everything." He smiled devilishly at Helen and poured drinks all around.

www.ingramcontent.com/pod-product-compliance
Lightning Source LLC
LaVergne TN
LVHW041606070426
835507LV00008B/150